In *A Year for the Books*, Katie and Maria Walther have crafted a practical guide to nurturing the reading identity of elementary and middle school students. The authors have brilliantly organized their text to follow the arc of our school year. As you read, you get the impression that Katie and Maria are trusted colleagues teaching next door, sharing "just-in-time" helpful tips and suggestions that you can implement in your class right away. Teachers who follow the year-long plan laid out in this text will go beyond teaching their students how to read; they will build a community of readers.

**—Christy Hermann Thompson**
**2nd-grade teacher and coauthor of *Hands Down, Speak Out:***
***Listening and Talking Across Literacy and Math***

Katie and Maria Walther furnish practical and concrete ideas for establishing reading routines that serve to rejuvenate both students and educators throughout the academic year, ultimately nurturing a deep-seated love for reading. They champion the celebration of student agency, modeling how to translate classroom literacy beliefs into actionable strategies that empower students as confident, capable readers. This book is essential reading for educators seeking an effective, straightforward plan to create inclusive, identity-centered literacy experiences that transcend basic reading instruction.

**—Dr. Rachael Mahmood**
**CEO Equity Teacher Leader, LLC**

Maria Walther has always conveyed a great appreciation and an immense knowledge of children's literature. Now she is joined by her daughter, Katie, and the journey continues into the upper grades. *A Year for the Books* is an essential guide for elementary and middle school teachers who want to put literature at the center of their literacy programs. Full of practical ideas, tips, and pictures from classrooms, this easy-to-navigate book includes a variety of literacy skills and strategies that will help teachers reach every student.

**—Susan Lovell**
**District Elementary Teacher**
**Peace River South (SD59), British Columbia, Canada**

Reading this book is like being welcomed into the classroom of the teacher next door and walking away with a gold mine of realistic strategies to try. This book is grounded in the latest research, organized into accessible bite-sized pieces—open to any page for a morsel to ponder and a researcher who's "got your back" to support the work teachers do in their classrooms. The authors provide an overview of a whole year, focused on creating spaces and routines for every learner to see themselves as readers, including strategies for engaging families in order to promote positive literacy identity both in and outside of the classroom. If you're looking for ways to promote the love of reading in your classroom, you've found the right book!

**—Sara Kerns**
**Instructional Coach**
**Cherry Creek School District, Denver, Colorado**

Authors Katie and Maria Walther begin this book with an educational truth: "Teaching is a lot like being on an uphill hike." Well, there they are, waiting for you at the trailhead on the first day of school, adeptly guiding you through the hike of the rest of the year. Their direction helps to equip both novices and masters to set strong grounding principles that will benefit all readers throughout the year. I strongly urge you to let Katie and Maria guide you through a year of reading successes for the students in your classroom.

**—Travis Leech**
**Literacy consultant and coauthor of *Patterns of Power***

# A YEAR FOR THE BOOKS

# A YEAR

# FOR THE

# BOOKS

Routines and Mindsets
for Creating Student-Centered
Reading Communities

PODCAST
FOR EVERY CHAPTER

# KATIE WALTHER
## AND
# MARIA WALTHER

Routledge
Taylor & Francis Group
NEW YORK AND LONDON

A Stenhouse Book

Cover design by Cindy Butler
Interior design by Jill Shaffer

First published 2024
by Routledge
605 Third Avenue, New York, NY 10158

and by Routledge
4 Park Square, Milton Park, Abingdon, Oxon, OX14 4RN

*Routledge is an imprint of the Taylor & Francis Group, an informa business*

ISBN: 9781625315670 (pbk)
ISBN: 9781032680491 (ebk)

DOI: 10.4324/9781032680491

Typeset in Odile Book
by Eclipse Publishing Services

Access the PDCast: www.routledge.com/9781625315670

**For Mom**. Thank you for being the most wonderful model of a mother, friend, and teacher. I feel so
fortunate to have you by my side on this journey.

—KW

**To educators** who, with fortitude, continue to
support their students and each other during
these challenging times.

—MW

# CONTENTS

Acknowledgments .................................................. xiii

**INTRODUCTION** **Get Ready, Get Set . . . Let's Get Started!** ........................... 1

Get Ready: A Year Together .................................... 1

Get Set: Grounding Principles ................................. 1

Staying on Course: A Quick Book Tour ......................... 6

Let's Get Started: Before School Begins ....................... 9

Make Every Decision Count ................................... 11

**CHAPTER 1** **Make the Most of Your First Day** ............................ 13

Welcome Reading Community Members ....................... 14

▶ Try This! Start with Small-Group Book Bins ............... 14

▶ Try This! Pose a Book Title Challenge .................... 17

Communicate Beliefs Through the Physical Layout of Your Classroom ........ 21

▶ Try This! Showcase Books Around Your Room ............ 22

▶ Try This! Display Powerful Quotes from Thought Leaders ........ 24

Kick Off Routines ........................................... 26

▶ Try This! Post a Visual Schedule ......................... 27

▶ Try This! Notice and Celebrate Student Agency and Independence ....... 28

Get to Know One Another .................................... 32

▶ Try This! Watch and Listen During Read-Aloud Experiences ......... 32

▶ Try This! Engage in an Introduction Circle .................. 35

Launch a Yearlong Partnership with Families/Caregivers ........ 38

▶ Try This! Gather Insights by Using a Family Questionnaire ......... 38

▶ Try This! Record a Video Introduction .................... 39

**CHAPTER 2:** **Follow Up During the First Few Weeks** ..................... 45

Familiarize Readers with the Books in Your Classroom ......... 46

▶ Try This! Explore Different Kinds of Books ................ 46

▶ Try This! Speed Date with Books ......................... 49

Collaborate on Shared Values ................................ 52

▶ Try This! Discuss How Students Want Their Classroom to Feel ......... 52

▶ Try This! Ask, "What Do We Value?" ..................... 54

**Develop Routines**..................................................58

▶ Try This! Model Text-Focused Conversations During Read-Aloud ........58

▶ Try This! Reflect on Known Routines ...........................62

**Cultivate Community** ...............................................64

▶ Try This! Create Identity Equations .............................65

▶ Try This! Conduct a Community Literacy Survey ................66

**Connect with Families/Caregivers**.................................69

▶ Try This! Display Students' Photographs ......................70

▶ Try This! Compose Family Letters .............................71

CHAPTER 3   **Build on Your Foundation: First Semester** ...................77

**Surround Independent Reading with Support**.....................78

▶ Try This! Gather Multifaceted Data to Intentionally Support Readers .....78

▶ Try This! Overcome Roadblocks to Conferring...................82

**Translate Beliefs into Actions**.....................................86

▶ Try This! Match Learning Experiences to Beliefs ...............86

▶ Try This! Plan with Beliefs at the Forefront ...................89

**Demonstrate and Practice Routines** ..............................92

▶ Try This! Create a Predictable
Teach-Demonstrate-Practice-Reflect Cycle .....................92

▶ Try This! Establish a Daily Reading Routine.....................94

**Elevate Community Through Literacy** ..............................99

▶ Try This! Strengthen Community During
Small-Group Collaborative Conversations ....................100

▶ Try This! Use Multimodal Text Sets to Spark
Collaborative Learning and Conversation ....................102

**Confer with Families/Caregivers** .................................104

▶ Try This! Explain the Child's Stage of Reading Development ...........105

▶ Try This! Use a List of Talking Points...........................106

CHAPTER 4   **Keep the Momentum Going: After Winter Break** ...................111

**Reenergize Supported Independent Reading** .......................112

▶ Try This! Refresh the Classroom Library .......................112

▶ Try This! Recommit to Regularly Scheduled Book Talks ..............114

Revisit Beliefs, Actions, and Goals . . . . . . . . . . . . . . . . . . . . . . . . . . . . . . . . . . . . . 119

▶ Try This! Make Resolutions . . . . . . . . . . . . . . . . . . . . . . . . . . . . . . . . . . . . . . . . 120

▶ Try This! Invite Student Self-Reflection on Shared Values . . . . . . . . . . . . . 120

Reintroduce Routines . . . . . . . . . . . . . . . . . . . . . . . . . . . . . . . . . . . . . . . . . . . . . . . . 124

▶ Try This! Put Learners in Charge. . . . . . . . . . . . . . . . . . . . . . . . . . . . . . . . . . . . 124

▶ Try This! Create "Do" and "Don't" Comic Strips . . . . . . . . . . . . . . . . . . . . . 126

Release Responsibility to Community Members . . . . . . . . . . . . . . . . . . . . . . . . . 128

▶ Try This! Launch Reader of the Day . . . . . . . . . . . . . . . . . . . . . . . . . . . . . . . . 128

▶ Try This! Encourage Student-Led Book Talks . . . . . . . . . . . . . . . . . . . . . . . . 129

Create Family/Caregiver Engagement Opportunities . . . . . . . . . . . . . . . . . . . . 131

▶ Try This! Set Up a Read to Me! Program. . . . . . . . . . . . . . . . . . . . . . . . . . . . 131

▶ Try This! Host a Gallery Walk . . . . . . . . . . . . . . . . . . . . . . . . . . . . . . . . . . . . . 133

CHAPTER 5 **Think Outside the Box: Spring Toward the Finish Line** . . . . . . . . . . . . 139

Broaden Supported Independent Reading. . . . . . . . . . . . . . . . . . . . . . . . . . . . . .140

▶ Try This! Get Readers Hooked on a Series . . . . . . . . . . . . . . . . . . . . . . . . . .140

▶ Try This! Extend Reading Practices Beyond the Classroom . . . . . . . . . . . . .144

Hold True to Your Beliefs . . . . . . . . . . . . . . . . . . . . . . . . . . . . . . . . . . . . . . . . . . . . .149

▶ Try This! Plan Belief-Driven Events and Celebrations . . . . . . . . . . . . . . . . . .150

▶ Try This! Treat Test Preparation Like a Genre or Unit . . . . . . . . . . . . . . . . . .152

Innovate on Routines. . . . . . . . . . . . . . . . . . . . . . . . . . . . . . . . . . . . . . . . . . . . . . . .156

▶ Try This! Integrate Poetry and the Arts . . . . . . . . . . . . . . . . . . . . . . . . . . . . . .157

▶ Try This! Remix Routines to Increase Engagement . . . . . . . . . . . . . . . . . . . .160

Refresh Positive Community . . . . . . . . . . . . . . . . . . . . . . . . . . . . . . . . . . . . . . . . . .163

▶ Try This! Sprinkle in Kindness . . . . . . . . . . . . . . . . . . . . . . . . . . . . . . . . . . . . .163

▶ Try This! Look Back to Move Forward . . . . . . . . . . . . . . . . . . . . . . . . . . . . . .164

Promote Student-to-Caregiver Communication . . . . . . . . . . . . . . . . . . . . . . . . .167

▶ Try This! Curate a Collection of Reading Memories. . . . . . . . . . . . . . . . . . . .168

▶ Try This! Engage in Community Book Matching . . . . . . . . . . . . . . . . . . . . . . .169

## Appendixes

A2.1  Someday List . . . . . . . . . . . . . . . . . . . . . . . . . . . . . . . . . . . . . . . . . . . . . . . . . . 175

A2.2  Community Literacy Survey. . . . . . . . . . . . . . . . . . . . . . . . . . . . . . . . . . . . . . . 176

A2.3  Photograph Request Letter. . . . . . . . . . . . . . . . . . . . . . . . . . . . . . . . . . . . . . . 178

A3.1  Thinking About My Reading . . . . . . . . . . . . . . . . . . . . . . . . . . . . . . . . . . . .179

A3.2  READ-O: Primary Grades . . . . . . . . . . . . . . . . . . . . . . . . . . . . . . . . . . . . . .180

A3.3  READ-O: Middle Grades . . . . . . . . . . . . . . . . . . . . . . . . . . . . . . . . . . . . . . 181

A3.4  Reading Bucket List: Primary Grades . . . . . . . . . . . . . . . . . . . . . . . . . . .182

A3.5  Reading Bucket List: Middle Grades . . . . . . . . . . . . . . . . . . . . . . . . . . .183

A3.6  Collaborative Conversation Anecdotal Note Sheet . . . . . . . . . . . . . . .184

A3.7  Stages of Reading Development . . . . . . . . . . . . . . . . . . . . . . . . . . . . . . .185

A4.1  Reader of the Day Family/Caregiver Letter . . . . . . . . . . . . . . . . . . . . .186

A4.2  Read to Me! . . . . . . . . . . . . . . . . . . . . . . . . . . . . . . . . . . . . . . . . . . . . . . . . . 187

A4.3  Gallery Walk Visitor's Guide . . . . . . . . . . . . . . . . . . . . . . . . . . . . . . . . . .188

A4.4  A Day in Our Classroom: Elementary . . . . . . . . . . . . . . . . . . . . . . . . . . .189

A4.5  A Reading Day in Our Classroom: Middle School . . . . . . . . . . . . . . . .190

A5.1  Summer Family/Caregiver Letter . . . . . . . . . . . . . . . . . . . . . . . . . . . . . .191

**Bibliography** . . . . . . . . . . . . . . . . . . . . . . . . . . . . . . . . . . . . . . . . .193

**Credits** . . . . . . . . . . . . . . . . . . . . . . . . . . . . . . . . . . . . . . . . . . . . . 203

**Index** . . . . . . . . . . . . . . . . . . . . . . . . . . . . . . . . . . . . . . . . . . . . . . 205

# ACKNOWLEDGMENTS

Just as teaching thrives on the power of collaboration, writing a book is so much more rewarding when done in community. We would like to express our gratitude and appreciation to the many partners who supported us as we worked together to create *A Year for the Books*:

**To our partners in thought . . .** Katherine Phillips-Toms, Karen Biggs-Tucker, Colette Sims, Valerie Hazelton, and all of the dynamic educators, teammates, and PLC members we've been lucky to collaborate with over the years. It's been an energizing learning experience to ponder and plan with all of you.

**To our partners in the classroom . . .** our students. You inspire us to keep learning, reading, and growing each and every day.

**To our partners in innovation . . .** National Council of Teachers of English, International Literacy Association along with all of their state and local affiliates. The opportunities you provide to learn from and with educators from around the world helps to breathe new life into our literacy practices and reconnect with our "why."

**To our partners in books . . .** teacher-librarians, public libraries, and independent bookstore owners who work in our schools and our cities, especially Anderson's Bookshop, Book Bar, Denver Public Libraries, and Aurora Public Libraries. You make these our happy places! We also appreciate the many trade book publishers who strive to create the best books for readers and share them with us in advance: Candlewick Press, Chronicle Books, Penguin Random House, Scholastic Press, and Simon & Schuster.

**To our partner in writing . . .** Terry Thompson. Your belief in the two of us and in this project was unwavering. We thank our lucky stars that you are our editor and admire your ability to keep the ball rolling while at the same time encouraging, suggesting, and celebrating along with us.

**To our partners in podcasting and publishing . . .** Nate Butler, Shannon St. Peter, Cindy Butler (we love our cover!), Jill Shaffer, and everyone at Stenhouse. We are grateful for your dedication and encouragement throughout this loooonnnng journey from idea to reality.

**To our partners in life . . .** Lenny Walther and Brian Denison.

# Get Ready, Get Set . . . Let's Get Started!

## GET READY: A YEAR TOGETHER

Teaching is a lot like being on an uphill hike. You start out in August quickly gaining elevation (perhaps a bit faster than you'd like) and continue to put one foot in front of the other until you've reached the top of the peak in May or June. Occasionally you can slow down to admire the view or take a quick break, but those days are often few and far between. In this book, we're going to hike next to you and stay there from day one until the last day of school. Together, we'll ponder and reflect on the multitude of instructional decisions that go into inspiring independent readers and creating a vibrant literacy community. We've trained for this and are ready to keep pace with you. We'll offer the wisdom that comes from being an elementary educator for nearly forty years (Maria) and the fresh outlook from someone who has taught middle schoolers for less than a decade (Katie). We hope that our insights and the wealth of ready-to-implement strategies in this resource will not only put a bounce in your step but also give you more time to take those necessary breaks and pauses. Our goal is that you end the year feeling energized, rather than exhausted, and ready to celebrate making it to the summit with the reading community you've cultivated . . . one decision at a time.

FIGURE I.1
*Maria and Katie learning together at CCIRA 2019.*

## GET SET: GROUNDING PRINCIPLES

The seed for this book was planted in February 2019, when our dear editor, Terry, attended one of Katie's first professional presentations at the Colorado Council of the International Reading Association (CCIRA) conference. Her session was geared toward early-career teachers, like herself, and in it she synthesized what she had learned about literacy teaching up to that point from experience, study, and a lot of conversations with colleagues and with her mom, Maria (see Figure I.1). Drawn to the idea of exploring independent reading and learning communities from the joint viewpoint of two teachers with varied perspectives and experiences, Terry suggested we think about sharing what and how we've learned together over time.

1

Both of us have been fortunate in our careers to have found thinking partners who pushed us to question, reflect, and grow as professionals. When Katie started teaching, we also had each other. Our passion for teaching readers has been fueled by professional conversations. So, with Terry's suggestion in mind, we decided to start recording those conversations to see where they would lead. The result is the book you now hold in your hands, and the accompanying PDCast collection. Our goal was to capture the spirit of our decision-making discussions and write down the words we wished we had been able to formulate when our beliefs about the importance of independent reading were wavering. In other words, we aimed to boil down what we had learned thus far from mentors, our students, and especially each other. In the fall of 2019, we started on the long journey of writing a book. And then, well, the pandemic happened. As educators and writers, we limped along trying to make sense of what we were learning from our new realities. The positive outcome of this extended time to reflect and write is that we were able to weave in what we discovered about teaching during and after a global pandemic. Through our conversations and writing, some themes and guiding principles began to emerge. All of this culminated in five foundational principles that ground our decisions and act as the tent poles for each chapter (see Figure I.2). With these grounding principles guiding our way, we are better able to make high-impact choices for the literacy learners in our care.

FIGURE I.2

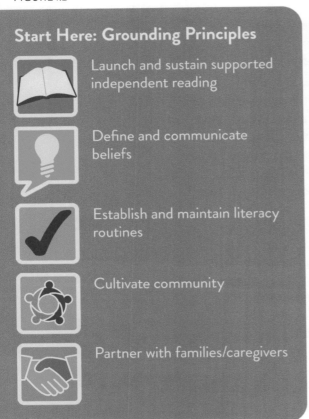

**Start Here: Grounding Principles**

Launch and sustain supported independent reading

Define and communicate beliefs

Establish and maintain literacy routines

Cultivate community

Partner with families/caregivers

### Grounding Principle #1:
### Launch and Sustain Supported Independent Reading

Whether you spend your days with kindergartners, middle school learners, or students in between, we believe that our most important role as literacy educators is to join readers on their unique path toward living a literate life. That is why we consider how to successfully launch *supported independent reading* even before our students arrive and how to keep it front and center throughout the year. When you organize your classroom space and prioritize time to read, students have the opportunity to internalize and apply the skills and strategies you've highlighted during your whole-group learning experiences.

Before we jump into our rationale for this grounding principle, let's all get on the same page by clarifying what we mean by supported independent reading. Over the years, our vision of supported independent reading has been shaped by literacy mentors like Pam Allyn and Ernest Morrell (*Every Child a Super Reader*, 2016), Nancie Atwell (*The Reading Zone*, 2007), Kelly Gallagher (*Readicide*, 2009), Penny Kittle (*Book Love*, 2012), Donalyn Miller (*The Book Whisperer*, 2009), Debbie Miller and Barbara Moss (*No More Independent Reading Without Support*, 2013), and Gholdy Muhammad (*Cultivating Genius*, 2020), just to name a few. We've reflected on, discussed, and dabbled with their ideas. Just as we encourage you to do with the strategies found in this book, we filtered their wisdom through our unique teaching lenses to create book experiences that were responsive to the students in our care. For us, supported independent reading happens when students have daily, or as close to daily as possible, dedicated time to read self-selected texts. The teacher's role is to surround this dedicated reading time with consistent support. Teachers support readers in the following ways before, during, and after they've enjoyed quiet time with a text:

- Create a reader-friendly environment.
- Offer easy access to a wide range of reading materials at school and to take home.
- Promote a wide variety of texts, including those created by and accurately representing people from marginalized and under-represented communities.
- Provide multiple avenues for students to read and access texts in the classroom and at home. Converse with students about texts, their reading goals, their literacy lives, and their lived experiences.
- Teach skills and strategies that will help learners continue to grow as readers, thinkers, and literate citizens.
- Reflect on what they've learned from students and adjust accordingly.

Since it gives students a voice in what they are reading, supported independent reading invites students to take ownership of the learning process. As you observe learners engaging with books and sit beside them to converse about their reading lives, you are strengthening bonds. In each chapter that follows, we will share concrete ways to sustain your community of readers as they grow and learn throughout the school year.

### Grounding Principle #2: Define and Communicate Beliefs

Clearly, we believe in the importance of launching and sustaining supported independent reading as a key component of powerful literacy instruction. This belief stems from the fact that, as literacy educators, our overarching goal is to walk alongside our students on their journey to becoming literate citizens. But if we, as the teachers, are the only ones in the classroom who are aware of our goals and beliefs, then we're missing an opportunity to create a shared vision of how our daily classroom routines connect to living a literate life outside of school. In order to help students clearly see this connection, two things have to happen. First, we engage in ongoing reflection to define our own beliefs about teaching and learning (we share our current beliefs in Chapter 1). When we use the term *beliefs* throughout this book, we're referring to our philosophy of or mindset regarding what it means to teach and learn alongside a community of readers. Second, we collaborate with students to establish shared classroom values. Coming to consensus on shared values helps students see the bigger picture and move toward collective understandings and goals around being a literate citizen (we offer some ideas for doing that in Chapter 2). Working together as a community toward the same goals in a belief-driven literacy classroom encourages a sense of camaraderie. What's more, using these shared goals as a jumping-off place supports students as they set their own individual goals. Belief-driven teaching also gives us a firm footing when we want to push against mandates and other quick fixes that stand in the way of making sure our literacy instruction is research based and focused on the needs of the learners in our care.

### Grounding Principle #3: Establish and Maintain Literacy Routines

With our beliefs about teaching and learning established, the next step is making them come alive in daily classroom life. When defining and communicating our philosophy about teaching and learning, we task ourselves and our students with big thinking related to the overarching goal of living a literate life. Connecting these abstract beliefs to the realities of day-to-day classroom instruction is where establishing and maintaining literacy routines come in. We've found that consistent routines are the most explicit way to translate our beliefs about teaching and learning into action. To that end, we make decisions related to our literacy practices by asking ourselves if-then questions like these:

- If we believe supported independent reading is a crucial part of reading development, then how do we show this through our daily literacy routines?

- If we believe all students are readers, then what routines need to be in place to uphold this philosophy?

You will find threads of if-then questions like these sprinkled throughout this book to guide you in solidifying the connection between your philosophy about teaching and learning and the classroom practices you encourage.

Not only do literacy routines exemplify our mindset, but they also create predictable, consistent learning experiences so that students know what to expect from day to day. Once these routines are firmly established, they provide stability so that readers and teachers can focus on the big ideas of each learning experience rather than getting caught up in the logistics. In the chapters that follow, we highlight practices specifically designed to breathe life into independent reading as well as those that nurture readers, such as read-aloud, book talks, collaborative conversations, conferring, small-group work, and maintaining a dynamic classroom library. Reliable routines are an essential component of a cohesive reading community, another principle that guides our work.

## Grounding Principle #4: Cultivate Community

A vibrant literacy community is built one day at a time over the course of a school year. As teachers, we strengthen the bonds with and among our learners one interaction at a time. With the passing weeks and months, the students in your classroom mature and change. For that reason, we organized this book to take you through a year of reader-focused decision-making. Together, we'll ponder how to make small changes to your approach in order to bring students together based on shared values and consistent routines. Making intentional decisions about how we tend to our safe, caring literacy community results in a positive and fruitful experience for everyone.

When cultivating community, we begin by understanding and celebrating the individual reading identities of all our students. Once we know students as readers, we can honor their strengths and assist them when they have challenges. Through a variety of reading experiences, we spark collaborative conversations that build comprehension, forge connections, and spark curiosity. Then we nudge curious learners to seek out and work to appreciate the varied perspectives found in the texts they are reading and among their classmates' ideas. Being aware of various perspectives and ideas helps learners read with a critical eye and, at the same time, supports a stronger reading community. To round out the classroom community, we put students in charge so that they gain a shared ownership of the learning. We also work to promote a literacy community outside of the classroom, which leads to our final principle: partnering with families and caregivers.

## Grounding Principle #5: Partner with Families/Caregivers

Our commitment to creating opportunities for equitable family engagement is an ongoing work in progress. We rely on the wise advice we've received by reading the work of scholars and practitioners whose ideas we've included in the "Why . . . ?" boxes in each chapter. We know it is essential for our students' families and caregivers to clearly see that their funds of knowledge (Moll et al. 1992) are a valued part of the classroom community. To that end, we look for innovative ways to reach out to our students' caregivers and invite them to interact with their child's educational experience in the ways that work best for them. We view family members/caregivers as the experts who have a wealth of information about their child and their child's unique learning styles. By partnering with them, we build a collaborative support system for each of our students, allowing us to meet them where they are and move them forward.

## STAYING ON COURSE: A QUICK BOOK TOUR

With these five grounding principles providing the framework, we've structured this book in a deliberate fashion so that you can easily access ideas when you need them. As we travel in chronological order through the school year, each chapter of the book focuses on a pivotal time in the scope of a year. We begin in Chapter 1 by outlining the deliberate decisions that go into a joyful and engaging first day with readers. We follow this up in Chapter 2 by considering the importance of taking the first few weeks of school to cement a foundation that will provide ongoing support to readers. Then, in Chapter 3, we tackle some dilemmas and decisions that seem to bubble up during the first semester. Chapter 4 is where we channel the after-winter-break energy and use it to propel us into the second semester. Finally, in Chapter 5, we spring toward the end of the school year and bring ideas full circle as we intentionally prepare readers for a literate life beyond the confines of the school year. Within each chapter we've designed features that will help you plan instruction, learn from varied voices in the education field, engage in professional conversations, and reflect on the impact your instructional decisions are having on your students' reading growth. These features include:

### PDCast Preview

Because we are aware of the realities of a teaching day, we wanted to offer a companion to this book that you can access while on the go. So, for each chapter, we offer an accompanying PDCast. Listen in to hear what's bringing us joy, to learn about our process for tackling dilemmas and making decisions at that particular point in the school year, and, of course, to discover a few books that might interest your readers. Learn while you commute, walk, meal-prep, or do your laundry!

A preview in each chapter will detail what we discuss in the PDCast, so if any of the ideas spark your interest, head over to that particular episode in the "A Year for the Books" PDCast collection to hear a little more.

For transcripts of all the PDcasts included in this book as well as links to your favorite podcast platforms, go to Routledge.com and search for *A Year for the Books.*

## Why . . . ?

We rely on literacy mentors and educational research to guide our decisions and practices. Therefore, for the five grounding principles in each chapter, we include a "Why . . . ?" section that provides a rationale for the importance of incorporating that guiding principle at that particular point in the school year. For more information, flip to the bibliography to see the full references. Use those books, articles, and blog posts to support your decision-making, further your professional learning, or provide food for thought during a team meeting or whole-school discussion.

## Try This! Ideas for Elementary and Middle School Readers

The ten "Try This!" sections in each chapter feature classroom-tested strategies that you can implement right away and revisit down the road. For each of the five grounding principles, we offer two "Try This!" recommendations. The first "Try This!" offering in each section is a bit more focused on supporting elementary-age readers, and the second "Try This!" suggestion is geared toward middle school readers. To help you identify which is which, the "Try This!" sections are designated by one of these two icons:

 **Ideas for Elementary Grade Readers**

 **Ideas for Middle School Readers**

However, we want to be crystal clear that most of these ideas will work as is (or are easily modified) for *any* grade level. That means you have fifty ideas to pick and choose from when deciding what will work best for your community of readers. As we have learned from years of conversations about the strategies we use when teaching readers from the early elementary grades to middle school, there are more similarities than differences!

Finally, each "Try This!" section follows a predictable three-part format to guide you in integrating our suggestions into your unique learning context:

- **Gather:** The information in the "Gather" section will help you to prepare by answering some or all of the following questions:
  - What materials will you need?
  - Are there any informal observations that might help guide your decisions?

- What ideas or questions should you ponder to prepare on your own or in a professional learning community (PLC)?
- Which texts might work well for this literacy learning experience?

■ **Get Started:** The procedure in the "Get Started" portion will provide helpful details on how to implement this literacy learning experience with the students in your classroom.

■ **Where This Might Lead:** This is our favorite section, as it prompts you to consider how each literacy learning experience might be enhanced or expanded. Use the suggestions you find here as a jumping-off point to modify and extend the experience for your own group of readers.

## Keep It Simple

With everything that falls on a teacher's plate each day, we believe in the power of keeping it simple. So, we wrap up each grounding-principle section with a suggestion of how to do just that. The insights found here are not grade specific, and we encourage you to flip directly to this feature if you are ever feeling overwhelmed with trying to "do it all."

## Back Pocket Wisdom

You know that moment when you walk into another teacher's class-room and observe something small they are doing that will make your teaching life ten times easier? We've been collecting those moments over the years and share them with you in a feature we call "Back Pocket Wisdom."

## TIY: Try It Yourself!

We've often left a professional learning experience with our wheels turning—energized and ready to rethink a particular aspect of our literacy instruction. Then the reality of our busy schedule sets in, and the ideas stay right where we put them, in our notebook or saved in a Google Doc. We've discovered, from experience, that unless you take the time to process what you've heard, either on your own or with a colleague, new learning tends to get lost in the school-year shuffle. To support you in implementing the strategies you've found compel-ling, we've included a "TIY—Try It Yourself" feature to conclude each chapter. This feature is especially helpful if you're reading this book as part of a book study with colleagues. As with all of the ideas we've packed into this book, use this feature in a way that makes the most sense for you and your readers.

The book's yearlong structure and easy-to-follow layout are designed to support you as you dip in and out of these pages throughout the year. But we know that the decision-making begins long before the students arrive. With that in mind, before you dive into Chapter 1 and the first day of school, we invite you to take a moment and ponder some foundational ideas as you get started.

## LET'S GET STARTED: BEFORE SCHOOL BEGINS

It's the week before school begins. We walk into Katie's classroom to find everything in the middle of the room—tables, books, shelves. Even her twinkly lights have been removed from the ceiling (yes, Katie's school allows mood lighting) (see Figure I.3). Knowing they were painting over the summer, Katie was prepared for the chaos, but it's still a shock. Whether you're setting up your classroom for the first time, moving down the hall, or just looking to update, getting started is always the most challenging part. Because both of us rely on checklists to help us stay on track, we've included a sample checklist of ideas to ponder and materials to prepare before your students arrive on the first day (see Figure I.4 on the following pages). As you read through it, notice how the checklist parallels the grounding principles we introduced earlier as the structural foundation for each of the coming chapters. For further ideas, many of the items on this checklist are also detailed in the chapters that follow.

FIGURE I.3
*It's the week before school starts, and everything is in the middle of the room.*

FIGURE I.4

| PONDER AND PREPARE PRIOR TO DAY ONE | |
| --- | --- |
| **Grounding Principle** | **Try This!** |
| Launch and sustain supported independent reading | ▪ Organize and/or freshen up your classroom library. Donate or discard outdated and tattered texts. Examine your texts with a critical eye to make sure they represent a variety of voices and do not contain any harmful stereotypes or misrepresentations of individuals or groups of people.<br>▪ Showcase a few books you think your students will enjoy.<br>▪ Display quotes from varied authors, leaders, or influencers.<br>▪ Place a book or stack of books at each student's place to generate discussion about reading at meet-and-greet or on the first day. |
| Define and communicate beliefs | ▪ Think about what the physical layout of your classroom communicates to students who will spend a year there. Will they see themselves and the rich variety of people in the world represented in the images and books in the classroom? Can they identify what is important to you as a teacher?<br>▪ View the classroom from a student perspective. Sit where they will be sitting. Make sure materials are accessible at their height level (this is especially important for young learners). Consider class size and how easily students will be able to navigate the spaces.<br>▪ Leave plenty of blank wall space for student-created or co-created artifacts of learning. |
| Establish and maintain literacy routines | **Classroom Library**<br>▪ Design a system for book checkout and return to provide ongoing book access for all students.<br>▪ Make a "book hospital" basket for damaged books.<br>▪ Label all books in some way to indicate they are from your classroom book collection (especially important when students switch classrooms).<br>**Literacy Routines**<br>▪ Create areas or flexible spaces for:<br>  • Independent reading and learning<br>  • Read-aloud<br>  • Whole-group demonstrations and modeling<br>  • Partner and small-group work<br>  • Literacy centers or stations |

## PONDER AND PREPARE PRIOR TO DAY ONE

| Grounding Principle | Try This! |
|---|---|
| <br>Cultivate community | ■ Display a few artifacts from previous years' students, like short pieces of writing, words of advice, book recommendations, and so on.<br>■ Ask the previous year's teachers how to pronounce students' names and if any child prefers a particular nickname. (It's essential that you confirm with students both the correct pronunciation and any nicknames, as their name preferences may have changed over the summer.)<br>■ Arrange seating or designate spaces so that students can converse with one another. |
| <br>Partner with families/caregivers | ■ Introduce yourself to families and caregivers. (It's helpful to get this done before the bustle of the first week.)<br>■ Invite families/caregivers to introduce their child in a way that works best for them by providing options like a Google Forms survey, video recording platform, paper-and-pencil survey, and so on.<br>■ Talk with colleagues about the most effective ways they've found to engage in ongoing communication with caregivers. We've had success setting up a safe, online information-sharing platform like RemindApp or an easy-to-use social media account to keep families informed of classroom happenings. If you do this, be sure to follow your school system's technology guidelines and provide easily accessible tutorials for caregivers. |

## MAKE EVERY DECISION COUNT

So, there you have it: our grounding principles, the layout of the book, and a few ideas to ponder before school even begins. Now it's time to lace up your hiking boots and step onto the trail. From the first day to the last, we'll be cheering for you as you stroll alongside your community of readers. We appreciate you trusting us to accompany you on the journey to support independent readers and collaborate with your students to create a vibrant literacy community. Together, let's make every decision count!

**Back-Pocket Wisdom: Ponder and Prepare Prior to Day One**

■ Create anecdotal notes sheet to record initial observations.

■ Devise a method for organizing meeting notes and your to-do list. We found that keeping one small notebook for both works well and helps us keep track of tasks that need to be completed. We especially love tearing out the pages of the to-do's once they're completed!

## CHAPTER 1

# Make the Most of Your First Day

*Welcome community members with reading interactions that spark joy.*

Love to talk about teaching? Join us to think through how we prepare for the first day of school. In Episode One, we share the deliberate decisions that go into a joyful and engaging first day in a literacy classroom, ponder the messages we want to send to students, and problem-solve for strategies to support learners who need additional attention on day one.

*Listen to "A Year for the Books" PDCast Episode One here.*

The first day. Anticipation. Excitement. A flutter of butterflies. Whether you are new to the profession or reflecting back over decades of first days, we find that the start of school stirs up similar thoughts and emotions. In the back of our minds and the corners of our classrooms, there are always a few summer projects that didn't get checked off the list. And what about those crazy school dreams where we're late or can't find our classroom? With all of this swirling in our brains, we somehow manage to make sure everything is prepared just so. Then the bell rings and the kids come streaming through the hallways. Like us, they're filled with nervous enthusiasm. How do you harness this first-day energy and use it to your advantage as you shine the spotlight on books and reading? To answer this question, we'll share some insights and ideas you might experiment with on the first day of school to launch your learners into a year of student-centered literacy experiences. Let's start by chatting about how to kick off supported independent reading.

## WELCOME READING COMMUNITY MEMBERS

First impressions are important. We strive to welcome learners into our reading community with a clear purpose in mind—creating simple yet meaningful literacy experiences where they can gather some seed ideas about what it means to be a reader. We also know the reality of the first day. From the time students arrive until the dismissal bell rings, time goes whizzing by. So, how do you achieve this goal within the frenetic energy of the first day of school? You plan reading interactions that will spark enthusiasm, interest, and joy.

### Why Launch Supported Independent Reading on the First Day?

- Introducing independent reading on the first day of school provides students with immediate access to the books in your classroom collection and the learning opportunities those books provide, conveying to learners that they will have autonomy and ownership over their reading journey (Hunter 2012).

- By talking about books, reading, and reading habits on the first day of school, you communicate to students that they are entering a reading environment (Francois 2015).

### Try This!
### Start with Small-Group Book Bins

When teachers come to observe Maria as she is teaching, one question she commonly hears is, "How do you get your kids started with supported independent reading?" To answer that question, Maria refers to the professional book that she leaned on when she began dabbling with reading workshop—*Reading with Meaning* (Miller 2002). In her book, Debbie Miller suggests starting the year with small-group book bins before transitioning to individual book boxes. Maria finds this to be the most successful way to launch independent reading for elementary school readers.

FIGURE 1.1
*Start the year with small-group book bins.*

Year after year, as children enjoy the books in the bins, she observes that starting out with small-group book bins has the following benefits:

- Provides easy access to texts in a manageable way
- Familiarizes readers with the books in the classroom library
- Sparks authentic, book-related conversations
- Presents students with opportunities to practice sharing and compromising when two children want to read the same book
- Gives teachers time to observe learners interacting with books and with their peers

## GATHER

If this sounds like something you might be interested in trying in your classroom, decide how many bins you will need for your seating arrangement. We would suggest one per table or group. So if you have six tables or groups, you'll need six bins. If you are going to use plastic milk crates, look for the kind with a solid piece of plastic on the bottom, as it will prevent wear and tear on your books. Stock the bins with a variety of books that will be accessible and interesting to the learners in your classroom. Be mindful to include books that reflect the lived experiences of your learners and books that offer readers a glimpse into the rich variety of lived experiences of people across the world (Sims Bishop 1990). Stock small-group bins with the types of texts found in Figure 1.2.

FIGURE 1.2

| TEXTS FOR SMALL-GROUP BOOK BINS | |
|---|---|
| **Primary-Grade Readers** | **Middle-Grade Readers** |
| Popular easy-reader series | Short texts like magazine articles, collections of short biographies, "browsable nonfiction" with short blocks of text like the Dorling Kindersley (DK) Eyewitness series (Stewart and Correia 2021), and so on. |
| Popular picture book series | Picture books that build background for upcoming curricular units |
| Concept books (alphabet, colors, numbers, shapes) | Short-story collections |
| Wordless and nearly wordless books | Poetry anthologies |

(continued on next page)

FIGURE 1.2 (continued)

| TEXTS FOR SMALL-GROUP BOOK BINS | |
| --- | --- |
| **Primary-Grade Readers** | **Middle-Grade Readers** |
| High-interest nonfiction books | Curriculum-related nonfiction books |
| Graphic-format texts | Graphic novels |

## GET STARTED

To introduce the small-group bins, bring a bin to an area where all the children can see. State your purpose by saying something like, "I've collected books in these bins that I thought you might enjoy reading." Show a few titles, then add, "As I get to know you as readers, you can help me add and change the books. We'll also rotate the bins so that everyone gets a chance to read the books in each bin." Depending on the age and experience of your readers, you might want to continue with a quick demonstration on different ways to read a book. Begin by posing a question such as this: "Let's say you can't read all of the words in the book yet. What could you do?" Based on student responses, you might share and demonstrate one of the following ways to read a book:

- Tell the story they see in the pictures.
- Retell a familiar story: "Oh, look! I've heard this story before. I know how it goes, so I'll tell it to myself."
- Read the familiar words.
- Learn from images and nonfiction text features like maps and diagrams.

In the days that follow, you can show them the other ways. The key here is to keep your introduction brief so that students have time to read. As students read the texts in the small-group bins in the ways that work best for them, trust that their book interactions will help them do the following:

- Engage in joyful reading
- Develop print concepts
- Raise awareness of reading preferences
- Strengthen story sense
- Enhance background knowledge
- Participate in conversations
- Expand oral language
- Broaden vocabulary knowledge

The benefit of familiarizing readers with small-group book bins right from the start is that you can pull out the bins throughout the day and in the upcoming weeks to reinforce the message that reading is an enjoyable way to pass the time.

## WHERE THIS MIGHT LEAD

Observe students' interactions with the books and use what you learn to plan responsive mini-lessons. When you notice a particular child engaging in a reading behavior or positive social interaction, jot down a note for yourself. Invite that child to demonstrate what you saw them do or say as they co-teach a mini-lesson with you. Make a deliberate effort to select students who may need an extra boost of confidence. These are helpful mini-lessons:

- The care and keeping of books
- Strategies for selecting the best books
- How to stick with a book from the beginning to the end
- What to do if two children want to read the same book
- Reasons to reread a book

Keep track of the lessons, along with the co-teacher's name, so that students can reach out to an "expert" when they need some help.

### Try This! Pose a Book Title Challenge

▶ During her first few years of teaching, Katie and her students took part in Book Speed Dating (see page 49 in Chapter 2) on the first day of school. Book Speed Dating worked well; however, Katie wanted to branch out and try something a bit different. Her goals for the first day are for students to engage in a learning experience where they collaborate with their class-mates, discuss books and reading, and apply the liter-acy skills that they will be using all year. To meet these goals within a fifty-minute class period, she invented the Book Title Challenge. This challenge invites read-ers to arrange words from book titles in innovative ways to create their own poem or story.

### GATHER

Earlier in the chapter, Maria suggested placing small-group book bins around the room. Not only does this immediately generate discussion around books, but it is

**Back Pocket Wisdom: Small-Group Book Bins**

To keep your small-group book bins fresh in the coming days and weeks . . .

- Rotate the bins from one group to the next every few days.

- Remove books that aren't of interest to your students.

- Add recent read-aloud favorites to the bins.

- Task students with adding their preferred books from the classroom or school library.

- Assign a junior librarian to straighten up the bins at the end of each day.

FIGURE 1.3

*Gather stacks of books for the Book Title Challenge.*

also the perfect setup for the Book Title Challenge. If you choose not to use small-group bins, perhaps consider Katie's method. She prepares for the Book Title Challenge by placing a stack of eight books all from the same genre on each pair or group of desks. However, you could easily facilitate this first-day experience using a stack of books from different genres as well. If you're in need of book suggestions or additional titles to add to your stacks, reach out to your school librarian, public librarian, or PLC members.

## GET STARTED

Once the book stacks are in place and students are in the room, display the directions that appear in Figure 1.4 and explain that their task is to create a poem or story using words from the book titles. To differentiate for your range of learners, the directions offer variations on the challenge, from least difficult to most complex. As soon as students understand the instructions, let them get to work! Circulate among the groups to observe how learners interact with their classmates, to find out if they have read any of the books, and to chat about the books you've enjoyed from each stack.

---

### Book Title Challenge

Choose a challenge with your group:

Write a poem or a story:

A.   Using ONE word from every book title in your stack and any other words you like

B.   Using EVERY word from the titles of the books in your stack and any other words you like

C.   Using EVERY word from the titles of the books in your stack and NO OTHER words

*Bonus: Create a poem or story that fits within the genre of books that your stack represents.*

---

FIGURE 1.4

*Sample directions for the Book Title Challenge.*

## WHERE THIS MIGHT LEAD

To conclude the challenge, either stop after a designated amount of time or simply observe when students seem to be wrapping up. Then invite groups to share some or all of the writing they've composed and celebrate their creativity. Depending on your school's schedule, composing and a quick share time may be all you can squeeze into one class period (all of Katie's classes only had a few minutes to share). But if you find yourself with extra time, share some informal teacher book talks about the titles in the stack that sparked interest or facilitate student book talks about the ones they've already read and would recommend. If you chose to do a genre-based Book Title Challenge, you can revisit the activity later in the year using a different genre.

### Keep It Simple: Gradually Add Books to Your Classroom Library

A classroom library brimming with engaging books is a necessity for creating a vibrant reading community. Sadly, very few school systems provide teachers with adequate funding to make this vision a reality. Figure 1.6 on the following page illustrates a few ideas to help you gradually fill your classroom with books in economical ways. A smart way to keep your library fresh is to rotate books in and out as the year progresses. You can do this in a variety of ways. Start by looking at your curriculum. What are some of the main topics your students will be studying? Sort books by these categories and store them until the time comes. Alternatively, you can rotate books in and out by seasons. If book storage is an issue, we've found that plastic milk crates that double as seats work well (see Figure 1.5).

FIGURE 1.5
*This handy milk crate seat doubles as book storage.*

As you are stocking your shelves, think about the messages the books communicate. We strive to create an inclusive reading experience for all students, and so we aim to fill our shelves with texts that highlight the beauty and accomplishments of folks from all walks of life. As you add books to your collection, seek out texts that accurately represent and/or are created by people from marginalized and underrepresented groups. Think critically about books you already have and weed out the ones that contain harmful stereotypes or inaccurate representations

*Access ILA classroom library equity audit here*

of groups of people. Books like these can cause harm to students. It is helpful to download and consult a classroom library equity audit like the ones that are available from the International Literacy Association or the trade book publisher Lee and Low.

FIGURE 1.6

### FILL YOUR BOOKSHELVES

Join your local public library branch or the branch in your school community. Many public libraries have online systems where you can order the books you want and they'll have them waiting. Often they also have an increased book limit for teachers. In your classroom, designate a separate spot for library books so that they don't get mixed up with your book collection.

Search for organizations that offer book grants. Collaborate with colleagues to apply for grants and complete the necessary paperwork.

Find a used-book store that will give you in-store credit for books. Then bring in all of your older or unread books and use the store credit to freshen up your shelves.

Set up an account with a company that offers book orders for students and use the bonus points or rewards you earn from student orders to purchase books for your classroom.

Send an email to community members asking them to donate any books they have at home that are no longer being read.

Reallocate unused books. If your school has a book room or book closet, discuss with your colleagues if there are any books from the shared collection that are not being used and would be better distributed among teacher's classrooms.

Engage in a book swap. If you have a lot of mystery books and your neighbor has a large collection of realistic fiction, ask if they would be interested in a book swap. To do this, select some books your students have already read and place them in a bin. Label the bin and each of the books with your name (e.g., "Books on Loan from Ms. Walther's Classroom"). The other teacher does the same. Swap bins, keep the books in your room for a few weeks, and then return them.

Develop a relationship with your local independent bookstore. Sometimes they receive advance reader copies (ARCs) that they will donate to classrooms. Once these books are in your library, keep an eye out for class favorites so you can include the final, published editions in your library.

If you attend a local, state, or national literacy conference, plan ahead. On the last day, vendors will often sell books at a reduced rate or give away books for free.

## COMMUNICATE BELIEFS THROUGH THE PHYSICAL LAYOUT OF YOUR CLASSROOM

Setting up a classroom for the beginning of the year is one of our favorite back-to-school activities. We love working together to problem-solve and come up with new ideas each year. The setup process is an excellent time for professional conversations and learning. Whether working alone or in collaboration as you're sliding furniture around and organizing books, you get the opportunity to reflect on and discuss how you want students to feel when they enter your room and how they can use the materials most effectively to become literate citizens. While these thoughts and conversations often lead to build-

**FIGURE 1.7**
*A classroom library is essential for creating a vibrant reading community.*

ing a contraption to fit a small space or moving the same table back and forth several times, they also support you in creating a classroom environment that communicates your beliefs to anyone who walks through the door.

When we use the term *beliefs* throughout this book, we're referring to our philosophy or mindset of what it means to teach and learn alongside a community of readers.

**FIGURE 1.8**
*Collaborating to solve dilemmas and make decisions about classroom layout is valuable professional learning.*

### How Does the Physical Layout of Your Classroom Communicate Your Beliefs?

■ As students walk into our classroom for the first time, they soak in the visual information they see. Essentially, they are "reading the room." By intentionally setting up the classroom in a way that showcases reading as important and valuable, students will immediately understand the core values of the classroom (Gallagher and Kittle 2018).

■ Besides understanding the importance of reading, learners are also getting a sense of the tone of your classroom when they see the layout. We want to make sure this tone is welcoming, inclusive, and safe (NCTE Committee Against Racism and Bias in the Teaching of English 2018).

### Try This! Showcase Books Around Your Room

For years, Maria's classroom library was housed in one corner of her classroom. Why? Because that is how it appeared in the professional books she was reading and in her colleagues' classrooms. After a while, she began to notice that having all the books in one place not only caused a traffic flow problem but also failed to communicate her belief that books permeate the school day. So she began to experiment with spreading books around the room: a bin here, a shelf there, a basket in the corner. Slowly her classroom became a "library classroom" rather than a classroom with a library in the corner. But it wasn't until a speaker at a conference asked the audience to think about the first item students saw when they looked in your room that she realized her small mistake. When she went back to her classroom and looked, she found that the first things her students saw were the garbage can and recycling bin. That aha moment led to some furniture rearranging, and from that day forward, books are always prominently showcased around her room—especially right by the door.

FIGURE 1.9

*Think about what students see as they walk in the door—is it books?*

### GATHER

Find the furniture or supplies you will need to display books around your classroom and near the door. The options could include:

- Low-cost bookshelves from discount stores or garage sales. You can also make shelves using two milk crates and a board.
- Bins, baskets, and other assorted containers. Try not to overload bins—it makes them too heavy to carry from place to place.
- Easels or book stands.
- Rain gutters or spice racks attached to the wall.
- Discarded display cases from stores that are going out of business.
- A-frame or tiered book shelves, with the books' front covers facing forward.
- Photocopies of book covers that represent varied voices and reflect diverse experiences, to post on your door.

### GET STARTED

Walk into your teaching space from the hallway. Notice what stands out. Think about the message the physical arrangement of your classroom furniture communicates. Consider ways that you could creatively display books around your

FIGURE 1.10
*Add book bins
to literacy centers.*

FIGURE 1.11
*Creatively use the space you have
to spread books around your room.*

room and near the door. In Figure 1.10 you can see how Maria stocks her literacy centers with book bins, and in Figure 1.11 Katie uses the space underneath her whiteboard to house both supplies and novels. When you break free from the "classroom library in the corner" mentality, you'll find nooks and crannies all over your classroom that are perfect for a collection of books.

## WHERE THIS MIGHT LEAD

Think about other places in your teaching space, hallway, school, or community where you and your colleagues could showcase books from a wide range of creators.

- Teachers post the books they are reading or have completed on or outside their classroom door.

- Administrators carry a book under their arm while walking around the building (Miller and Sharp 2018).

- Create a bulletin board or space to highlight soon-to-be-published books.

- Set up a StoryWalk® outside your school.

- If your school has a monitor or other display device near the front entrance, add popular books to the rotating pictures.

**Back Pocket Wisdom:
Showcasing Books**

Here are ways to showcase books on the first day:

- Display the books you plan to read aloud in a prominent place.

- Place a book or a book stack at each child's spot.

- At the end of the day, view a book trailer for an upcoming read-aloud.

- Include pictures of what you are reading or upcoming whole-class reads on your classroom website or a virtual landing page.
- Change your email signature to include what you are currently reading.

### Try This! Display Powerful Quotes from Thought Leaders

▶ White, cisgender women make up more than 70 percent of teachers, as evidenced by the data collected by the National Center for Education Statistics during the 2017-2018 school year: more than 76 percent of teachers surveyed identified as white, and 79.1 percent of teachers surveyed identified as female (Irwin et al. 2022). We are two of the teachers within that 70-plus percent. Therefore, we are keenly aware that many students who walk into our schools and classrooms do not see themselves represented in the educators with whom they spend their days. If they are middle schoolers, it is likely that they have experienced this lack of representation for years. Consider this fact when critiquing the physical layout of your classroom, and ensure that underrepresented groups of the global majority are visible in the posters, images, books, and quotes that are displayed around the room (Muhammad 2020). Here we'll focus on one small step toward broadening representation—curating a collection of powerful quotations.

### GATHER

Research and compile wise words about books, reading, and literacy in general from some of your students' favorite authors, leaders in literacy, historical figures, and present-day influencers. Be sure that the majority of the quotes are from people from underrepresented communities. The website Goodreads is an excellent place to find quotations from books.

### GET STARTED

Turn these quotes into mini-posters by creating a slide deck that includes a photograph of the author, leader, or influencer along with their exact words. Place each person's information on its own slide. Print and display the posters around your classroom (see Figure 1.12).

FIGURE 1.12

*Curate a collection of powerful quotations by people from underrepresented and marginalized communities.*

## WHERE THIS MIGHT LEAD

While introducing herself to her students by sharing her background and interests, Katie mentioned that she loves the musical *Hamilton*. She then asked them if they could find some of the hidden *Hamilton* references around their classroom. She was shocked by how many students immediately pointed to the small poster, somewhat hidden underneath the whiteboard, with a quote from Lin-Manuel Miranda, the creator of *Hamilton*. Clearly, without any explicit mention or discussion, students had already noticed these posters around the classroom. This underscores the importance of being intentional when deciding what to hang on your classroom walls. To extend students' learning beyond noticing the quotations, do a rotation activity where small groups of students dive deeper into a quote or two and think about the meaning. Follow this up by providing time for interested students to curate their own literacy-related mini-posters containing inspiring quotes to add to the classroom collection.

### Keep It Simple: Overplan, Prioritize, and Stay Flexible

Planning for the first day typically occurs after you've had some time away from school. Because of this, we've found that our day-one plans are usually a little ambitious. Somehow, we forget how long everything takes. Our advice is: Be prepared by planning enough learning experiences for a full day or period, but stay flexible because chances are that some of those experiences could get spread over the next few days. Here are some tips we've found helpful when sketching out our first day with students:

- Collaborate with colleagues. Make a menu of first-day activities from which each of you can choose. Record your ideas in a shared document so that you can add notes as you reflect on and brainstorm ways to improve them for the coming years.

- Critique your planned activities. Ask yourself, "Does this literacy activity reflect my beliefs about student learning?"

- Have materials at your fingertips. Make a few extra copies of any student materials just in case you get a new student or two at the last minute.

- Prioritize the learning experiences you want to share—do them early in the day or period.

- Be prepared to change your plans in response to your students' needs.

## KICK OFF ROUTINES

Why wait until the second day, second week, or beyond to launch your literacy routines? Both of us have had success engaging in the same routines on day one that we plan to continue throughout the year. Does the first-day version of the practice look like it will in October or April? No. But we view this like a sneak preview or snippet of what's to come. In the elementary grades, Maria tries to squeeze in as many routine parts of the day as possible (see Figure 1.13). For instance, you can weave social-emotional learning (SEL) activities into your first-day literacy routines by planning learning experiences where students work with partners or in small groups. Then, as opportunities arise, coach students on social skills such as turn taking, fair play, and using kind words and actions. In middle school, Katie keeps her first-day agenda simple (see Figure 1.14) to allow plenty of time for purposeful talk. She focuses her first-day energy on getting to know her learners while they explore books by weaving in routines such as turn-and-talk or collaborative group work. By doing this, you get an overall sense of each class period's group dynamics so that you can begin to adjust and problem-solve accordingly. Whatever age student you are working with, think about how you can plan your first day to most closely match what students will see in the days and weeks to come.

FIGURE 1.13

### First Day of First-Grade Schedule

Morning message, shared reading of poem, read-aloud experience (see page 32)

Brain Break: Play a name game

Reading Workshop: Introduce small-group book bins (see page 14)

Lunch/recess

Read-aloud experience

Writing Workshop: Introduce book making

Recess

Word Study: Letter and word exploration

Special classes

Math Workshop: Math manipulative exploration

FIGURE 1.14

## First Day of Seventh-Grade Agenda

| What? | I can get to know my classmates as readers |
|---|---|
| Why? | To begin creating a reading community |
| How? | • Introduction Circle (see page 35)<br>• Book Title Challenge (see page 17)<br>• Book Title Challenge Sharing |

### Try This! Post a Visual Schedule

"When is it time for lunch?" "Do we have P.E. today?" "Is it snack time yet?" We're guessing you've heard similar questions in your classroom. Starting on the first day, instead of answering these questions ourselves, we point to resources in our classroom that will help learners find their own answers. One of these resources is a visual schedule—in other words, a schedule with key words and recognizable icons that is posted in an easy-to-access location. Although it seems like a simple solution, posting a visual schedule can make your day run more smoothly by helping both you and your students stay on track. In addition, reviewing your schedule at the beginning of the day and revisiting it throughout the day is supportive for those students who are still learning how to adjust to transitions.

### GATHER

Create schedule cards with visual icons to post on the board or display electronically (see Figure 1.15 on the following page). In addition to the whole-class cards, make a set or two of smaller cards for individuals who may benefit from manipulating their own schedule. To sneak in a little math instruction and enhance the schedule pictured in Figure 1.15, pair the schedule with cards featuring a clock that shows the analog time for key events like lunch, special classes, and dismissal.

### Why Kick Off Routines?

■ When we begin the year by "implementing regular rituals and routines," we foster a safe and predictable learning environment where "students know what to expect from their teachers and their day" (Souers and Hall 2016, 104). By starting these routines on day one, learners will feel more at ease stepping into the classroom on day two because they have an overall sense of the rhythm of their day.

■ Introducing students to daily routines within the first day shows learners that the reading routines in the classroom will be important and "save[s] management time" as students become familiar with the routines (Gallagher and Kittle 2018, 26).

FIGURE 1.15

*Post and review a visual schedule.*

## GET STARTED

As you go through the first day together, introduce each literacy routine by giving a kid-friendly rationale and quick description. Once students are engaged, don't let any routine go on too long. Leave them wanting more. Say something like, "Kids, I have some bad news. I can see you are really enjoying your books, but reading time is over for today. Good news! We'll have it again tomorrow." Throughout the day, review the schedule periodically, inviting children to say "Check!" when activities have been completed. This procedure gives them a sense of accomplishment and an understanding of where they are in the sequence of their day. It is also wise to point out that sometimes you might run out of time for scheduled activities, but you will try to squeeze them in the next day. When saying this, Maria always assures her first graders that they will never run out of time for lunch, special classes, or dismissal. This helps to ease some anxiety!

## WHERE THIS MIGHT LEAD

When students know that they can count on seeing a visual schedule each day, it increases their independence because they are able to answer their "when is it time for" questions with a quick glance. You can facilitate this agency by replying to their questions with this type of response: "Reeya, can you check the schedule and let us know what we still have to do before we eat lunch?" As the year progresses, offer students the opportunity (one student per week) to pick their favorite learning activity (not recess, lunch, or special classes) and do that twice on Fridays or another day that works with your plans. This practice gives you insights into students' preferred learning activities. In addition, it puts the students in charge of the decision-making. When reviewing the schedule on each child's special day, say something like, "Today we're doing Chayce's readers' workshop. He's going to get you started by showing you something he discovered in his book."

### Try This! Notice and Celebrate Student Agency and Independence

As you step into routines, purposefully make small shifts in the feedback phrases you share with students to spotlight their agency and independence. When you do this, you move from spending your first day going over a laundry list of agreements, expectations, or values to communicating your beliefs through your words and actions. This is beneficial for all learners but is particularly important if your students see multiple teachers in one day because they've probably heard similar expectations at least one other time. In addition, we believe inviting students to experience the routines for a few days can provide necessary context when you work together to co-create shared agreements about those routines. In short, it is unnecessary to state all of your classroom beliefs and expectations on day one; noticing and naming when students are positively contributing to the learning community can easily establish routines with minimal effort (Johnston 2004).

## GATHER

To align your feedback with the beliefs you want to infuse within your classroom teaching, start by listing your guiding principles in one column of a T-chart. Then write down specific phrases that would clearly reinforce each belief (see Figure 1.16). We've found it's helpful to keep these feedback phrases handy on a clipboard or a sticky note attached to our laptop as a constant reminder of the language we want to use to promote students' agency.

FIGURE 1.16

### PHRASES TO CELEBRATE STUDENT AGENCY

| Our Beliefs About Teaching and Learning | Feedback Phrases |
|---|---|
| We believe everyone is a reader. | ■ I noticed that this group of readers is . . .<br>■ [Student's name] is modeling the reading skill of . . . |
| We believe that reading feeds our hearts and minds. | ■ I see you that can't stop reading that book! Great news. We're going to have time to read almost every day.<br>■ I can tell by the look on your face that you really like that book. What makes it special to you?<br>■ It looks like you're enjoying that nonfiction book about _____. Did you learn anything new? |
| We believe everyone's voice should be heard. | ■ Thank you for actively listening as [student's name] spoke.<br>■ [Student's name], I noticed when you shared your thinking you . . .<br>■ Please repeat what you just said a bit louder so everyone can hear you. |

(continued on next page)

FIGURE 1.16 (continued)

| PHRASES TO CELEBRATE STUDENT AGENCY | |
| --- | --- |
| **Our Beliefs About Teaching and Learning** | **Feedback Phrases** |
| We believe that we learn from each other. | ▪ You connected your thinking to your friend's idea. Can anyone add something else?<br><br>▪ [Student's name], that was an example of adding different thinking to the discussion in order to help us consider all perspectives. |
| We believe talking and writing help us understand what we've read. | ▪ I overheard you saying _____. That shows me you really enjoyed/understood/care about that book.<br><br>▪ I saw you jot down some things you wanted to remember in your notebook. That's the same thing I do when I want to remember something I've read! |
| We believe mistakes are learning opportunities. | Note: These are demonstration phrases to share when you've made a mistake. We find it is better to wait until you've built a relationship with students to determine whether you can comment on and appreciate what they've learned from their mistakes.<br><br>▪ Wait! I made a mistake. We're all going to make mistakes this year. Let's see what we can learn from them.<br><br>▪ That didn't go exactly like I wanted it to. I'll try again tomorrow using what I learned today. |

## GET STARTED

Focus your energy on students who are following your school's core pillars and/or demonstrating the reading routines you would like to establish. Get in the habit of using descriptive feedback phrases similar to these:

▪ Isaiah, thank you for patiently waiting to share your noticing about the read-aloud until we found a stopping point. That helps us all stay focused.

▪ Havana, that's a smart idea to write down the name of the book title you are interested in reading so that you remember it for the future.

▪ Maniya and Xavier, I noticed when you did a turn-and-talk, you were facing one another and took turns so each person could share their thinking.

Descriptive feedback phrases signal to the rest of the class the types of routines and behaviors that you will be celebrating in your classroom throughout the year. Keep these small celebrations going throughout the school day (even when your patience wears thin). Remember to refer to your clipboard or sticky note of feedback phrases to help you stay on track and ensure readers are inherently learning about the routines of the literacy community.

## WHERE THIS MIGHT LEAD

Although it takes a lot of mental energy on your part, this positive and specific feedback will go a long way. Each time you point out and explain the impact of an action or the value of a thoughtful comment, you reinforce the underpinnings of your belief-based literacy routines. If you make a conscious effort to notice and celebrate, you will see the following benefits for all the members of your reading community:

- **Promoting students' agency.** Learners develop an "I can do this myself" attitude.

- **Fostering healthy relationships.** Students internalize the values and beliefs, so you spend less time managing behavior and more time for learning alongside readers.

- **Transferring ownership.** When readers frequently hear feedback about the shared agreements, they begin to see their role in maintaining a vibrant learning community.

- **Creating a positive classroom environment.** Positivity is contagious! When you focus your mental energy on noticing agreed-upon behaviors, kids will begin to do the same.

- **Championing an asset-based mindset.** It is healthier and more uplifting to train your brain to look for and celebrate students' approximations rather than zeroing in on what they can't do yet.

As the days and weeks go by, you will have opportunities to be more explicit by demonstrating and practicing classroom routines so that students know exactly what to expect. In future chapters, we'll offer suggestions about how to help students clearly articulate the shared classroom beliefs they have been learning from each other and from the feedback you began offering from the start.

## Keep It Simple: Use Proximity, Music, and Visual Signals Rather than Words

Do you remember what Charlie Brown's teacher, Miss Othmar, sounded like in the *Peanuts* television cartoons? "Wah wah woh wah wah." If you don't remember the cartoon, give it a quick Google. Anyway, as teachers, many of us like to talk, but too much verbal clutter can be overwhelming for students and begin to sound just like Charlie Brown's teacher. When stepping into routines, try to think of other ways to get your message across without words. Some that work well for us include:

- **Proximity.** Circulate around the room, standing near students who need a little extra attention.
- **Music.** Play snippets of songs as transitions from one activity to the next. (Learn more about this in Chapter 3 on page 98.)
- **Visual signals.** Teach students words in American Sign Language or create your own visual signals.
- **Auditory signals.** Curate a collection of soothing sound effects like chimes, falling rain, and the like to play for transitions. Another simple way to create auditory signals is by snapping, clapping, or tapping rhythms for children to join in and imitate.

### GET TO KNOW ONE ANOTHER

After a two-month visit, Aadvik's grandparents left to go back home to India. Lana is trying out for the school play at four o'clock. Emotion-filled events such as these can impact your students' classroom life. With each interaction grounded in caring learning communities, listening hearts, established culturally responsive practices, and trauma-informed care, we develop relationships with students so that they feel comfortable sharing their ups and downs. In the reading realm, knowing students' celebrations and struggles can provide insight into the types of books that will touch their hearts. Along with learning about your students, you also want to make space in your day for students to informally connect with each other so that when they are working with partners or in groups, they are on their way to developing a rapport.

### Why Take the Time to Get to Know One Another?

- When readers feel valued and seen, they become empowered and more connected to the reading work happening in the classroom (Allyn and Morrell 2022).

- Reading communities promote relationships among students. Together, avid book enthusiasts see that reading is useful and enjoyable. Those who haven't yet found the joy in leading a literate life benefit from the consistent positive messages about reading (Miller and Lesesne 2022).

### Try This! Watch and Listen During Read-Aloud Experiences

There is something magical about the first time you read aloud to a new group of students. Perhaps it's the energy and excitement that happens when you gather children together to share book joy. You can learn a lot about your students' personalities if you slow down the pace of the read-aloud experience and make time to notice students' behavior and listen to their comments. Well-chosen books elicit a range of feelings. Watch for these emotions reflected in the faces of your students. The read-aloud setting is also ripe for observing students' ability to focus, interact with their peers, demonstrate listening comprehension, and communicate their thoughts and ideas.

## GATHER

Your opening read-aloud experience sets the stage for many that will follow. Selecting first-day books is something we consider with great care, but we're also mindful that our final decision takes into account the kids in front of us. To do this, gather a preselected first-day book stack, and then gauge the mood of the class before making your final decision. The books in Figure 1.18 are a few you might find in our stack.

FIGURE 1.17
*The read-aloud setting is ideal for observing students.*

FIGURE 1.18

## PICTURE BOOKS IN OUR FIRST-DAY BOOK STACK

| Picture Book | Summary |
| --- | --- |
|  Gibberish (Vo 2022) | Dat (rhymes with *bat*) and Mah have traveled a long way to get to their new home. Before Mah puts him on the school bus, she prepares him by telling him that when people talk it will sound like gibberish. Mah is right—and, in addition to the gibberish, no one says Dat's name correctly. Then Dat meets Julie, who takes the time to communicate with Dat and also learns how to say his name. |
|  Hurry, Little Tortoise, Time for School! (Finison 2022) | It's Little Tortoise's first day of school, so she paints on her racing stripes, grabs her Super Tortoise lunch box, and is on her speedy way: *Plonk-a-plunk, plonk-a-plunk.* First Cheetah races by: *Sha-shoom!* Cheetah is followed by a llama, a group of monkeys, a pangolin (we think!), and a snail. Just as Little Tortoise is nearing the school, Cheetah races by and knocks her over, shell side down. Fortunately, her teacher, Mr. Sloth, is also a slow mover. Together, they arrive just in the nick of time. But a surprise awaits . . . you'll have to read the book to find out! |

(continued on next page)

FIGURE 1.18 (continued)

## PICTURE BOOKS IN OUR FIRST-DAY BOOK STACK

| Picture Book | Summary |
|---|---|
| *Isabel and Her Colores Go to School* (Alessandri 2021) | Isabel prefers speaking *español* to speaking *inglés* and is worried that might be a problem on her first day of school. Isabel feels "small and lost" until a girl named Sarah tries to befriend her. The two have trouble communicating until it is time to color. Isabel draws a picture of herself and Sarah to communicate the idea of friendship, and it works. |
| *This Is a School* (Schu 2022) | A school is a community that grows, celebrates, transforms, and works together. Detail-oriented readers will enjoy choosing a child to follow through the book, like the girl with the green turtle shirt, the boy with the yellow glasses, the girl with pigtails and polka dots, or the boy with the orange shirt. Notice that the girl with the turtle shirt gets to be a turtle in the play. |

### GET STARTED

As you're reading, pause here and there and invite students to share what they notice. To keep comments focused on the book, start by modeling your own. For instance, while reading Young Vo's book *Gibberish* (2022), you might comment, "I notice Dat and his mom are the only characters that are drawn as humans. What do you notice?" As you're engaged in reading, thinking, and talking about the book, notice which children do the following:

- Lean in as if hanging on every word
- Jump into every conversation quickly
- Sit quietly while others talk around them
- Display evidence of comprehension through their facial expressions
- Understand the humor in the book

While children are listening and conversing, try your best to jot down a few notes. Reflect on what you notice to guide future read-aloud conversations.

## WHERE THIS MIGHT LEAD

Think about how you can use the behaviors you observed during your first few read-aloud experiences to demonstrate expected behaviors or as inspiration for a quick mini-lesson or feedback phrase (see Figure 1.19).

FIGURE 1.19

| WHERE FIRST-DAY READ-ALOUD OBSERVATIONS CAN LEAD | |
|---|---|
| **If You Notice Listeners Do This . . .** | **Say This . . .** |
| Lean in as if hanging on every word | I noticed that Madi is always leaning toward me as I'm reading. I can tell she's actively listening. What are other clues that signal that your friend is actively listening? [Possible responses: They look at you, ask questions, nod or smile, and so on.] |
| Jump into every conversation quickly | Sometimes I have an idea that I want to share and it pops right out of my mouth. When this happens during read-aloud, I take away everyone else's thinking time. What are some strategies we can use to stop ourselves from shouting out our thoughts? [Possible responses: raise our hand and wait our turn, listen to two other people's thoughts before sharing our own, notice who isn't talking and ask them what they think, and so on.] |
| Sit quietly while others talk around them | Have you ever been in a group where someone never gets a chance to talk? What can you do when you notice this is happening? [Possible responses: ask the person what they are thinking, say "I'd like to hear what _____ has to say," pause before speaking to give the person a chance to gather their thoughts, and so on.] |
| Display evidence of comprehension through their facial expressions | When I look at Mekhai's face, I can tell he's worried about what might happen next. His facial expressions show me that he's comprehending [or understanding] what's happening in the book. That's why I like to face you while I'm reading, so I can look for signs of comprehension. |
| Understand the humor in the book | Alejandro, I notice that you were laughing during this part. Can you share why you thought it was funny? |

### Try This! Engage in an Introduction Circle

If you teach multiple classes like Katie does, you are well aware of how quickly the class periods fly by. Between altered schedules, mandated activities, and assisting students as they find their classes (and use a combination lock!), there is limited time remaining to fully engage with each learner. In her first years of teaching, Katie always planned to administer a reading interest survey on the first day as a way to get to know learners as readers, but year after year this important activity got pushed to the following days. She finally realized that she should just plan to do the survey later in the week because her students' time was better spent engaging in an Introduction Circle at the beginning of their first class period together.

While calling students' names to take attendance is a practice that is ingrained in many middle school and high school buildings, we know that "mispronouncing students' names, albeit unintentionally, may have lasting effects" (Souto-Manning et al. 2018). So, with the help of her PLC and seventh-grade team, Katie developed a plan to allow students to voice their own names on the first day.

## GATHER

To prepare for the Introduction Circle, print off a list of names so that you can take notes during the circle. Also, determine a space in your classroom where students can all sit or stand in a circle. Katie has students stand around the desks on the edges of the classroom. If this is not feasible, see if you can head out into the hallway or another open space in your building for this quick activity.

## GET STARTED

On the first day, begin each class period with an Introduction Circle where students say their names and share something about themselves. Share the purpose of this welcoming event with an introduction like, "We're doing this so that we can learn a little bit about each other and also hear how to pronounce each other's names correctly. In the future, if someone in our classroom or school is not pronouncing your name correctly, please stop them and take a moment to teach them how to say it the way your family does."

After saying their name, you can either ask students to share something as simple as their favorite snack or invite a more literacy-focused response with one of these prompts:

- Name a book, author, or genre you enjoy.
- Tell us your favorite book that was turned into a movie.
- Would you rather write to entertain others or to inform others?
- Where is your preferred spot to read, write, or think?

Give students a minute or two to think about their response before sharing, and remind students that this is an ideal time to practice the active listening skills they will use all year. Begin the circle by introducing yourself. When you share, if you feel so inclined, include your pronouns in your statement so that other students who feel comfortable can share their pronouns as well. Then go around the circle and begin to get to know your reading community members.

If you notice a student is hesitant or unwilling to share, give them the option to skip and share at the end. If they still don't feel like introducing themselves, find a time to touch base with them to learn the reasons behind their hesitancy.

## WHERE THIS MIGHT LEAD

While the circle is going, take notes of name pronunciation and pronouns. Mark which students you may need to individually ask for clarification on the pronunciation of their name. If students have name pronunciations that take a bit more practice, record a voice memo of the student saying their name so that you can listen and rehearse. When you begin class by encouraging students to introduce themselves, everyone in the classroom is able to start the second day of school with a better knowledge of how to pronounce the names of the members of their new learning community.

### Keep It Simple: Find Doable Ways to Document Your Observations

Both of our "Try This!" examples involve jotting down your observations of students' behaviors and interactions. Keeping a record of your noticings and wonderings sets you up to create a more student-centered, asset-focused learning environment. However, we are well aware that the first day of school is a challenging time to pause and take detailed notes. Therefore, it is helpful to find a quick documentation system that works for you and your learning context. Figure 1.20 has a few options for you to try.

FIGURE 1.20

| A VARIETY OF WAYS TO DOCUMENT OBSERVATIONS | |
|---|---|
| Make an easy-to-use anecdotal note sheet | Create a one-page grid with a box for each student's name along with space to jot down observations. Place the grid on a clipboard with a writing tool attached. |
| Create a classroom diagram | Draw an image of your classroom layout on a sheet of paper. Then take notes on the happenings in the different locations of your classroom. Reflect on how the physical layout of your learning environment impacts students' interactions. |
| Take pictures | Take pictures of students, their work, and/or their peer interactions. Review the photos at the end of the day. Notice their facial expressions, body language, and other indicators of engagement. |
| Video and/or audio record | If students are introducing themselves or sharing, take a video or audio recording to reference later. |
| Enlist help | If you happen to have a support person or other colleague willing to help out, invite them to document anything they notice about your learners. |

## LAUNCH A YEARLONG PARTNERSHIP WITH FAMILIES/CAREGIVERS

In the book *Butterflies on the First Day of School* (Silvestro 2019), Rosie is worried about starting school, but at the end of the story the reader discovers that Rosie's mom has butterflies too. We often talk about the fact that both students and teachers are nervous on the first day of school. But we can't forget another key stakeholder—families/caregivers. Whether their child is starting kindergarten or entering middle school, many caregivers are just as anxious as their learners on the first day. One way to help ease their case of butterflies is by reaching out to caregivers on or before day one. This initial contact can alleviate some stress as they send their children off to a new year of learning.

### Why Launch a Yearlong Partnership with Families/Caregivers?

■ Introducing yourself to families/caregivers early on in the school year helps to build a foundation from which to grow a positive partnership (Mapp, Carver, and Lander 2017).

■ Caregivers have many things to juggle at home, so informing them about classroom routines and schedules early on can help them to feel confident about how they can best support their learners (Serravallo 2020).

### Try This! Gather Insights by Using a Family Questionnaire

One way to ease minds is to open the lines of communication on or before the first day of school. Reaching out to caregivers to learn more about their child sends the message that they have valuable information to share and you want to hear what they have to say. When you make the effort to gather information about your students directly from those who care for them, you honor and learn about their backgrounds. To that end, you can prepare and send a family questionnaire. Knowing that caregivers are busy, aim to ask no more than four or five questions. Keep in mind that you can always send short follow-up surveys later in the year to gather additional information as needed.

## GATHER

Work with your colleagues to compose a few questions that will help you get to know your learners' families/caregivers and show that you want to form a learning partnership. Some questions that have worked well for us include:

- Who are the special people in your child's life?
- What do you enjoy doing together?
- What are your hopes for your child this year?
- What is the best way to communicate with you about your child?
- Share anything you would like me to know about your child's culture and/or traditions.
- What else do you want me to know about your child?

## GET STARTED

Once you've settled on your set of questions, provide the questionnaire in different formats and languages according to the needs of your students' families/caregivers. If you create the questionnaire in Google Forms, it will populate a spreadsheet for organized whole-class viewing. Use what you learn from families/caregivers to spark informal conversations and tailor your book suggestions.

## WHERE THIS CAN LEAD

There is nothing worse than taking the time to complete a survey and wondering whether someone is actually going to read your responses. To alleviate this feeling for families/caregivers, reply with a child-specific email, something like, "Thanks for taking the time to fill out the questionnaire. I read that [child's name] enjoys swimming. I'm a swimmer too. I'm looking forward to learning with your child this year." This quick email is another way to foster the school-to-home connection.

### Try This! Record a Video Introduction

Although elementary school learners may have one classroom teacher, they interact with a variety of school personnel. Certainly, middle schoolers who have different teachers for each subject see even more staff members. Imagine this from a caregiver's point of view: "Mr. Who? What does he teach again?" "Ms. What? What day do you work with her?" Because of this reality, a comment that Katie hears quite often at back-to-school night or during the first round of caregiver-teacher conferences is "I just wanted to come meet you so that I could put a face with a name." Oftentimes simply seeing you in person helps ease family members' beginning-of-the-year jitters. So why not help them put a face with a name right away? One suggestion for doing just that is recording an introductory video to send home to your students' families/caregivers.

## GATHER

Even with all of our recent experience using virtual meeting platforms to communicate, recording a video to share with families/caregivers can still be somewhat nerve-racking. Sketching out an outline or plan makes the filming process go more smoothly. To do this, think about the key information you want to share with families/caregivers before the start of the school year, and then make a list of topics in the order that you want them to appear in the video (see Figure 1.21). Remember that the goal of this video is to give families/caregivers a sense of who you are, so stay focused on introducing yourself! You can share more about your literacy curriculum at a later date.

FIGURE 1.21

| SAMPLE OUTLINE FOR VIDEO INTRODUCTION | |
|---|---|
| Name, grade level, content area | Katie Walther, seventh grade, language arts |
| Background | Grew up in Aurora, Illinois, and now teaches in Aurora, Colorado |
| Hobbies/interests | Loves to read and spend time outdoors (hike, walk, bike, and so on) |
| Education | Loyola University Chicago (undergrad) and University of Colorado Denver (graduate) |
| Quick classroom tour | Bookshelves, literacy notebook spot, flexible seating, and so on |
| Contact info | Email, school phone |

## GET STARTED

Grab your school computer, phone, or any other filming device and record your introduction, using your outline to keep you on track. Remember, your video does not have to be perfect! In fact, it is better if it isn't overly practiced or produced. Families/caregivers will be happy to learn a bit more about you even if you stumble over your words. Once you have the recording done, post the video to your school's learning platform and email it home to families/caregivers. If it is possible, turn on the caption feature, so that the written words appear along with your spoken ones.

## WHERE THIS CAN LEAD

After you've shared your video, the natural follow-up would be to gather insights about your students' families/caregivers using a family questionnaire, as we suggested earlier in this section. Alternatively, you could offer families/caregivers the option of responding to your video by working together with their child to create a unique introduction of their own (see Figure 1.22). If you are a middle school teacher, collaborate with your grade-level teammates and send home one note so that each family only has to produce one introduction that you can all access. Finally, if you find that your students' families/caregivers respond positively to and enjoy the video format for communication, continue to send video updates throughout the school year.

### Keep It Simple: Use Clear Language, Avoid Educational Jargon

Is your email inbox overflowing? What do you do when you get an email that goes on and on? We usually close it and say to ourselves, "I'll read that one later." It is wise to keep this reaction in mind when communicating with your students' families/caregivers, especially when you begin sending notes home about literacy instruction. We tend to want to share as much as we can about the learning experiences that are happening in our classroom along with ways families/caregivers can follow up at home. But too much information at one time can be overwhelming. If you have a lot you want to share, consider breaking it into sections and sending the information home a little at a time. Review your family communications with these suggestions in mind:

- Get to the point quickly (within the first line or two of an email).

- Organize ideas using bullet points rather than full sentences or paragraphs.

- Use clear, straightforward language. Avoid using terms that are unfamiliar to folks who aren't educators; if you must use educational terms, pair them with a concise definition.

FIGURE 1.22
*Introduction Directions for Families/Caregivers*

Dear Families/Caregivers,

Now that you've learned a bit more about me through my introduction video, I would love to know more about your learner. Please work with your child to create an introduction in a way that works best for your child (video, drawing, photo collage, poem, and so on). If you and your child choose to record a video, try to keep it short (1–2 minutes). Include any information you want me to know. Here are some ideas to get you started. The introduction is due on _____.

- Their name, how to pronounce it, and why it is special
- The names of family members (including any pets)
- Hobbies and interests outside of school
- Goals for this school year

Happy creating!
Your Child's Teacher

- Use images to illustrate ideas whenever possible.
- Create and post quick tutorial videos for frequently asked questions.
- Ensure that the platform you're using offers options for translation.

In this chapter and in those that follow, we will include exemplars of family communications. Use these examples as they appear or, better yet, adapt them to match the needs of the families/caregivers in your learning community.

As much as you plan and prepare for the first day, know that there are usually some hiccups and unexpected occurrences. If this happens, view it as an opportunity to model flexibility, a sense of humor, and the fact that mistakes are learning opportunities. Our first-day motto is "Keep calm and go with the flow!" Speaking of going with the flow, when you turn to Chapter 2, you'll see how the first day flows into the first weeks of school.

# TIY—Try It Yourself!

**Are there any ideas from this chapter or PDCast that would be helpful in your classroom?**

**Which ideas would you modify to better fit your teaching context?**

**Did this chapter or PDCast spark any questions, reflections, or new thinking?**

## CHAPTER 2

# Follow Up During the First Few Weeks

*Nurture the seeds of the routines and practices you sprinkled across day one.*

Love to talk about teaching? Join us to think through the decisions that we make during the first weeks of school. In Episode Two, we map out how to introduce the concept of literacy and authentically incorporate social-emotional learning. Then we problem-solve around the ever-present issue of time—there's just never enough of it! Finally, we end with a few book talks to inspire readers as the school year takes off.

*Listen to "A Year for the Books" PDCast Episode Two here.*

Deep breath. You've made it through the first day with learners. Moving forward, you'll nurture seeds of the routines and practices that you sprinkled across day one. For us, planning the first few weeks of school is always energizing because we can dabble with new ideas that we dreamed up over the summer and implement strategies we discovered during professional learning experiences. As you dig in, you'll begin to see students' knowledge about themselves as readers sprout up here and there. In this chapter and the accompanying PDCast, we offer ideas and strategies designed to help students' reading lives take root while keeping in mind the reality of the hectic initial weeks. Give yourself permission to take it slow and let your students' reactions be your guide. Anticipate that the ideas we share here may stretch beyond the first few weeks; that's okay. You're cultivating a community from the ground up, and that takes time, tenacity, and vulnerability. Try to view any missteps that occur as opportunities to learn and grow professionally.

## FAMILIARIZE READERS WITH THE BOOKS IN YOUR CLASSROOM

Speaking of growing professionally, before you look toward continuing to build familiarity with texts and routines, take a moment to reflect on your students' first-day reading experiences. As you welcomed readers into the classroom, you might have introduced small-group book bins or facilitated a Book Title Challenge. What went well? Based on your students' responses, what are the practices you want to continue? Are there any that need a bit of tweaking? Use the answers to these questions to help guide your continued work with readers. In an interview, Dr. Linda Darling-Hammond reminds us that we need to be responsive to the students in our care because "a single way of doing things is never enough" (Lacina and Griffith 2021, 675). Keep Linda's wise advice in mind as you move forward with independent reading. Be mindful of the fact that it is supportive for learners to review or repeat reading experiences (perhaps in a new way) to better understand the connection between new activities and prior learning. For that reason, revisiting something you did on the first day in a different way reinforces students' grasp of the literacy habits and behaviors you are introducing.

### Why It's Important to Build on the Launch of Supported Independent Reading

- The scientific research is clear: instructional practices that are hallmarks of supported independent reading, such as student choice and process-oriented feedback, kindle motivation and, in turn, improve reading comprehension (Duke, Ward, and Pearson 2021).

- Children need time and practice as they learn how to take care of the books in their classroom. Your classroom library will be the hub of activity during supported independent reading and will work best if you take the time to establish routines for its use, care, and upkeep (Hunter 2012).

### Try This! Explore Different Kinds of Books

A high-priority goal is to get to know each reader in your care so that you can guide them in choosing books that will interest them and support their reading development. While gathering intel on your readers, you'll want to find out which types of texts they enjoy. One way to do this is to create an inquiry experience, where students work in partnerships or small groups to identify the genre of a book. While students are gaining familiarity with genres, a standards-based learning goal, you'll have time to learn more about their reading preferences.

## GATHER

To get the most bang for your buck when selecting mentor texts for your beginning-of-the-year literacy lessons, look for dual-purpose picture books. Our definition of a dual-purpose picture book is one that will grab and keep your students' attention while also including content you can leverage to invite inquiry, make teaching points, or use as a springboard to extend the learning. In other words, dual-purpose books are engaging texts with high entertainment value that will lead to a joyful reading experience. In this particular case, what you're looking for in a dual-purpose mentor text is a book that introduces the concept of genres in a fun and engaging manner. Here are two titles that fit the criteria:

- *This Is Not That Kind of Book* (Healy 2019)
  Summary: Little Red Riding Hood and her pals, capital A and an apple from an alphabet book, set off through the book to try to figure out what type of story it is. Along the way, readers discover books about friendship, joke books, mysteries, and more in this comical introduction to genres.

- *We're in the Wrong Book* (Byrne 2015)
  Summary: Bella and Ben, the characters from *This Book Just Ate My Dog* (2014), get bumped off the page and end up on a journey through books of different genres, including comic books, and fairy tales.

In addition to selecting a read-aloud text, plan the easiest way for pairs of students to gather a small stack of books. Some possibilities include:

- Learners self-select two or three books from the small-group book bins.

- You assemble stacks of books representing various genres and learners pick two or three books, each from a different genre stack. To help students easily differentiate among genres, we would suggest that stacks include the following types of books:
  - Alphabet books
  - Counting books
  - Photo-illustrated nonfiction texts
  - Stories with make-believe characters
  - Familiar traditional tales
  - Graphic-format texts
  - Joke/riddle books

If you can't find enough of the different types of books in your classroom book collection, collaborate with colleagues to make shared stacks that you can rotate from room to room. Take advantage of your school's book room (if you have one), or reach out to your school or public librarian to have them help you curate the sets you need. Whichever strategy you choose to gather additional titles, make sure that all of the books are labeled so that once every class has done the activity, you can return the books to their respective homes.

### GET STARTED

- Read aloud and discuss a book that introduces genres.

- Using the books in their stack, students work with their partner to look for clues that will help them identify the genre of each book. Share that the goal of this exploration is to use the book parts to determine the genre, not to try to read the whole book. There will be time for that later! Once they've identified the genre, learners collaborate to create a sticky-note label. Their label can be designed with pictures and/or words. If this is your students' first experience learning about genres, celebrate their approximations. For instance, they might label a nonfiction book a "fact book" or an alphabet book a "letter book." Chances are some of their labels will be more fitting than the formal ones!

- After all of the books are labeled, each student selects one book from their stack and finds a peer from a different group to compare and discuss their genre designations. Repeat as time and interest permit.

- As students are circulating, chat with them about the types of books they prefer and record any insights you gain.

- Make sure to take a few photos of students' sticky-note labels, as they may come in handy for future genre discussions or to use as labels for classroom library book bins.

FIGURE 2.1

*Graph students' genre preferences.*

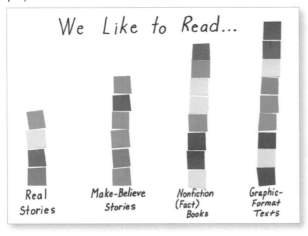

### WHERE THIS MIGHT LEAD

Let's say your informal chats with students during this activity didn't give you enough information about their genre preferences. You can continue this conversation by surveying the class and co-creating a graph or other visual representation of their preferred genres (see Figure 2.1). Another way to discover students' individual reading preferences is by administering a reading interest survey. There are many reading interest surveys available to use or modify. In the primary grades, we found that simply asking students to identify things they like helps us find books they will enjoy. To do this, supply each student with a blank piece of paper and show them how to divide it into fourths. Then ask them to draw and/or write about four things they like. Use the results of this no-fuss survey to identify preferences and find books about those particular topics.

### Try This! Speed Date with Books

If you are an avid book collector, you probably remember the scene from the Disney movie *Beauty and the Beast* where the Beast gifts Belle his massive library. It's one of those scenes that make book lovers' eyes turn into hearts. To introduce Book Speed Dating, play this scene and tell students, "While this classroom doesn't have *quite* as many books, the ones you see around you are all yours to enjoy this year. Today you are going to start to familiarize yourselves with some of them."

### GATHER

To get ready for Book Speed Dating, place a differ-ent book on each reader's desk. If possible, do this prior to students entering the classroom so that they see it right when they come in. As you select titles, choose books from a variety of genres and those created by authors with varied voices. If you do not have enough books in your classroom library for a full class set, reach out to your teammates, school, or public librarian to borrow a few books. Another alternative that requires fewer books is to plan to have learners complete this activity in pairs or small groups.

### GET STARTED

Begin by introducing the concept of a Someday List, which is simply a running list of books stu-dents might want to read in the future (Miller 2009). Students can keep a Someday List in their literacy notebooks (see Figure 2.2), on an elec-tronic document, on a blank sheet of paper, or on the printable Someday List in Appendix A2.1. From there, ask readers, "How do you preview a book to see if you are interested in reading it?" Record their responses on a chart or electronic document so that other students can use the same strategies (see Figure 2.3 on the following page).

FIGURE 2.2

*Printable: Someday List (top); Student Work Sample: Someday List in Literacy Notebook (bottom)*

**Previewing A Book**

- read back
- read 2 lines
- skim pages
- table of contents
- read reviews/summaries
- title/cover
- inside flap
- genre
- author

FIGURE 2.3
*Anchor Chart:*
*Previewing a Book*

When students have their Someday Lists at the ready and know how to preview a book, announce that it is time for Book Speed Dating or time to Scan the Stacks (Walther and Biggs-Tucker 2020). In most classrooms, just the mention of the word *dating* will cause a ripple of anticipation and a few giggles. You might choose the name Scan the Stacks if the practice of dating conflicts with any of your students' or caregivers' cultural beliefs. Explain that similar to speed dating, students will have one to two minutes to get to know each book and, if it piques their interest, jot down the title on their Someday List.

After you've answered any questions and students feel confident in the process, set a timer for two to three minutes, and begin. At the end of each timed interval, students pass their books or move seats and the dating continues. While students are familiarizing themselves with the books, take note of the books that are added to readers' Someday Lists and those titles that get overlooked.

Getting acquainted with books can be a somewhat stationary, quiet experience. Here are a few ideas to incorporate talk and movement:

- After they've previewed a few books, invite learners to turn and talk with a partner about the most interesting book they found so far.

- When time is up, ask a few students to share the one title they are most excited about reading. If you are familiar with the book, do a quick, informal book talk in case others missed it. If book talks are new to you, we share some tips in Chapter 4 on page 114.

- If learners came across any books they have already read and enjoyed, give them an opportunity to do a quick, spoiler-free book talk.

- Save a few minutes at the end of the experience for students to do a gallery walk of any books they want to revisit or any books they missed.

- If time allows, encourage students to get up and peruse the other books in your classroom library.

## WHERE THIS MIGHT LEAD

Book Speed Dating is a practice you can revisit periodically over the course of the year. Use it to familiarize students with books you add to your classroom library or to highlight titles from one specific genre. It is also a quick way to introduce students to a selection of book club books so that they can choose which one they want to read.

### Keep It Simple: Offer Short Texts

In your personal reading life, there may be moments where you want to take a break from reading an entire book. Perhaps you just finished a thought-provoking text and you need time to ponder. Or maybe you forgot to bring a book with you to an appointment. Similarly, your students may find themselves without a book or the desire to start a new one. When this happens, preparing alternative reading options is a smart way to help learners continue their daily reading habit. One easy solution is to curate a collection of news articles and other short texts for students to have at their fingertips. These texts could be presented on paper or loaded onto available tablets or e-readers for students to borrow. During the first weeks of school, point these out to students and introduce them as an alternative reading option if learners forget or finish their book. Every two or three weeks, swap out or reload the short reads so that students have fresh, engaging options. Here are a few of our favorite places to find high-interest news articles and other short texts:

- Articles from Newsela.com
- Kelly Gallagher's Article of the Week
- Infographics and Quick Reads from KidsDiscover.com
- Back of cereal boxes (ask families/caregivers to send these in)
- Children's magazines like *National Geographic Kids* or *Zoobooks* (ask your librarian if they have back issues that you can have or borrow)
- Poetry for kids from PoetryFoundation.org or Poets.org

*Download articles from Kelly Gallagher's Article of the Week here.*

If your classroom is short on storage space, use an idea Katie learned from a colleague: attach file folders to the wall and place the news articles and other short texts in the folders (see Figure 2.4). If you're teaching middle grade or middle school learners, remember the importance of continuing to share and promote picture book reading. You can find fascinating picture books about almost any topic, and these short texts are ideal for building background knowledge and vocabulary for readers of all ages.

FIGURE 2.4

*Place short reads in folders around your room.*

## COLLABORATE ON SHARED VALUES

You've intentionally arranged your learning space to communicate your beliefs. Now that the students have arrived, it's time to include them in the conversation. The more learners see their ideas and experiences reflected in the everyday happenings of the classroom, the better. In fact, we've found that when we make it a point to ask our students for their suggestions about classroom dilemmas, they routinely come up with solutions that are more insightful than those we considered. Setting aside time to create shared agreements about the learning environment will pay off in the weeks and months ahead.

### Try This! Discuss How Students Want Their Classroom to Feel

▶ For many students, the beginning of the school year is an emotional roller coaster. Over the course of a day, they might be missing their caregivers, worried about something that is going on at home, hesitant to share ideas in class, excited about meeting new friends, or anxious about eating lunch in a noisy lunchroom. As you build relationships with your learners, offer support as they learn to articulate their emotions so that you can help them develop healthy ways to regulate them. The ability to identify and understand feelings is one of the hallmarks of self-awareness. In this experience, we blend a social-emotional learning experience that focuses on feelings with co-creating shared classroom values. We believe the more you can weave social-emotional learning into your literacy instruction, the better (CASEL 2023). After all, literacy learning is a social endeavor.

### Why Collaborate on Shared Values?

■ When we collaborate with our students to create shared values, it establishes an environment of "trust and agency" for everyone in the community (Beechum 2020).

■ Teachers who engage in as much dialogue as possible and invite students' voices into the conversation are better able to gauge what students are thinking and how they are processing what's happening in their classroom (Fisher, Frey, and Hattie 2021).

### GATHER

■ A book to read aloud that highlights feelings and emotions. Here are a few you might try:

  ● *I Feel! A Book of Emotions* (Medina 2022)
    Summary: In the third book in her I Will series, Juana Medina shares fourteen different emotions. The book ends with the conversation-starting statement "All feelings are valid. It is what we do with them that matters."

- ***The Many Colors of Harpreet Singh*** (Kelkar 2019)
  Summary: Harpreet wears a different-colored patka depending on his mood—yellow when he's feeling sunny and red when he needs to be brave. When Harpreet's mom announces that they're moving for her new job, he's worried. At his new school, Harpreet wears white because he doesn't want to be seen. When Harpreet finds and returns Abby's smiley-face stocking cap, the two become friends and he gets back to wearing bright colors again.

- ***Out of a Jar*** (Marcero 2022)
  Summary: Llewellyn likes scary things, but he doesn't like to be scared. He tries to get rid of his fear and it keeps coming back, so he puts his fear in a jar and locks it away in the basement closet. Soon he is locking all of his emotions away in separate jars: sadness, anger, loneliness, joy, and disappointment. Eventually there isn't any room in the closet for another jar and all of the repressed emotions burst out. Once they are free, Llewellyn is relieved and learns to face his feelings and share them with others.

- ■ Sticky notes, whiteboard, or electronic document to record students' ideas

## GET STARTED

To keep this activity brief and engaging, we suggest splitting it into two separate bursts of instruction:

- ■ First, read aloud and discuss a book about feelings. Talk about the different emotions that you and your students have experienced during the first few weeks of school.

- ■ Later, refer back to your previous discussion. Explain to students that you are going to be living and learning together for a whole year and you want their classroom to make them feel comfortable. Ask children, "How do you want our classroom to feel?" Give each child a sticky note to draw or write their answer. Collect the sticky notes and compile them into a collective class chart (see Figure 2.5). Refer to the chart as you continue to build a shared understanding of the climate of the classroom.

FIGURE 2.5
*Anchor Chart: How We Want Our Classroom To Feel*

## WHERE THIS MIGHT LEAD

You can build on this experience by highlighting the connection between the emotions listed on the chart and the actions that students choose in order to keep the classroom feeling that way. For instance, you might point out things like, "If we want our classroom to feel welcoming, we'll help each other," or "If we want our classroom to feel happy, we'll use kind words." Refer to the chart as you give students descriptive feedback on their actions by saying something like, "Erin, I noticed that you and Kaavya took turns while you were acting out that book. You're helping our classroom feel playful."

### Try This! Ask, "What Do We Value?"

By the middle grades and certainly in middle school, most students are quite familiar with classroom beliefs, agreements, and routines. Thus, simply asking learners to generate a list of agreements can sometimes lead to rote responses that the students think their teachers want to hear. Getting creative with different ways to approach generating shared beliefs can elicit independent and original thinking from classroom members. As we pointed out in the introduction, although we designed the ideas in the chapters to span from the elementary grades to middle school, many overlap and there are no rules about which activities work best at a particular grade level or in a particular learning context. You could easily use Maria's idea of How We Want Our Classroom to Feel with upper-grade learners. Or you could try a different strategy that we like to call What Do We Value? With this approach, students are asked to determine what they value in both students and teachers. This list acts as a jumping-off point for classroom routines that the community continues to build throughout the school year.

### GATHER

Begin by doing a quick check for understanding to ensure that students have a firm grasp of the meaning of the word *value* and how to determine a value by having a conversation similar to the one that follows:

> **MS. WALTHER:** Let's begin thinking about this concept of values so that we can discuss and formulate our classroom values. Look around our classroom. What would you say I value?
>
> **BRIE:** Books!
>
> **MS. WALTHER:** What evidence do you have for that thinking?
>
> **BRIE:** There are bookshelves all over the classroom.
>
> **MS. WALTHER:** Brie, thank you for supporting your thinking with evidence! So, Brie notices there are a lot of books in the classroom.

Who can expand on that thinking with a different value word that relates to having a lot of books? Some value words might be *kindness*, *respect* . . .

**ASRIEL:** Knowledge, because you can learn from books.

**MS. WALTHER:** Brie and Asriel, smart thinking! I value knowledge. What else?

**TRINITY:** Organization, because there are calendars and schedules and labels around the room.

**MS. WALTHER:** You're noticing evidence, Trinity! Anything else?

Now that learners are in the mindset of noticing and naming values, read aloud a text with a plot or characters that showcase a variety of values and will prompt strong discussion. We chose the picture books in Figure 2.6 because they are set in a school. This offers readers the opportunity to connect the values the characters display in the book to those they determine are important in their classroom.

FIGURE 2.6

## PICTURE BOOKS TO DEMONSTRATE VALUES

| Book Title | | What does the main character value? | What does the teacher value? |
|---|---|---|---|
| | *The Arabic Quilt: An Immigrant Story* (Khalil 2020) Summary: Kanzi and her family immigrated to America from their home country, Egypt. On her first day in a new school, Kanzi's classmates laugh when they overhear her mother using an Arabic term of affection. Seeing Kanzi upset, Mrs. Haugen, Kanzi's teacher, reassures her that being multilingual is beautiful. | Culture, family, friendship, creativity, honesty, being multilingual | Understanding, tolerance, inclusion, curiosity, creativity |
| | *My Very Favorite Book in the Whole Wide World* (Mitchell 2021) Summary: Despite Henley's best efforts, he can't seem to find a book that makes reading easier and more fun. Then his teacher, Mrs. Joy, gives him "the worst homework assignment ever": to bring his favorite book in the whole wide world to share with the class. Henley goes to the library and the bookshop, but he leaves both empty-handed. Henley's mother reassures him that the best stories come from within, inspiring Henley to write and share his own book. | Play, community, responsibility mom's advice, literacy | Reading, books, students' stories, hard work |

### GET STARTED

Read aloud the picture book, and then identify the values students notice based on the characters' actions. Connect the read-aloud to the community-building experience by telling readers that, with their input, you will be compiling a list of classroom values to guide your literacy learning throughout the school year. From there, move into a discussion of what students value both in students (themselves and their peers) and in teachers. Ask a few learners to share their thinking to get everyone's ideas flowing. Once ideas are bouncing around the room, give each student two sticky notes and have them label one with the heading *Students* and the other with the heading *Teachers*. Invite them to write one to three things they value in teachers and one to three things they value in students on the labeled sticky notes. Designate a spot in the room for students to post their sticky notes.

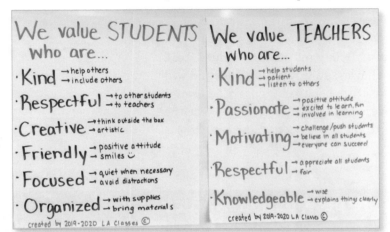

FIGURE 2.7

*Anchor Chart: Co-created Values*

After sticky notes are posted, read them over to identify common threads and ideas. Compose a rough draft of values and discuss revisions and edits with students. Agree upon the final draft in some "official" manner. Then post the chart in a visible spot so that both you and your students can review and reference it throughout the school year (see Figure 2.7).

### WHERE THIS MIGHT LEAD

Here are two different ways you could innovate as you co-create a classroom values chart:

- Split students into two groups. Have group one review the sticky notes that name student values and group two review the sticky notes that name teacher values. Ask each group to come to consensus in order to compile a shared list of values. If you have large class sizes and splitting your class into two big groups seems unmanageable, half of the class can work on the values in two smaller groups and the other half of the class can browse and check out books from the classroom library. Then, at a predetermined time, switch.

- Katie's teammate Val had the genius idea of making this activity electronic, and remote-teaching friendly, by asking students to brainstorm their values in Google Forms. She then put student responses into a word cloud generator to show the most commonly stated values from all students (see Figure 2.8).

Whichever way you choose to formulate and display your shared values, their power comes in making sure they are more than just a decoration on the wall (or slide). To do this, periodically review the shared values during your morning meeting, when new students join your community, before having a substitute, or when student behaviors signal the need for a refresh. View the values charts as a living document that you and your students can revise as the year progresses.

## Keep It Simple: Take Your Time, Be Creative

Shared beliefs are the foundation on which your classroom routines and practices will stand. Taking the time you need to co-create them is important. In both "Try This!" examples, we made time for belief identification by integrating it with other important read-aloud experiences. This helps students see it as part of the learning process, rather than an add-on or extra. If you are teaching upper-grade learners, approach this belief creation with creativity, keeping in mind that this is likely not your students' first time doing it. You could suggest sharing ways to co-create beliefs at a cross-grade-level articulation meeting. This will provide all the educators in your school community an opportunity to gather innovative ideas and check that they're not duplicating something that students have already done a few times.

### Back Pocket Wisdom: What Do We Value?

If you work with different groups of students across your day, it may not be realistic to create a values chart for each class, as you only have so much room to hang charts. To solve this problem, take notes for a rough draft for each group and then put it all together in a collective final copy that represents all your groups. If chart-hanging space is at a premium, another alternative is to display and review the values electronically as part of your daily slide deck. It is also helpful to make a printable copy to send home to families/caregivers or include in information you share with new students.

FIGURE 2.8
*Compile students' online responses into a word cloud generator to show the most commonly stated values.*

### DEVELOP ROUTINES

Like the back cover blurb of a book, students have had a sneak peek into the story of their literacy lives in your classroom. On day one, they dabbled with some daily literacy routines. You may have taken suggestions from Chapter 1 and posted a daily schedule or used feedback phrases to celebrate students' agency and independence. Moving forward, you'll gradually fill in the details as you demonstrate and practice all of the elements that, when put together, create the narrative of a caring and cohesive place to learn.

## Why Develop Routines?

- It takes time to develop strong habits and the stamina for silent reading. Students need to engage in the routine of independent reading day after day over an extended period, and from one grade to the next (Hiebert 2014).

- When we prioritize routines that support the instructional practice of independent reading, we move closer to the end goal, which is to nurture "habitual readers with conscious reading identities" (NCTE 2019, 1).

### Try This! Model Text-Focused Conversations During Read-Aloud

Powerful literacy instruction is multifaceted and dynamic. It looks different from day to day and year to year. Why? Because the most effective teaching is responsive to the needs of the students in front of you. As you're planning your first week and beyond, view each interaction you have with your learners as a literacy-building event. Whether you're chatting with students as they enter the room or are huddled with a small group puzzling over the theme of a text, be confident you are guiding learners toward independence. An essential literacy event in both of our classrooms is interactive read-aloud. When you read aloud to students and invite them to join in the discussion, you are laying the groundwork for the thinking and internal conversations they will have with themselves as they read on their own. As an added bonus, you are giving them a leg up in becoming a person who knows how to have a meaningful two-way conversation.

### GATHER

To get ready for an interactive read-aloud experience, select a picture book that will provoke conversation. We've included a few suggestions in Figure 2.9. Decide where you want students to sit while you read aloud. We prefer reading aloud while the kids are gathered together on the floor. If your class size or available space makes this impractical, consider having students stay in their seats and project the book using a document camera so that they can see the details. If listeners are going to join you on the floor and need a bit more structure, strategically assign learning spots and use stick-on dots to help them remember their place for learning (see Figure 2.10 on the following page). You may also want to pair them with a turn-and-talk partner. Plan on changing both their learning spots and turn-and-talk partners on a regular basis so that students have opportunities to learn from all of their peers.

FIGURE 2.9

| PICTURE BOOKS TO SPARK CONVERSATIONS | | |
|---|---|---|
| **Book Title** | **Summary** | **Sparks Conversation About . . .** |
| *Dress-Up Day* (Gómez 2022) [Spanish edition available] | A little girl is ready for dress-up day in her mom-made bunny costume and, unfortunately, wakes up sick. The next day, she decides it would be a good idea to dress up anyway, but her classmates are unkind to her. Luckily, Hugo shows up dressed like a carrot and, together, they inspire all of their friends to join in the fun. | ▪ How the main character dealt with disappointment<br>▪ Why characters' feelings change |
| *Friends* (Sosa 2022) | This warm and cheerful picture book brings to light the fact that our friendships are precious. Sometimes relationships are fleeting, and in other cases they last a lifetime. Either way, friendships comfort, teach, and bring joy and laughter to our lives. | ▪ How friendships begin, change, and sometimes end<br>▪ Characteristics of trusted friends |
| *People Are Wild* (Meganck 2022) | Unique and amusing! This book begins with an illustration of an elephant and her calf looking across the savannah at a mother and child. The text reads, "Mama, what is that?" The elephant answers the question by sharing all the reasons to stay away from humans. The illustrations depict the similarities between animals and humans. Backmatter includes a brief paragraph of kid-friendly facts about each animal pictured in the book, a map indicating where the animals live, and their ranking on the endangered animal continuum. | ▪ Point of view<br>▪ Backmatter in a nonfiction book |

FIGURE 2.10

*If needed, strategically assign learning spots for interactive read-aloud.*

## GET STARTED

During read-aloud experiences, communicate your belief that learning is a social endeavor by posing prompts or asking questions that encourage dialogue. Start with these:

- Ask your friend what they're thinking. Listen to see if you can add something to what they said.
- Listen to your neighbor share their opinion. Share the reasons your opinion is the same or different.
- Ask your classmate three questions before you share what's on your mind.
- Is everyone's voice being heard? Talk with someone you haven't heard from in a while.

Then use Figure 2.11 to prompt additional interactions as you read aloud your favorite titles. Keep in mind that the goal of an interactive read-aloud experience is to provoke as much peer-to-peer conversation as possible.

FIGURE 2.11

| HOW TO SPARK INTERACTIVE READ-ALOUD CONVERSATIONS | | |
|---|---|---|
| **BEFORE READING** | | |
| **When you notice . . .** | **Ask or say . . .** | **This leads to thinking or conversation about . . .** |
| A wrap-around cover (a cover where the illustration spans across the spine) or two separate illustrations on the front and back cover | "Look at the cover and back of this book. Take turns with a classmate pointing out and talking about something you notice. Discuss any predictions you may have at this point." | - Making predictions based on the exterior illustrations<br>- Using the cover illustration to gauge interest in the book |
| A back cover blurb | "Listen to me read this blurb. Talk with a friend about how it might help you better understand what is going to happen in this book." | - Previewing the book<br>- Writing blurbs for books that don't already have them |
| Interesting end papers | "Take a look at these end papers in the front of the book. After reading, we'll come back and compare them to the end papers found in the back of the book to ponder their connection to the story." | - Book design and illustration study<br>- Reading the whole book |

## BEFORE READING (continued)

| When you notice . . . | Ask or say . . . | This leads to thinking or conversation about . . . |
| --- | --- | --- |
| Table of contents in a nonfiction book | "Let's preview this book by reading the table of contents. Are there any topics that you can't wait to learn more about? Share them with someone nearby." | ■ Previewing an informational text<br>■ Selecting the sections of an informational text that will help answer their questions about the topic |

## DURING READING

| When you notice . . . | Ask or say . . . | This leads to thinking or conversation about . . . |
| --- | --- | --- |
| A character expressing emotion through words or illustrations | "Can you infer how this character is feeling? Share your clues with a neighbor. Ask them if they agree." | ■ Character traits<br>■ Characters' actions and reactions<br>■ How characters' feelings change over the course of the story |
| Sensory language | "Can you imagine the setting [this character's experience]? Tell someone which words helped you to do that." | ■ Visualizing while reading<br>■ Importance of word choice |
| Key details in a nonfiction book | "How did those details help you better understand the topic? Exchange a fact you learned about the topic with a classmate." | ■ Paying attention to details<br>■ Determining which details are important |

## AFTER READING

| When you notice . . . | Ask or say . . . | This leads to thinking or conversation about . . . |
| --- | --- | --- |
| A strong theme or big idea | "What do you think the author wanted you to learn from reading this book?" What are your clues? Ask a shoulder partner what they learned." | ■ Using text clues to infer the theme<br>■ Understanding the author's purpose |
| A surprise or unresolved ending | "What was your opinion of the ending? Trade ideas with a friend. Would you have ended the story a different way? What do you predict might happen next?" | ■ Noticing plot structure<br>■ Thinking beyond the story |
| Backmatter (author or illustrator note, additional information, glossary of terms, and so on) | "How will reading this information enhance your understanding of the book?" | ■ Enhancing the reading experience<br>■ Extending learning beyond the book |

If the idea of collaborative discussion is appealing to you, Maria has written extensively about how to spark dialogue during the read-aloud experience in *The Ramped-Up Read Aloud* (2019) and *Shake Up Shared Reading* (2022).

## WHERE THIS MIGHT LEAD

Provoke conversations across your school day or about certain topics using multimodal texts like video clips, images, podcasts, artifacts, primary sources, or other objects that will spark wonder and, perhaps, debate. In addition to being responsive to the range of learners you work with, providing time for learners to engage in discussions about a variety of inputs gives them more opportunities to strengthen their speaking and listening skills.

### Try This! Reflect on Known Routines

As we mentioned earlier in this chapter, by upper elementary and middle school, most students are quite familiar with the routines and structures of a classroom environment. So, rather than focusing on front-loading expectations before learners practice routines, we suggest using a whole-to-part scaffolding approach. Think of this approach as similar to how swim instructors teach young children. They begin by getting swimmers comfortable by playing in the water. Later, when they see that children are feeling more confident, the instructor brings them together to offer modeling and feedback on the basics, like how to blow bubbles with their faces in the water or float on their backs. In the same way, your students will begin to get comfortable with different classroom practices that you haven't had a chance to fully teach. Then, after they've experienced a classroom structure for a day or two, invite learners to reflect on their experience. There are a variety of ways students can reflect on routines. Our favorite is a simple protocol called Looks Like, Sounds Like, Feels Like, and Why.

### GATHER

Throughout the next few weeks of school your students will engage in various literacy experiences. Remember to offer descriptive feedback to students upholding the classroom values and displaying the habits and behaviors of readers. Observe and notice which structures are familiar to students and which may need a bit more scaffolding or a clearer definition of their purpose. As you make these observations, compile a list of the two or three most important or relevant practices you want students to discuss and reflect on. Some of these practices might include supported independent reading, interactive read-alouds, shared reading interactions, whole-class discussions, turn-and-talks, book clubs, and book talks. We love a good list! In this case, making a list of all the classroom routines students need to know can help you be more strategic in your planning.

With your list in hand (see Figure 2.12), devise a plan to discuss each routine with students at a future time when it is relevant and after students have had the opportunity to try it out. For example, after students browse the classroom library for the first time, discuss how to check out books. Or when you notice readers without books or nearing the end of their books, schedule some time to show how to return books and find short reads (see page 51). A more responsive approach to introducing routines can help you and your learners feel less over-whelmed with a long list of routines at the beginning of the year and can provide each structure with greater relevance.

FIGURE 2.12

*Make a list of classroom routines you want to introduce and devise a plan for doing it.*

## GET STARTED

Now that you have a strategic plan for discussing routines with students, tar-get the first routine by coming together as a class to complete a Looks Like, Sounds Like, Feels Like, and Why? chart. Explain to learners that the purpose of this chart is to clarify their actions during that literacy experience.

Introduce what each section means by saying something like this: "Now that we've enjoyed a few read-alouds [or whatever literacy practice you've selected], let's reflect on and discuss that structure and the routines that are involved when we enjoy that experience together. In the Looks Like section, we will jot down what someone would see if they walked into our classroom during read-aloud time. Similarly, the Sounds Like section will include dif-ferent sounds and language they would hear. Feels Like is the most abstract, out-of-the-box thinking section. We will write how we want to feel emotion-ally during our read-aloud experiences. Finally, in the Why? section we will include our thoughts on why it's important to participate in this particular literacy routine."

After explaining each section of the chart, open up the discussion so students can add suggestions to each section based on their experiences. We've found that students are quite comfortable identifying what literacy routines look like and sound like, so you can usually complete these parts quickly. This will give you time to focus on what the practice feels like and why it is important. These sections are essential, as they give students a sense of purpose when engaging in the experience. The Why? section can be

## Independent Reading

**Looks Like ☺**
- everyone looking at books (Christian)
- quickly writing down homework (Felicity)
- checking out a book (Brian)
- listening to audiobook (Eli)
- students reading independently (Dillon)

**Sounds Like ♪**
- pages turning (Sy'Rai)
- quiet (Felicity)
- audiobook playing

**Feels Like ♡**
- In the book (Clara)
- calm (Rylee)
- putting your feelings into the character (Natalie)
- entertaining
- going into another world

**Why?**
- expand vocabulary (Claire)
- build reading stamina (Brian)
- get in the mood for LA (Reese)
- learn something (Jishnu)
- makes you want to read more if it's a book you enjoy (Addie)
- faster reading (Eli)

**FIGURE 2.13**
*Anchor Chart: Independent Reading*

especially illuminating, allowing you to both hear why students believe they are engaging in certain literacy practices and help them to see the real-life implications of these practices. Keep track of students' thinking and compile it into a chart that you post somewhere visible in the classroom (see Figure 2.13).

### WHERE THIS MIGHT LEAD

Once readers are familiar with the chart structure, put the students in charge by having them collaborate with partners or small groups to create their own charts. Then assign a few students the task of compiling all of the thinking into a class chart. With students in charge, the Looks Like, Sounds Like, Feels Like, and Why? protocol can spill into other areas of your teaching day, including hallway expectations or how to welcome any new students.

### Keep It Simple: Stop, Reflect, Regroup

▶▶ We would love to be able to tell you that after students have tried out the literacy routines and you've collaborated to identify their expected characteristics, they will go smoothly for the rest of the year. In our experience, however, that is not always the case. Classroom dynamics are constantly changing, so we need to be prepared with a plan when they do. If classroom practice is not going as planned, don't be afraid to stop the action and calmly say, "This is not going the way we planned. Let's talk about what we notice and share ideas about how we might do this differently as we continue." Often this focused redirection will help students regroup and get back on course.

### CULTIVATE COMMUNITY

When you have 120 students or more, like Katie and many other middle school teachers do, getting to know each and every one of them can be a bit daunting. While not quite as overwhelming, the same is true in a busy elementary classroom with thirty or more students. That is why we like to plan plenty of time to cultivate community by nurturing relationships among learners and, of equal importance, students' relationships with us, their teachers. However, rather than planning out-of-context community-building activities, we believe it is more authentic to center these experiences around literacy so that students see the connection between community and literacy right away. Here are a few tried-and-true ideas to weave together literacy and relationship building.

### Try This! Create Identity Equations

During the 2020–2021 school year, Maria collaborated with a colleague to design and co-teach a virtual after-school literacy experience for students. The goal of the fourteen-week class, called Beyond the Page, was to use picture books as a springboard to engage students with literacy in innovative ways. The challenges were the fact that the class was taught through the screen and that the learners spanned grades one through five. The rewards were the opportunity to build a cross-grade-level literacy community and learn from a smart group of students. The idea that appears here was created by that group of students, who took our planned activity in a new direction. Enjoy trying out what we learned from them.

> ## Why Cultivate Community?
>
> ■ Part of creating a productive reading community is getting to know your students as readers so that you can use your understanding to "adjust curriculum and plan scaffolds and interventions to move students forward" (Robb 2010, 67).
>
> ■ Encouraging students and community members to build relationships based on reading can help to make reading a norm in your classroom community and beyond (Miller 2014).

### GATHER

Our original goal for this learning experience was to have students write equations to communicate concepts. To get them thinking in this direction, we shared the picture book *This Plus That: Life's Little Equations* (Rosenthal 2011). After reading the book aloud, we modeled a few of our own equations. Soon after we shared our equations, ideas like these began to pop up in the chat:

> ice cream + hot days = summer
>
> cuddly + fun + furry = dog
>
> building + kids = school

Then, without any prompting, a student changed the direction and wrote this equation:

> crafting + dancing = me

That's all it took for the students to begin crafting their own identity equations, making them longer and longer:

> Kit Kats + drawing + reading + summer + spicy chips + social media + personal computer = me

In fact, one fourth-grade learner wrote a page-long identity equation in their literacy notebook.

## GET STARTED

If writing identity equations sounds like something that your students would enjoy, you can start out in the same way by reading aloud a book with equations. Then model creating your own identity equation. After you've checked for understanding, provide students with time and materials to create their identity equations. If you're working with beginning writers, demonstrate how they can use pictures to create equations. Plan time for writers to share equations with partners, in small groups, and/or with the whole class. Post the equations along with a photo of each child so that students can revisit them to better learn about their peers.

## WHERE THIS MIGHT LEAD

Think about other ways you might use equations later in the year. You could build on their individual identity work and invite students to write equations for words like *school*, *friends*, *home*, and/or *family*. Students can formulate literacy-focused equations to summarize a book, describe a character, compare and contrast settings, or process theme development. You might even carry this over to content area instruction, with Laura Purdie Salas's *Snowman – Cold = Puddle: Spring Equations* (2019). Finally, if you are interested in using these equations with older readers, consider tying in what they are learning about mathematical equations. How could they find meaningful ways to include parentheses, exponents, or other elements of algebraic expressions (see Figure 2.14)?

FIGURE 2.14
*Student Work Sample: Identity Equation*

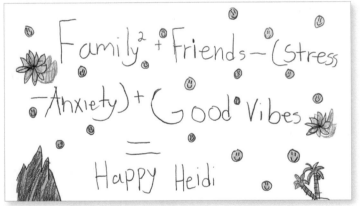

### Try This! Conduct a Community Literacy Survey

In *Cultivating Genius*, Gholdy Muhammad (2020) reminds us that before we can begin teaching students about leading literate lives, we need to define the term *literacy*. Keeping her advice in mind, we created an experience where learners expand their current definition of some of the key elements of language arts (reading, writing, listening, speaking, and researching) by surveying classmates and community members about their literacy practices. By conducting a literacy-based survey, learners make connections with their school and community members while gaining a deeper understanding of the importance of literacy in everyday life.

## GATHER

Start planning this experience by determining a literacy-related question that your students could pose to community members. Katie and her colleagues settled on this question: "On a daily basis, which one of the following literacy skills do you use most often: reading, writing, listening, speaking, or researching?" Alternatively, you could work with learners to co-create a question. Some other possible survey questions include the following:

- Which of the following literacy skills helps you to feel most successful: reading, writing, listening, speaking, or researching?
- Which of the following literacy skills do you use most at work or school and which do you use most at home: reading, writing, listening, speaking, or researching?

If you work in a middle school, once you've decided on your question, check in with the science or social studies teachers to determine if they have a specific survey method they use in their classrooms, so that students are seeing consistency across content areas. If not, we provide a sample survey in Appendix A2.2.

## GET STARTED

With your survey question in mind, introduce students to the five elements of literacy and say that they will be practicing their researching skills in order to better understand how all the elements show up in the school community. Then model how you would ask someone the survey question, and invite students to get to know their classmates by surveying each other.

To get to know members of the community at large, assist learners in brainstorming a list of trusted adults in the building and in their community that they could survey. Then, so as to not overwhelm your colleagues, determine appropriate times for students to ask their survey questions: administrators at lunch, other teachers during passing periods, dean's/counseling/office staff before and after school, family members at home, extended family over the phone or via text or email. Give students ample time to complete their research. It is helpful to extend the data collection over a weekend so that students have more time to survey their trusted adults outside of the building.

Once students' data collection is complete, the analysis and discussion begin. Show students how to compile all of the classroom data in one place (see Figures 2.15 and 2.16 on the following page). Then open the floor for analysis of the data and student notes by posing these questions:

- What do you notice?
- What can we learn from these data?

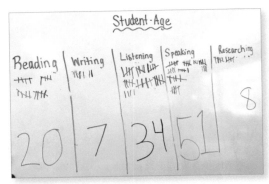

**FIGURE 2.15**

*Students tally the student-age data from the Community Literacy Survey.*

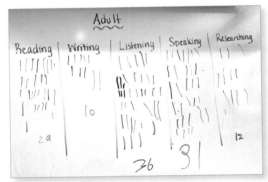

**FIGURE 2.16**

*Students tally the data gathered from adults from the Community Literacy Survey.*

- How do members of our community use literacy skills?
- What information are we missing from these data? What else might we want to learn?

In Katie's classroom, this discussion focused on how many people mentioned speaking as being a skill they use often and, then, why this is an important skill to practice in the language arts classroom. Wherever the discussion leads, students will be learning more about the role literacy plays in their school and community!

## WHERE THIS MIGHT LEAD

Once the community data are compiled and discussed, the results can become a reference point as you engage in different literacy practices throughout the year. However, if you and students are wanting to continue to explore these literacy ideas, offer an extension opportunity with the two ideas in Figure 2.17. To bring the activity full circle, present the data to the community by having students create a short video detailing their findings to send home and/or to be included as a part of a back-to-school or literacy night hosted by your school. This way stakeholders can see how the results of the survey came to life in your classroom.

**FIGURE 2.17**

| EXTENSION OPPORTUNITIES FOR THE COMMUNITY LITERACY SURVEY | |
|---|---|
| **Option A:** Image with Caption | **Option B:** Chart or Graph with Caption |
| Create an image to represent the data the class has discussed. The image can be abstract or realistic. Create a caption connecting the image to the data (see Figure 2.18). | Create a chart/graph to represent the data. Create a caption connecting the chart/graph to the data (see Figure 2.19). |

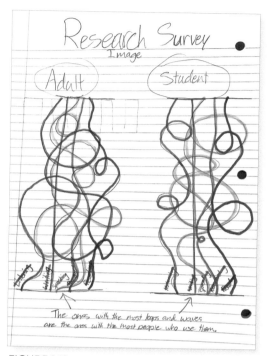

FIGURE 2.18

*Student Work Sample: An Image and Caption Representing Community Literacy Survey Results*

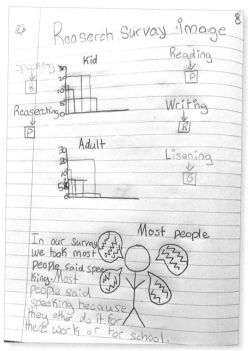

FIGURE 2.19

*Student Work Sample: A Graph Representing Community Literacy Survey Results*

### Keep It Simple: Chat with Your Students

Reflect on how your own relationships develop. Most of our friendships began with a connection, often through a shared interest, and then took shape one conversation at a time. Keep this in mind as you bond with students and cultivate community. Instead of getting bogged down or overwhelmed trying to create a multitude of community-building experiences, focus on a few high-impact activities. Then prioritize chatting with your students. Give yourself the freedom to enjoy each other's company, knowing that informal conversations are the best way to discover shared interests, uncover connections, and find common ground—the underpinnings of a strong relationship.

## CONNECT WITH FAMILIES/CAREGIVERS

When we think about cultivating community in our classroom, we tend to focus on making sure that all of our students feel safe, welcomed, and supported. While this focus is the number one priority, in our diligence to create an inclusive classroom learning environment we sometimes lose sight of the importance of extending this same warm welcome to the other important stakeholders—students' caregivers and families. Here we offer a few suggestions of doable ways to connect with families/caregivers. We hope these recommendations spark even more ideas that are specific to your unique learning context.

### Try This! Display Students' Photographs

▶ Look around your living space. What items make it feel like home? For us, it is being surrounded by photographs of memorable times with family and friends, places we've visited, and images of family members who have passed away. To make your classroom feel more like home for your students, create a space for them to display a few photographs. Students' photographs can lead to planned or impromptu conversations that help learners to get to know one another and you to get to know more about their lives outside of school.

### GATHER

Send a note home requesting that students bring or electronically transmit a photograph of someone, something, or some place that is special to them (see Appendix A2.3). If students and their families/caregivers don't feel comfortable doing this, take a photo of the student with comforting people in their lives, like their favorite teacher in the building or clusters of their friends in the learning community.

Note that in some cultures people do not want to have their photograph taken at all. Specifically, the concern is with their face being photographed. If this is the case, instead of photographing the child, ask them to identify an item or place that is representative of them and display that image.

Decide on the best way to display the photographs. Some options include dollar-store frames, donated frames, or even student-decorated paper frames. If frames will take up too much space, search online for an inexpensive hanging photo display with strings and clips (we found one that holds thirty photos); this setup makes it easy to swap out photos throughout the year. If families/caregivers are okay with you stapling or putting a tack in the picture, you can designate some bulletin board space for this display.

### Why Connect with Families/Caregivers?

■ When welcoming families/caregivers into the classroom, we have an opportunity to learn more about each student's background and are able to tap into the students' individual funds of knowledge to inform classroom practice as the year progresses (Moll et al. 1992).

■ By opening our classrooms either virtually or in person during the first week, community members begin to feel a sense of ownership and understanding around the daily routine and learning of their readers (Henderson and Mapp 2002).

## GET STARTED

Before you display the photos, plan a time for photo sharing. Decide whether you want students to show their photos to the whole class, if they are comfortable doing so. If you choose to do whole-class sharing, we suggest highlighting a few students at a time; this method may stretch over a week or so to give everyone a chance. Another time-efficient alternative is to divide your class into four groups. First the group members share their photos with one another. Then, one by one, each group goes on a gallery walk to learn more about the rest of their peers' pictures.

## WHERE THIS MIGHT LEAD

Refer to the photographs to make connections between topics you are studying and experiences pictured in students' photos. The pictures are also helpful when matching kids to the books in your classroom collection. If a student's photograph includes a multigenerational family, recommend books that feature characters with similar family structure. If they have a pet, offer some nonfiction books about that animal. You get the idea! Finally, when writers are stuck, an image can provide a seed idea for a story or lead to some research—even if that photograph belongs to one of their classmates.

### Try This! Compose Family Letters

While teacher-to-family communication is crucial in helping students become lifelong readers and writers, it is also important to center students in the dialogue between school and home. So if you have already sent home your teacher welcome video, now is a great time for students to compose their own communication to go along with it. Moreover, a letter from their child can help caregivers feel connected to daily classroom life and act as another avenue for creating strong bonds between families/caregivers and school.

## GATHER

You will begin this activity by familiarizing students with the letter-writing format. To do this, either gather letters from previous students to use as demonstration texts or use a picture book like those listed here to introduce the purpose and structure of a friendly letter:

- *Dear Substitute* (Scanlon and Vernick 2018)
  Summary: The girl in this book responds to having a substitute by writing letters throughout the day. The narrator's expressive letters and Chris Raschka's signature art illustrate her range of feelings, making this an ideal book to discuss how letters can relay how we're feeling about books, situations, and events in school.

- ***Little Red and the Big Bad Editor*** (Rector 2022)
  Summary: Red's grandma sends her a brand-new cape that is as "scarlet as a ripe tomato." So she scribbles a thank-you note (even though she hasn't learned how to compose a friendly letter yet) and sashays off to Granny's. As we might expect, she encounters Mr. Wolf. When he leans in close, he notices the letter, pulls out his pencil, and makes his first edit—finger spaces between the words. Just as he's about to eat her, Red shoves a cinnamon muffin in his mouth. The story continues in the same fashion, with Mr. Wolf adding beginning capitals (and mysterious ending marks) along with the opening and closing of the letter. This book would work well as a mentor text for primary-grade writers.

Ponder how you would like to have students write and deliver their letters, in order to determine what other supplies are needed (such as paper, family email addresses, and so on).

### GET STARTED

To begin, co-create a checklist of the elements of a friendly letter. As you study mentor texts, encourage students to identify what they notice about the format and content of a letter. Take notes on their observations so that writers will have a reference guide for how to structure their letter and ideas about how to make it interesting to read (see Figure 2.20).

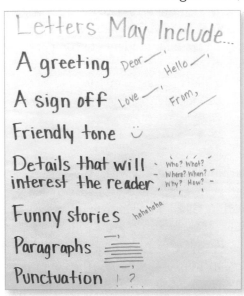

After the checklist is complete, clarify the purpose for their letter writing: "Today we will be writing our own letters to our families/caregivers so they can learn about the first few weeks of school and a little bit about your daily classroom life." To help students accomplish this purpose, brainstorm possible ideas or, if needed, provide prompts to help students get started (see Figure 2.21). With a clear purpose in mind, students can begin drafting their letters.

FIGURE 2.20
*Co-create a checklist to guide students' letter writing.*

FIGURE 2.21

## FAMILY/CAREGIVER LETTER PROMPTS

- After the first few weeks of _____ grade, I'm feeling . . .
- I've been reading _____. Let me tell you about it.
- I can't wait to read _____ because . . . [talk about books on your Someday List]
- My reading goals for this year are . . . You can support me at home by . . .
- I've already learned _____ about myself as a reader.
- This year, I'm most looking forward to . . .
- I'm still wondering about . . .
- Something you might not know about our classroom is . . .

In terms of delivering the letters to families/caregivers, your methods may vary depending on your school community. See Figure 2.22 for a variety of ideas that you can mix and match depending on what will work best. Remember to take pictures or make copies of a few letters to save as mentor texts for next year.

FIGURE 2.22

## OPTIONS FOR DELIVERING FAMILY/CAREGIVER LETTERS

| If . . . | Then . . . |
|---|---|
| Your school has a back-to-school night or open-house event | Set the letters out on desks for families/caregivers to pick up and read. For families/caregivers who cannot attend, send the letters home with the students, take a picture of the letter to send in an email, or mail the letters home. |
| Students have a take-home folder | Place the handwritten or printed letter in their folder. |
| Students have access to a school email account and computers | Guide students in sending their letter via email. This option helps familiarize students with the conventions of email communication. |
| Students have access to voice or video recording software (Voice Memo, Flipgrid, and so on) | Provide time for students to record themselves reading their letters and email the link to their families/caregivers. |

## WHERE THIS MIGHT LEAD

This letter not only acts as a way for students to take ownership of classroom communication but also gives you a glimpse of learners' feelings toward school as well as an informal assessment of their writing abilities. Take some time to skim the letters and make anecdotal notes about what writing mini-lessons you may want to forgo or enhance based on the students' current writing abilities.

### Back Pocket Wisdom: Honor Multilingual Learners' Language Preferences

Encourage students to write the letter in the language that is used most often in their home or in which they are most comfortable. If students have stronger oral fluency in that language, help them to record themselves on a phone or computer and send the letter in an email or voice memo.

### Keep It Simple: Use Your Camera or Jot Down Some Notes

 After a few years of teaching (or a few decades, in Maria's case), families'/caregivers' faces and names can begin to blur together. To solve this problem, Maria started taking photos of family members/caregivers as she met them. For instance, if your school hosts a back-to-school night, ask permission to quickly snap photos of family members sitting in their child's seat, remembering that not all folks are comfortable being photographed. Or if you have any virtual meetings with families/caregivers, ask to take a screenshot so that you will be able to put a name to a face in the future. Once you have these photos, label them and compile them into a folder to use for reference throughout the school year.

If family members prefer not to be photographed, another strategy to help you put faces with names is to ask them to share three words that describe their child. As they are sharing the words, picture their child. Then jot down the three words next to their child's name on your class roster.

🍃 🍂 🍃

As this chapter draws to a close and we look toward Chapter 3, where we'll tackle the rest of the first semester, we hope you found some ideas that affirm your current practices and others that were supportive as you launched your literacy routines. It goes without saying that the first weeks of school are an exciting time to get to know learners and establish community reading practices for the school year. However, after summer break, it can also be exhausting to be back in the classroom. On Friday of the first week, we are usually in bed before 8:00 pm! So enjoy your days with students, but also remember to take some time for yourself before moving into the rest of the semester.

## TIY—Try It Yourself!

**Are there any ideas from this chapter or PDCast that would be helpful in your classroom?**



**Which ideas would you modify to better fit your teaching context?**



**Did this chapter or PDCast spark any questions, reflections, or new thinking?**

## CHAPTER 3

# Build on Your Foundation: First Semester

*Build on the foundation you've established during the first few weeks to create a reader-friendly learning environment.*

Love to talk about teaching? Join us to think through the decisions we make during the first semester. In Episode Three, we dig into strategies for conferring, consider different ways to hold on to classroom beliefs, and share practical ideas for supporting all readers. Because we are book enthusiasts, we end with a few book recommendations.

*Listen to "A Year for the Books" PDCast Episode Three here.*

It feels different to step into our classrooms after a month or so than it did on day one. Certainly there is more stuff strewn about! It doesn't take long to accumulate stray pencils, a forgotten water bottle, and half of a granola bar (yuck). Along with the homey clutter, there are treasures like colorful kids' drawings and sticky-note messages. All of this minutiae is evidence that you and your learners are settling into a comfortable learning environment. In this chapter, we've set out to share a handful of ideas that build on the foundation you've established during your first few weeks with learners. We've intentionally included routines and ideas that you can easily adapt to match the unique learning profiles of your students and modify for different purposes across the first semester.

We realize that, depending on where you are teaching, your school year might be divided into quarters, trimesters, semesters, or the like. To make sure we're all on the same page, we define the first semester as the time between the first day of school and winter break. It's an extended stretch of time to firmly solidify your students' understanding of the thought processes and actions of folks who lead literate lives.

## SURROUND INDEPENDENT READING WITH SUPPORT

During the first handful of weeks, readers continue to explore the books in your teaching space while you take the necessary steps to learn about their interests and preferences. Both of these foundational activities will continue throughout the year as you acquire new titles for your book collection and as your students' reading lives grow and change. In addition to these activities, we want to consider how to surround independent readers with support. For us, supported independent reading is all about guiding readers in the way that works best for them. We lean on Regie Routman's (2008, 62) definition of guiding readers as "any learning context where the teacher guides one or more learners through some aspect of the reading process: making sense of text, decoding and defining words, monitoring comprehension, determining author's purpose, and so on." Across the first semester, we focus on assisting individual readers by building on their assets and demonstrating whatever skills and strategies they need to move closer to independence. Knowing and guiding the *reader* is the key. Let's look at a few ways you can encourage readers as they settle into independent reading.

### Why Surround Independent Reading with Support?

■ Again and again, we learn that when students read for pleasure and enjoyment, their overall reading skills improve. Supporting and encouraging learners to develop their own reading lives is the best way to ensure their success throughout their school career (Gallagher 2009).

■ As students learn reading strategies, it is crucial for them to have consistent and sustained opportunities to practice these strategies on their own (Hiebert 2014).

FIGURE 3.1
*Surround readers with a network of strategic teaching moves.*

Read-Aloud · Shared Reading · Shared Writing · Guided Reading · Book Talks · Guided Writing · Book Matching · **Supporting Readers** · Conferring · Kid Watching · Interactive Writing · Mini-Lessons · Conversing

### Try This! Gather Multifaceted Data to Intentionally Support Readers

▶ For all readers, but especially those at the earliest stages, their success as independent readers is bolstered when they are surrounded by a network of strategic teaching moves (see Figure 3.1). When you make intentional teaching decisions to guide readers in a way that's tailored to them, you honor their unique learning styles. But how do you gather the data needed to boost your students' competence and confidence as readers? To begin, we acknowledge that the most impactful data provide us with multiple perspectives about our readers.

### GATHER

When getting to know our readers, we've had the greatest success when we rely on multiple sources of formative data rather than on one assessment or a single data point. As you collect insights about your readers, approach the work like a detective tracking down clues. Take an inquiry stance and begin by admiring what the reader is doing well (Goldberg 2016). Ask yourself, "How can I leverage their strengths to help them make the most of independent reading time?" Perhaps you notice a child who loves to organize the books in the small-group book box (instead of reading). Invite them to read three books and organize them in order according to how many stars they would give the book on a scale from one to five. In Figure 3.2, we offer ideas for gathering multifaceted data along with some possible next steps.

FIGURE 3.2

## COLLECTING MULTIFACETED READING DATA: CONTEXTS AND NEXT STEPS

| Data Collection Context | Focus | When It's Going Well, Try This . . . | When Readers Need Support, Try This . . . |
|---|---|---|---|
| Kid watching during independent reading | **Engagement** Notice: <br>■ How long readers stay engaged <br>■ What distracts them from reading <br>■ Where they seem most comfortable reading | Extend the time learners have for independent reading. In other words, let readers who are in "the reading zone" (Atwell 2007) continue to read while you meet with kids who need additional strategies to increase their engagement. | ■ Meet with individuals or small groups to select new books. <br>■ If students are reading shorter books, practice reading one book after another. Show them how to use a reading mat, where they physically move books from the green "start" side to the red "finished" side as they complete them. Then, as the arrow indicates, they return all the books to the start side to reread (see Figure 3.3). |
| Observations during conferences | **Reading Behaviors** Notice: <br>■ If they can articulate their reading preferences <br>■ Whether they have a reading plan <br>■ How they go about setting and achieving goals | ■ Invite readers to hold a student-led small group to teach their peers about something that is going well for them, such as finding books they love to read or keeping track of their reading. (See Figure 3.4 for other possible topics.) <br>■ Readers make a chart or individual signs detailing helpful hints for independent reading to post in the classroom. | Ask the reader, "What's challenging for you?" Based on their response, work together to identify an attainable goal (read for five minutes, start and finish three books). Offer tools and strategies to support that goal. Monitor and celebrate their progress. |

(continued on next page)

FIGURE 3.2 (continued)

| COLLECTING MULTIFACETED READING DATA: CONTEXTS AND NEXT STEPS | | | |
|---|---|---|---|
| **Data Collection Context** | **Focus** | **When It's Going Well, Try This . . .** | **When Readers Need Support, Try This . . .** |
| Conversations during interactive read-alouds | **Comprehension**<br><br>Notice:<br>■ Whether readers are comprehending at a literal level, able to answer *who, what,* and *where* questions<br>■ Whether readers are comprehending at an inferential level, able to answer *why, how,* and *what if* questions | Nudge readers to think beyond the book with follow-up questions that start like these:<br>■ "Why do you think . . ."<br>■ "Explain why . . ."<br>■ "What would happen if . . ."<br>■ "How might . . ." | Engage in short bursts of shared reading (Walther 2022) by revisiting key pages or parts of the text you read aloud to practice and apply comprehension strategies. |
| Small-group reading experiences | **Collaborative Conversations**<br><br>Notice:<br>■ Students' ability to connect with and build on their peers' ideas<br>■ Learners' willingness to listen to peers who have differing viewpoints | ■ Sit back and let students do most of the talking.<br>■ Jump in only when needed to get the conversation back on track. Use the opportunity to model conversational techniques like inviting quiet participants into the conversation by asking, "I'd love to hear what _____ is thinking about this idea." | To encourage participation in small-group conversations, provide learners with sentence stems like these:<br>■ "This book/character reminds me of . . ."<br>■ "An interesting fact I learned is . . ."<br>■ "I'm still wondering . . ."<br>■ "What did you think about this part?"<br>■ "I'd like to add on to _____'s thinking . . ." |
| Running records | **Strategic Actions**<br><br>Notice:<br>■ Readers' use of strategic actions when faced with an unknown word<br>■ Readers' fluency<br>■ Readers' ability to retell and/or answer questions about the text | Once the running record is finished, give descriptive feedback to celebrate and solidify what the reader is doing well: "I noticed you reread when the sentence wasn't making sense. That's what readers do!" | Select an instructional focus based on what you learned from your analysis and observations. Some might include:<br>■ Word identification<br>■ Comprehension monitoring<br>■ Fluency<br>■ Vocabulary knowledge and strategies<br>■ Comprehension strategy use (Duke 2020) |

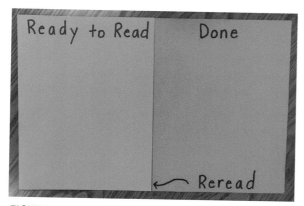

**FIGURE 3.3**

*Readers move books from the green "ready to read" side to the red "done" side as they complete them.*

### Student-Led Small-Group Topics

| Get Ready to Read | Find Texts You ♥ |
|---|---|
| • Choose a reason to read<br>  (Laugh, Learn, Ponder, Relax, Imagine)<br>• Set a reading goal<br>• Match your place to your purpose | • Know what you like<br>• Know where to look<br>• Know who to ask<br>• Decide if a text is right for you |
| **Think Together About Books** | **Build Your Reading Power** |
| • Notice things to talk about<br>• Ask your friends questions<br>• Build on your friends' thinking<br>• Ponder big ideas | • Read words<br>• Figure out what words mean<br>• Figure out what the text means |

**FIGURE 3.4**

*Invite readers to hold student-led small groups to share their expertise with peers.*

## GET STARTED

With your formative assessment data in hand, make a flexible plan for supporting readers either individually or in small groups. Flexibility and responsiveness are the keys to effective small-group reading instruction. This sentiment is echoed by researcher Nell Duke, who finds that "grouping flexibly and using a variety of grouping strategies can help teachers to see children more multidimensionally" (Duke and Varlas 2019). Keep in mind that your goal during these interactions is to shine a spotlight on one aspect of the reading process in a way that helps readers to apply it on their own. Whether meeting with individuals or small groups, we use the three-step process we learned from Jan Richardson (2016) (see Figure 3.5).

**FIGURE 3.5**

### THREE-STEP PROCESS FOR GUIDING READERS

| Focus | Text | Teach |
|---|---|---|
| Based on your formative assessments, identify an explicit instructional focus (a reading skill, strategy, or behavior) and state it at the beginning of a small-group reading lesson.<br><br>After spending time with an individual reader, collaboratively set a future focus/goal. | Select a text that matches students' interests and is ideal for practicing the skill, strategy, or behavior in context.<br><br>If conferring, use a book that students are currently reading or bring a mentor text along to the conference. | Demonstrate the focus skill, strategy, or behavior.<br><br>Provide time for students to practice. Observe the reader so that you can prompt, coach, and/or give descriptive feedback.<br><br>Wrap up the interaction by restating the focus or goal. |

## WHERE THIS MIGHT LEAD

Little by little, over the course of the first semester you'll gain insights into what makes each of your readers tick and add to your repertoire of techniques to meet them where they are and move them forward. One of the key ingredients in many of your interactions will be well-chosen texts. Remember the small-group book bins we introduced in Chapter 1? Now is an ideal time to help readers make the transition from small-group book bins to individual book collections. One way to do this is by curating a personalized set of books for each of your readers. Although this will take a bit of your planning time, it is worth it when you see kids' faces light up. Here's how Maria does it:

- Consider what you've learned about each reader from your multi-faceted data collection.
- Select a few books that match their current interests and that, based on formative assessments, you estimate they will feel successful reading independently.
- Place that stack on their desk or in their book container.
- If you have time, write a quick note to each reader (see Figure 3.6).

FIGURE 3.6

*Use what you've learned about your readers to create personalized book stacks.*

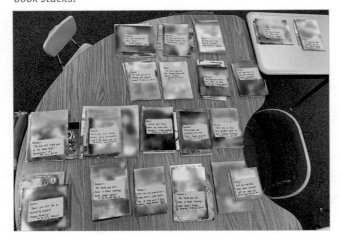

When readers are ready to select new texts for their individual book collection, teach them strategies for choosing "just-right" books. Then pull them together in small groups to shop for books based on their interests and stage of reading development. In the small group, ask students to tell a bit about a book or two that they enjoyed. Oftentimes this informal sharing of titles leads to book swapping. We've found that small-group book shopping is an efficient way to gather additional insights about your readers as they learn the ins and outs of strategic book selection.

### Try This! Overcome Roadblocks to Conferring

Whether it's short class periods, large class sizes, district-mandated schedules, classroom management challenges, or a combination of factors, finding time to confer with our middle-grade and middle school readers can sometimes feel like an unsolvable equation. If we continue to subscribe to Regie Routman's (2008) broader definition of guiding readers, we can address the challenging factors in this equation by implementing work-arounds to help us guide readers within the boundaries of our unique teaching contexts.

## GATHER

Before reading on, determine one or two of the most daunting issues that cause you to confer less often than you would like or to abandon the practice altogether. With these dilemmas in mind, read through the ideas found in the "Get Started" section that follows to find suggestions to use or modify as you guide readers throughout the first semester.

## GET STARTED

| Roadblock | Try This! |
|---|---|
| There's never enough time! *How do I fit everything into a language arts block or class period?* | Tie your conferring focus to your whole-class instruction for the day, week, or unit. Once readers have explored a concept in a mini-lesson or during group work, prompt them to return to their independent-reading books to apply their new learning.<br><br>For instance, if students are studying how setting impacts conflict while you're reading *Other Words for Home* (Warga 2019) as a class, ask them to notice if the setting impacts the conflict in the book they're reading on their own. When conferring, prioritize students who need extra support with this concept or may benefit from an extension of your whole-class learning targets. |
| I have large class sizes. *How do I reach all learners in a classroom of more than thirty readers?* | Confer with readers in small groups. Using your formative data, strategically place readers into small groups of four to six based on assets, needs, or a combination of both. While the other students read independently, meet with one group per day. Gathering together in small groups creates opportunities for students to support one another in their reading journeys. Here are some possible instructional focuses for grouping readers:<br>■ Applying decoding strategies<br>■ Expanding reading to new genres<br>■ Finding new books to read<br>■ Strengthening fluency<br>■ Comparing multimodal texts on a similar theme<br>■ Analyzing nonfiction text structures |
| The rest of the class needs my help. *How do I make time for conferring while also addressing other students' questions and needs?* | Set up, clearly demonstrate, and practice a system for students to use when they have non-urgent questions. This could look like reserving a space on a whiteboard where learners indicate they need to talk to you by writing down their name. As you transition between conferences, glance at the board and quickly check in with a student or two. Alternatively, students can place a brightly colored sticky note somewhere visible near their reading spot as a flag to let you know they need to talk when you have a minute. When you have systems like these in place, it lessens the interruptions that distract you from conferring. |

(continued on next page)

GET STARTED (continued)

| Roadblock | Try This! |
|---|---|
| I'm unsure of what to say or ask. *When I sit down to guide a reader, how do I know what to ask? How do I guide the conversation?* | Use the Thinking About My Reading response sheet (see Figure 3.7 and Appendix A3.1) to help you get conferring conversations started. To make a Thinking About My Reading response sheet, create a four-square grid. In each of the quadrants write a prompt that will encourage learners to think about their reading in different ways. We've included four prompts that have worked well in our classrooms, but feel free to tailor the ideas to match your instructional goals and your students' learning needs.<br><br>One day a week (or more if kids want to) readers can jot down a response to one of the four questions on a sticky note and place it on top of that quadrant of the chart. (If you have sticky notes that don't stick well, like the ones in our classrooms, you may end up stapling them to the grid to keep them from fluttering around the classroom.) When you sit beside a reader, use the ideas on their sticky notes as a nice jumping-off point for your conversation (see the student work sample in Figure 3.8). As the semester continues, students can keep adding sticky notes to their charts and even look for patterns in their thinking and reading habits. |
| I just came up with a great idea for how to make today's lesson better, and I need a few minutes to prepare or revise today's lesson. *How can I use independent reading time to work on the lesson and still make sure to fit in conferring?* | When this roadblock comes up, allow yourself that time to make the learning better for all students. Then intentionally use the transition times throughout your day to have informal conversations with readers. Here are some moments where we try to fit in a brief reading conversation:<br><br>■ As students get supplies for an activity or experience<br>■ Walking down the hallway between classes or to electives<br>■ When a student finishes a task before their peers<br>■ While learners are taking a Brain Break |

FIGURE 3.7

### THINKING ABOUT MY READING RESPONSE SHEET

| | |
|---|---|
| **ENGAGEMENT:** Rate your engagement with the text from 1–10. Explain your rating. | **CONNECTION:** Share something in the text that connects to your learning, your life, or what is going on in the world. |
| **EMOTIONS:** Jot down any emotions that came up while you were reading this text. What happened in the text to cause these emotions? | **ROADBLOCKS:** Did you run into any roadblocks while you were reading? What did you try? Is there anything I can do to help? |

## WHERE THIS MIGHT LEAD

After dabbling with a few of our suggestions related to your unique roadblocks, reflect on how the ideas have impacted your ability to guide readers. View roadblocks as opportunities for innovation. Talk with your colleagues about how they navigate different situations in their classrooms. Reach out to other professionals in your building who might have a different point of view, like the school social worker or special educator. They often have tricks up their sleeve that you haven't tried yet.

By identifying roadblocks and working to tackle them one at a time, you are taking small steps toward improving your craft. Don't expect change to happen overnight—reflective educators ponder and revise their teaching moves every day. Ask yourself, "What other roadblocks am I facing? What are some innovative ways to guide readers despite these roadblocks?" Use these two questions as you continually reflect and refine your practice to align with the needs of your readers and as those needs evolve throughout the school year.

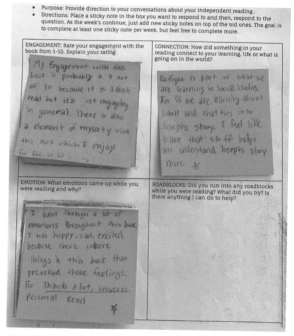

**FIGURE 3.8**
*Student Work Sample: Thinking About My Reading Response Sheet*

## Keep It Simple: Focus on the Reader

▶▶ Whether you're engaged in a reading experience with the whole class, meeting with a small group, checking in on student-led book clubs, listening in during whole-group book discussions, or sitting beside a reader, keep it simple by using these three questions to reflect on your interactions:

- What did I learn about this reader that I didn't already know?

- How can I use what I learned to support and challenge them?

- What else do I need to learn about this reader to better support them?

When you set your sights on answering these reader-focused questions during your interactions with students, the answers will lead you toward discovering the most impactful ways to deepen independent reading during the first semester.

**FIGURE 3.9**
*Focus on the reader.*

## TRANSLATE BELIEFS INTO ACTIONS

You've pondered how the physical layout of your classroom reflects your beliefs, and you've collaboratively worked with students to establish guiding principles. The next step is consistently working day in and day out to translate your beliefs about teaching and learning into intentional actions. In Chapter 1, we identified the following beliefs that are the foundation for our vibrant reading community:

- We believe everyone is a reader.
- We believe that reading feeds our hearts and minds.
- We believe everyone's voice should be heard.
- We believe that we learn from each other.
- We believe talking and writing help us understand what we've read.
- We believe mistakes are learning opportunities.

Our goal, as we continue learning alongside students, is to make it crystal clear when a classroom learning experience amplifies one of our beliefs. This can be as simple as saying, "Chat about the book you read today with a partner because talking with others makes you even smarter." In the sections that follow, we detail two decision-making processes that help us stay true to our beliefs.

### Why Translate Beliefs into Actions?

- When we translate our reading beliefs into actions, we help our students and ourselves see the shared vision that we aspire to each day. This shared vision can then act as a road map for navigating any hurdles or changes (Graham 2022).

- When classroom actions are rooted in deeply held beliefs and aimed at helping students gain true understanding, learners are able to see how literacy experiences are connected, extended, and related, with minimal teacher support. As learners see classroom beliefs show up as classroom actions, they can feel confident in applying these actions to new intellectual challenges and contexts (Wiggins and McTighe 2011).

### Try This! Match Learning Experiences to Beliefs

If the ideas in this book are ringing true but you're wondering when you'll find time in your jam-packed schedule for authentic reading experiences, we've been there. One statement you rarely hear at a school or district meeting is "Today we are going to take something off your plate." To change this narrative, Maria and her colleagues choose to begin their team meetings with something they call "brave abandonments." They cheer and celebrate when a colleague modifies or lets go of any action, small or large, to make more room for student-centered learning (cue the song "Let It Go!" from the movie *Frozen*). To find practices to bravely abandon, we suggest examining your current reading lesson or unit plans and, if necessary, moving away from surface-level activities and toward connected learning experiences that match your beliefs and make a difference for readers.

## GATHER

To begin, get together with a thinking partner or group of like-minded colleagues. These people may be your team members, other educators in your building, or a professional learning group that meets via an online platform. Select a specific unit of study or series of lessons that you want to analyze and streamline.

## GET STARTED

Follow the six-step process detailed here:

### Step 1: Determine the standards-based essential understandings.

As curriculum is passed from one teacher to another, we tend to focus on the *what* of teaching, the activities, rather than zeroing in on the deeper reason behind the planned learning experiences, the *why*. By taking a minute to uncover the essential understandings that underpin the learning sequence, you gain a clearer vision of exactly what you want to help readers understand and apply. Weigh the planned learning activities against that vision to determine which are impactful and which you can abandon.

### Step 2: Identify and prioritize big ideas.

Use the standards-based essential understandings to determine a big idea or two that you want readers to grasp. Then, rather than spending time planning separate surface-level activities, create a connected sequence of learning events tied to a big idea. This will help students organize and make sense of their learning.

### Step 3: Select short, multimodal texts.

With your big ideas in mind, evaluate the texts students are currently reading. Ask yourself, "Are the texts up-to-date? Do they match my students' lived experiences and reflect the rich diversity in the world around them?" When selecting texts to use to teach mini-lessons that demonstrate reading habits, skills, and behaviors, we suggest curating short multimodal texts like picture books, short stories, video clips, podcasts, song lyrics, and so on to keep the engagement high and the teacher-directed portion of the demonstration lesson short.

### Step 4: Plan engaging learning experiences that are tied to your purpose.

We subscribe to the "less is more" philosophy when planning learning experiences. Start with a well-chosen text, surround it with conversation, and extend that experience in some simple way—perhaps a blank piece of paper, sticky note, or electronic document for students to record their ideas. If you choose to access and use reading-related activities from an online site, keep in mind that web-based curriculum developers don't know your students or your learning context. On the surface, the activity you print out might meet the standards, but does it match your purpose and will it engage your learners? Before printing, think about these questions:

- Where does the activity fit in your connected sequence of learning events?
- Will it lead your students to a more in-depth understanding of the topic or concept?
- Will your students engage with literacy in a way that will have lasting impact?
- Can you do the same thing with carefully selected texts and a blank piece of paper?

### Step 5: Integrate as much as possible.

Look for ways to embed as much learning as possible into the learning sequence. Perhaps you have a unit on nonfiction text structures coming up. Would it be possible to tie it to your current science topic? Maybe students are reading and studying biographies—what an ideal time to integrate social studies. If you're looking for more ideas, Maria and her co-author Karen Biggs-Tucker detail a clear path toward integrating literacy instruction in their book *The Literacy Workshop* (2020).

### Step 6: Trust that volume reading works.

Be mindful to leave plenty of time for students to read, because volume reading makes a difference. Researcher and longtime advocate of volume reading Dick Allington sums it up in a review of recent research (Allington and McGill-Franzen 2021): once students develop basic proficiencies as readers, extensive reading activity—in other words, increased reading volume—leads to gains in reading achievement. Work with your colleagues to figure out how to carve out time for students to read each and every day.

## WHERE THIS MIGHT LEAD

Collaboratively planning connected learning experiences will add depth to your teaching. When you rely on your beliefs, professional expertise, and knowledge of your students to guide your teaching actions, you gain a deep understanding of the *why* behind your decisions. Knowing your rationale makes it easier to communicate with the stakeholders in your learning community. In other words, you will find yourself better equipped to explain your professional decisions to administrators during evaluation meetings, to questioning caregivers, and to colleagues who might wonder why you choose to prioritize certain learning experiences.

### Try This! Plan with Beliefs at the Forefront

During the first few weeks of school, you've intentionally invested time and energy in establishing classroom actions that match your beliefs. As the year gets busier and busier, it can be far too easy to lose sight of your guiding principles. The more that gets added to the calendar, the more your vision can fade into the background. When you are not regularly checking in on your beliefs, you can stray off course with your actions and classroom experiences. Making time during the first semester to design a user-friendly system to orient yourself toward the north star of your beliefs can help keep you on course for the rest of the year.

### GATHER

Refer back to the list of classroom beliefs that you established at the beginning of the school year. Add to those any schoolwide beliefs or those held by your professional learning community. We shared our beliefs on pages 29 (in Chapter 1) and 86 (earlier in this chapter). Next to your belief statements, list the possible actions that should show up in your classroom as a result of those beliefs (see Figure 3.10).

FIGURE 3.10

| TURNING BELIEFS ABOUT TEACHING AND LEARNING INTO ACTIONS | |
|---|---|
| **Belief** | **Action** |
| We believe everyone is a reader. | We will have ten minutes of reading time each day. |
| We believe that reading feeds our hearts and minds. | We will schedule time to talk about the texts we've learned from and enjoyed. |

(continued on next page)

FIGURE 3.10 (continued)

| TURNING BELIEFS ABOUT TEACHING AND LEARNING INTO ACTIONS | |
|---|---|
| **Belief** | **Action** |
| We believe everyone's voice should be heard. | We will build in time for students to have collaborative conversations during book experiences. |
| We believe that we learn from each other. | We will plan and coordinate student-led learning experiences. |
| We believe talking and writing help us to understand what we've read. | We will provide opportunities for students to reflect on their reading in various ways. |
| We believe mistakes are learning opportunities. | We will develop a system for revising our classroom work. |

## GET STARTED

Once you've settled on specific actions that will exemplify your classroom beliefs, create a tracking system to help you intentionally plan with these beliefs in mind. Design a manageable tracking system that aligns with your organizational style and planning methods. Katie's tracking system is simply an extra column in her weekly planning template where she lists the learning actions that she wants her students to engage in each week. Then, after planning with her PLC, she tweaks and modifies the plan to ensure that students' literacy experiences align with her beliefs about teaching and learning. Figure 3.11 provides an example of this tracking system.

## WHERE THIS MIGHT LEAD

Once you've tried a tracking system for a while, reflect and make any necessary adjustments. Ask yourself the following questions:

- Are there additional belief-based actions I might implement and keep tabs on based on the big ideas I've identified, learning targets for the unit, or a specific essential question?

- Am I being realistic about what students can accomplish in a week?

- How can I modify and adjust my expectations for weeks with holidays, snow days, standardized testing, and so on?

In short, use the tracking system as a flexible tool rather than a rigid structure.

FIGURE 3.11

## Beliefs into Actions Tracking System

**Essential Question:** How does learning about a different time period help me to better understand the world today?

**Learning Targets:**

- I can learn about a time in history in order to better understand a story.

- I can determine the main idea and supporting details of a text.

> The actions that Katie prioritized this particular school year were the five elements of literacy, opportunities for non-academic community building, book talks, and literacy notebook responses.

> Including a section to list what learning artifacts you will grade each week will help you to be realistic about your workload and honor work-life balance.

| MONDAY | TUESDAY | WEDNESDAY | THURSDAY | FRIDAY | TRACKING |
|---|---|---|---|---|---|
| Independent reading | Independent reading | Independent reading | Independent reading | Independent reading | • ~~Reading~~ |
| Mini-lesson on main idea and supporting details—Cuban refugee article | Poetry analysis (first-person accounts of being a refugee) | Mini-lesson on flashbacks | Community building | Book talks | • ~~Writing~~ <br> • Speaking <br> • ~~Listening~~ <br> • ~~Researching~~ <br> • ~~Community building~~ |
| Article of the Week response work time in small groups | | Flashback Question Challenge—questions related to refugee experience | Connections to myself and the world: *Refugee* [turn into literacy notebook work] | Mini-lesson review of main idea and supporting details | • ~~Book talks~~ <br> • ~~Notebook work~~ <br><br> What am I grading? <br> • Article of the Week response |

> The Article of the Week is a helpful resource that is available on Kelly Gallagher's website.

Download articles from Kelly Gallagher's Article of the Week here.

> Here Katie's PLC was planning an interactive whiteboard activity, but she believes in the power of notebook work. She modified this lesson to make sure the action showed up in the school week, while still reaching the same end goal as her colleagues.

> You will see that Katie did not get to every action this week. Give yourself grace as a teacher, but also use your system as a data point. Are you consistently letting one or two of your actions slip by? How can you change this in the future?

### Keep It Simple: Stay the Course

Just as your shared classroom beliefs guide students' actions, strive to stay true to your beliefs about teaching and learning when making instructional decisions. Our advice here is simple: stay the course. Avoid detours caused by comparing yourself to the perfectly polished "edustars" on social media, and evade roadblocks put in place by negative colleagues. Keep your eyes on the road by trusting your professional judgment and seeking out mentors and colleagues who push back on your thinking and give you energy. Finally, enjoy the ride as you focus on creating a caring environment where readers can thrive!

## DEMONSTRATE AND PRACTICE ROUTINES

Now that you and your learners have taken the beginning steps toward establishing literacy routines, it's time for them to become, well . . . routine. But how do you go from setting up routines to transitioning them into an everyday ritual? Just as you would when teaching anything from riding a bike to driving a car, you model, coach, and give learners plenty of time to practice, practice, practice. The goal is that with repetition and descriptive feedback, literacy routines become second nature. Once you get these routines running smoothly, you can focus your energy on fostering a community of literacy lovers. Read on for a few ways we demonstrate and practice routines in our classrooms.

### Why Demonstrate and Practice Routines?

■ Teachers who create a culturally responsive community for learning "design routines to emphasize interdependency and social connection." Affirming and communal routines build social networks among students. When routines are taught, modeled, and practiced, they create positive energy and eventually become an invisible part of the classroom culture (Hammond 2015, 146).

■ When we consistently practice the routines we've taken time to establish in the classroom, we are showing students that we value the routines that help us to establish or enhance our love of literacy (Routman 2019).

### Try This! Create a Predictable Teach-Demonstrate-Practice-Reflect Cycle

Teaching is unpredictable. Even when we feel like we've planned well and are fully prepared, anything can happen, from bathroom emergencies to fire drills to bears running loose in the neighborhood (if you teach in Colorado, like Katie). Unexpected occurrences are par for the course and have the potential to throw us off-kilter. Planning predictable learning experiences is one way to anchor your teaching so that you can stay on course when things go awry. A predictable sequence that works well when turning routines into rituals is teach-demonstrate-practice-reflect (see Figure 3.12).

## GATHER

To plan a cycle, answer the following questions:

- What do I want kids to do?
- What are the underlying skills/strategies they need in order to do it? (See Figure 3.13 for some examples.)
- How can I make the skills/strategies concrete for learners?
- How will they practice? Independently, in partnerships, in small groups?
- What success criteria will I use to confirm they have internalized the routine?

Once you have the answers, you're ready to begin planning the first cycle.

FIGURE 3.12

*Plan this predictable sequence of instruction when solidifying routines.*

FIGURE 3.13

| SKILLS AND STRATEGIES THAT SUPPORT READING ROUTINES | |
|---|---|
| **Routine** | **Underlying Skills and Strategies** |
| Read the whole time | ■ Knowledge of the different ways to read (see Chapter 1, page 16)<br>■ Habit of reading one book after another<br>■ Understanding of the various reasons to reread |
| Read in a quiet voice | ■ Clarity about expected voice levels<br>■ Awareness of own voice level |
| Read with a partner | ■ Ability to share the book<br>■ Ability to take turns<br>■ Ability to coach a peer using known strategies |
| Shop for new books | ■ Awareness of reading interests and preferences<br>■ Understanding of book selection strategies |

## GET STARTED

Knowing you only have a limited amount of time to get your message across before learners lose their focus, plan to be as clear as possible and avoid verbal clutter. Here are some sentence stems to try out that will keep your cycle focused:

- **Teach:** "Today we're going to learn how to _____."

- **Demonstrate:** "I'm going to show you how readers _____. What do you notice? Would someone like to come up and show the class what _____ looks like?"

- **Practice:** "Now you're going to try it with a partner. Remember, your goal is to _____." While readers are practicing, gather anecdotal data as you circulate by jotting down notes, taking photos, or recording video clips to use in future demonstrations. Along the way, give descriptive feedback by noticing and naming the child's reading behaviors. Say something like, "I noticed that when you finished the book, you started another one right away. That's what readers do."

- **Reflect:** "What went well today? What was challenging?" Gather students together for a brief reflection. If you make this a habit, you will find that the challenges children identify often turn into the content for your next cycle.

## WHERE THIS MIGHT LEAD

Repeat the cycle periodically throughout the semester as you notice that readers need a refresher or as new students join your reading community. Once students are familiar with the cycle, consider an asset-focused adaptation where you invite students to use the same process to teach their peers the skills and strategies at which they excel. Perhaps you have a student who is skilled at using book selection strategies. Talk with them about their process and then have them plan a teach-demonstrate-plan-reflect cycle to share their expertise with another student, a small group, or the whole class. If you teach the middle grades, invite children to teach younger students the strategies they've found helpful for keeping their reading routine going.

### Try This! Establish a Daily Reading Routine

So far, we've focused on familiarizing students with the texts in our classrooms by exploring different kinds of books through Book Title Challenges, book talks, and Book Speed Dating. Now it's time to put those texts to good use as you settle into a daily practice of independent reading. Turning this routine into an expected ritual in your classroom spotlights the importance of pleasure reading and offers all students time to improve their reading proficiency.

## GATHER

You're already well on your way to assembling the necessary materials and teaching practices that you need to support a successful independent reading routine. To sustain it across the first semester, we would suggest gathering your patience, ingenuity, and sense of humor, because you will need all three to guide readers over any bumps in the road that might crop up in the coming months.

## GET STARTED

We've found that scheduling a consistent time of day for students to read can help incorporate this routine. In Katie's classroom, independent reading time takes place during the first ten minutes of class. That way, students begin each language arts period by reading self-selected texts. Depending on your daily schedule, you might find it easier to carve out time at the end of your class period or even in the middle of your literacy block. Because your goal is to make time for volume reading, the key is slotting it into your schedule in a place where it won't get pushed aside when time is running short.

To signal the start of supported independent reading, Katie creates a calm reading environment (see "Back Pocket Wisdom" on page 97), and then it always magically gets quiet. Wait! That doesn't always happen?! Have you ever watched a video clip or read a professional book where once the independent reading routines were introduced everything goes beautifully—kids are reading, the teacher is conferring, and everyone is happy? Well, we teach in the real world, where that is not necessarily the case. So to help you sustain the reading routine all semester, we'll share some roadblocks that we've experienced in our classrooms and how we've used patience, ingenuity, and humor to help our readers get back on track (see Figure 3.14).

FIGURE 3.14

| TROUBLESHOOTING DURING SUPPORTED INDEPENDENT READING | |
|---|---|
| **When Readers Do This . . .** | **Try This . . .** |
| Forget or can't find a book to read | ■ Guide them to consult their Someday List or pair them with a reader with similar interests to see if they can help them find a book. If you notice a lot of readers having the same issue, host another Book Speed Dating event (see Chapter 2, page 49).<br>■ Point them toward your collection of short texts (see Chapter 2, page 51). |
| Flip through the pages quickly without taking time to read and comprehend the content | ■ Prioritize these readers on your conferring schedule. Work to find texts that match their interests and ability. For middle schoolers, consider introducing graphic novels like *Borders* by Thomas King (1993/2021), *Long Distance* by Whitney Gardner (2021), or the I Survived graphic novel series (Tarshis 2020–). Check in frequently to gauge their progress. |

(continued on next page)

FIGURE 3.14 (continued)

| TROUBLESHOOTING DURING SUPPORTED INDEPENDENT READING | |
|---|---|
| **When Readers Do This . . .** | **Try This . . .** |
| Abandon book after book | ■ Ask the reader to let you know before they give up on a book. Have a quick conversation to find out the reason and jot it down. Look for a pattern so that you can be strategic in your next steps. Notice whether the reasons are related to attention/stamina or book selection.<br>  ● If related to attention/stamina: offer shorter texts.<br>  ● If related to book selection: partner with your school librarian to find texts that you don't have in your book collection. |
| Refuse to read | ■ Refusal to read can be an indicator of many different underlying factors. Work to determine the root cause for the refusal. However, while you're doing this, remember that students are much more likely to follow the lead of their peers than to heed our nudges and prompting. So, rely on the fact that observing other readers through peer modeling will also be occurring and that this might just be enough to encourage the learner to join the reading community. In other words, sometimes we simply let the child sit and watch other readers while we observe and learn about the child. |

Troubleshooting done, now things can fall into serene quiet while everyone gets lost in a book, right? Well, not necessarily. In a responsive classroom, supported independent reading is a calm but active time. On any given day, you might see readers do any or all of the following:

- Settling down with a good book
- Shopping for a new book
- Recommending a book to a friend
- Adding a title to their Someday List
- Conferring with a teacher
- Discussing their reading with peers
- Reflecting in their literacy notebook
- Writing a book review to post

During independent reading time, view your classroom as a true "library classroom." Take on the role of coach and cheerleader as you help students fall in love with books!

FIGURE 3.15
*Display a few books with the covers facing forward.*

## WHERE THIS MIGHT LEAD

Once students become more comfortable with a daily reading practice and checking out books to take home from your school and classroom library, the natural next step is for students to set their own reading goals and/or track the books they read individually or collectively as a class. Invite students to set and reflect on reading goals. We find the 4Cs for effective goal setting (Dotson 2016) helpful when supporting students in determining personal learning intentions:

- Create goals that are specific, measurable, attainable, realistic, and time sensitive.

- Coach and support students as they develop an action plan.

- Check in frequently to monitor progress.

- Celebrate successes both big and small.

### Back Pocket Wisdom: Create a Calm Reading Environment

Here are a few simple ways to arrange a calm classroom environment primed for abundant amounts of reading:

- Mood lighting. Turn off some or all of the bright fluorescent lights and switch on small lamps or strings of lights, or let in the sunlight (if you're lucky enough to have windows).

- Quiet music. In Katie's classroom, the following Spotify playlists are on repeat to set the tone: Instrumental Study, Reading Chill Out, Positive Focus, and Reading Soundtrack.

- Soothing scenes. Provide ambience by projecting soothing scenes. We've found that the Netflix series *Fireplace for Your Home* is a go-to at any time of the year!

- Enticing books. Display books throughout the classroom to entice readers into picking up an engaging story or compelling informational book. Bonus points if the books are front-facing (see Figure 3.15).

- Comfortable seating. Think of the places where you enjoy reading, and recreate them in simple ways. Make small spaces on the floor where kids can snuggle in and read. Add a stack of plastic stepstools for footrests. Scatter a few pillows (with zip-off covers for easy washing) around the room.

To keep the momentum going over the course of the first semester, you might occasionally pose a book challenge where students track the books they're reading in different ways. These challenges engage some of your more competitively motivated readers. Some reading challenges we've found successful include:

- **Class reading challenges.** This strategy works well if you teach multiple class periods. To set up a class reading challenge, create a space in your room for readers to keep track of the books they've finished. Then develop a system, like color-coding, to indicate which class period the student is in. As students post their finished titles, they get ideas for future reads and see which books are the most popular (see Figure 3.16).

- **READ-O.** Create a reading bingo card where each space includes a reading goal for learners. Spaces could include "Read a science fiction book, "Read outside," or "Listen to an audiobook." Set a time frame for readers and challenge them to get as many READ-Os as possible in the allotted time (see Figure 3.17). You can find printable versions in Appendixes A3.2 and A3.3.

- **Reading bucket list.** We borrowed and modified this idea from adult reading bucket lists we've seen in local independent bookshops. To make a bucket list for your students, list ten to twenty different types of books that readers might be interested in reading, like a book with an imaginary main character or an informational book about a natural disaster (see Figure 3.18). Students' goal is to check off as many books from the list as possible or as time allows. (See Appendixes A3.4 and A3.5 for printable bucket lists.)

FIGURE 3.16

*Readers keep track of the books they've finished.*

You might find you have other students that are self-motivated and prefer to simply track their reading in their literacy notebook or an online book database. Be sure to take students like these into account when you are setting up book challenges.

### Keep It Simple: Play a Happy Tune

▶▶ Many years ago, Maria tasked Katie with clipping and editing a playlist of her favorite first-grade-friendly songs, like "Good Morning Baltimore" from *Hairspray* and "Ease on Down the Road" from *The Wiz*, to cue

**READ-O: Primary Grades**

Name: _____

| NONFICTION BOOK | FUNNY BOOK | ANIMAL BOOK |
|---|---|---|
| Title: _____ | Title: _____ | Title: _____ |
| Author: _____ | Author: _____ | Author: _____ |
| BIOGRAPHY | YOUR CHOICE! | GRAPHIC NOVEL |
| Title: _____ | Title: _____ | Title: _____ |
| Author: _____ | Author: _____ | Author: _____ |
| MAKE-BELIEVE BOOK | POETRY BOOK | CHAPTER BOOK |
| Title: _____ | Title: _____ | Title: _____ |
| Author: _____ | Author: _____ | Author: _____ |

**FIGURE 3.17**

*Challenge readers to get as many READ-Os as possible in the allotted time.*

**FIGURE 3.18**

*Readers check as many books off their bucket list as time allows.*

Name: _____

**Reading Bucket List: Middle Grades**

Directions: Pick ____ items off the reading bucket list. Write down the title and author. Once you have finished the text, put a checkmark in the "Finished" column. When you've completed the challenge, ask your parent/caregiver to sign the paper.

| | Book Title and Author | ✓ Finished |
|---|---|---|
| A book in a series you have never read | | |
| A book published this year | | |
| A book with a number in the title | | |
| A book written by someone under age thirty | | |
| A book of short stories | | |
| A chapter book that won the Sibert Medal | | |
| A chapter book that won the Newbery Medal | | |
| A book based on a true event | | |
| A book your parent/caregiver loves | | |
| A book published in the year you were born | | |
| A book set somewhere you want to visit | | |
| A book with a color in the title | | |
| A book by an author whose lived experiences are different from yours | | |
| A play | | |
| A novel in verse | | |
| A nonfiction book | | |
| An autobiography, biography, or memoir | | |
| Other (get this option approved by your teacher) | | |

Due Date: _____    Caregiver Signature: _____

transitions in the classroom. This process took hours and resulted in a custom CD (remember those?!) that was well used in Maria's classroom. Fortunately, there are now much easier ways to play a snippet of your kids' favorite music. The handy thing about having a song that signals it's time to shift from one learning experience to the next is that it gives you a moment to gather the materials you need while, at the same time, providing students with a quick Brain Break. In addition, musical transitions become yet another familiar classroom routine. Consider playing an energetic tune to lead students out of reading and into a mini-lesson, or ease them into reading time with the first few notes of a quiet, calming song. Find your favorite kid-appropriate tunes and give it a try. You'll be amazed at how music can smooth out your transitions and keep everyone smiling.

## ELEVATE COMMUNITY THROUGH LITERACY

Reflect on the communities that have been instrumental in your growth as a person and as a professional. What are the characteristics of those learning networks? When we think of the places where we've learned, the common traits that come to mind are shared goals, collaborative knowledge building, positivity, and celebration. How do we infuse these traits into our literacy learning community? In the "Try This!" examples that follow, we will show you how to design reading experiences that introduce students to the joys and advantages of learning in community.

## Why Elevate Community Through Literacy?

■ Teachers who focus on culturally relevant instruction expect a higher level of success for the entire class, focusing on collaboration rather than competition. Students learn with and from each other during both planned and informal interactions (Ladson-Billings 2021).

■ Students who work together in small groups to achieve collaborative goals deepen their understanding of the concepts they are learning and build intergroup relationships. Carefully orchestrated collaborative group work "crosses lines of social identity and academic achievement, supports equitable access to content knowledge and broadens participation" (Scharf 2018, 5).

## Try This! Strengthen Community During Small-Group Collaborative Conversations

▶ The ideas in this section are dual-purpose. First we share strategies to get kids collaboratively thinking and talking about books. Then we suggest some texts that spotlight the benefits of learning in a community. The ideas here build on what we've already shared about modeling text-focused conversations during read-aloud on page 58 in Chapter 2, and extend these conversations into the small-group setting.

### GATHER

Choose a stack of books that will spark discussions about learning with and from others. Here are a pair of picture books that have sparked rich conversations among a small group of students in our classrooms.

| Read This . . . | Talk About This . . . |
| --- | --- |
| *Fly!* (Thurman 2022)<br>Africa wants to take part in a double Dutch competition on Sunday to, as her brother shares, "show the world what she's made of." There is only one little problem: she has never played double Dutch before. After trying unsuccessfully to learn on her own, she asks her pals at school to help her out. Although none of them know double Dutch, each teaches her a skill that will transfer, like dancing, stepping, and hand-clapping. On Sunday, she shows everyone that she can "jump, fly, double Dutch to the sky." | ■ Goal setting<br>■ Willingness to learn<br>■ Seeking help from others<br>■ Positive attitude |
| *The Year We Learned to Fly* (Woodson 2022)<br>The story begins on a stormy spring day when a brother and sister are stuck inside and their wise grandmother tells them to use their "beautiful and brilliant minds." Using their imaginations, they fly over the flower-filled city. During the summer, when they are arguing about chores, their grandmother advises, "Stop being so mean about everything." So they fly over the city, leaving their anger behind them. When autumn arrives, they remember what their grandmother's been teaching them about their ancestors who used their brilliant and beautiful minds to fly. Winter brings a big change as the family moves out of their neighborhood. Because of their grandmother's teachings, they are ready to fly past "any new thing coming their way." | ■ Family relationships<br>■ Learning from family members<br>■ Life lessons<br>■ Overcoming challenges<br><br> |

## GET STARTED

- Gather a group based on interests, assets, or needs. If grouping by interest, choose a short text on a topic that matches the group's mutual interest. In this instance, an asset-based group would be learners who are adept at conversation, whereas a needs-based group might be those who are more comfortable talking in a small-group setting.
- Preview the text to find compelling parts where you can pause and discuss.
- Begin by reading the first part of the text aloud.
- Pose a question, and invite a child to start the conversation. Model what to do when they want to add on to what a friend says or pose a question in response: the child simply says their friend's name and shares their idea. Build on this by collaboratively deciding the best strategies for the following conversational etiquette:
  - "What do you do when two people start talking at the same time?"
  - "How do you monitor and balance the amount of time you are talking and listening?"
  - "What can you say when you notice someone is not getting a chance to talk?"
- To guide future teaching points or mini-lessons, collect observations on an anecdotal note sheet like the one that appears in Figure 3.19, which can also be found in Appendix A3.6.

FIGURE 3.19
*Record observations during collaborative conversations.*

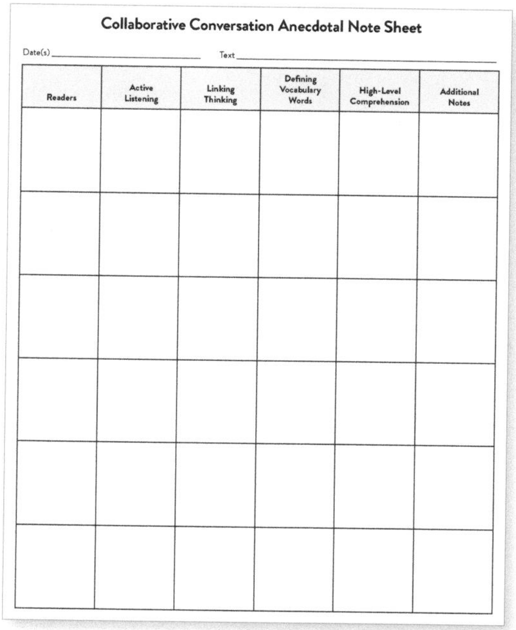

**Collaborative Conversation Anecdotal Note Sheet**

Date(s) ______ Text ______

| Readers | Active Listening | Linking Thinking | Defining Vocabulary Words | High-Level Comprehension | Additional Notes |
|---|---|---|---|---|---|
| | | | | | |
| | | | | | |
| | | | | | |
| | | | | | |
| | | | | | |
| | | | | | |

## WHERE THIS MIGHT LEAD

Once students are adept at collaborative small-group conversations with you by their side, transition to student-led book clubs. When setting up book clubs, we follow the advice Dr. Sonja Cherry-Paul and Dana Johansen share in their book *Breathing New Life into Book Clubs* (2019): give readers choice, guide readers in creating personal and collective book club goals, and set aside a specific time for clubs to meet and converse. Another helpful resource about book clubs is Sara Kugler's book *Better Book Clubs: Deepening Comprehension and Elevating Conversation* (2022).

## Try This! Use Multimodal Text Sets to Spark Collaborative Learning and Conversation

▶ We believe in creating community-building opportunities within the literacy practices that are already routine in our classrooms. So when deciding which texts you want to share with readers during the first semester, consider creating multimodal text sets that not only target reading goals but also open avenues for students to share their identities and collaborate with the members of their literacy community. The beauty of any multimodal text set is that they inherently meet many academic goals, including enhancing media literacy, encouraging large volumes of reading, and fostering synthesis skills. While these literacy-related goals are important, carefully selected text sets offer an added bonus: they draw students' attention to the overarching goals of creating a community of trust and respect within your classroom.

### GATHER

Identify your learning standards and/or reading goals for a unit or experience you are planning. Curate texts that meet your reading goals and will spark opportunities for students to collaborate and converse with their peers. Seek out texts in a variety of mediums and by creators with varied voices. See Figure 3.20 for a sample text set curated by Katie's PLC for a unit focused on how one's environment impacts their identity.

### GET STARTED

Once you've assembled a text set, think about how you can you maximize the power of the individual texts to encourage collaboration and conversation amongst your learners. Create experiences where students read, listen to, or view the texts and then are able to connect those texts to their own lives and identities in various ways. For example, when seventh graders listened to the TED Talk listed in Figure 3.20, each child created a reflection (Figure 3.21). Then they shared these reflections with one another in order to understand their peers' different perspectives.

FIGURE 3.20

| ENVIRONMENT IMPACTS IDENTITY MULTIMODAL TEXT SET | | |
|---|---|---|
| Essential Question: How do people's environments impact their identity? | | |
| Text | Connection to Essential Question | Community-Building Questions |
| "Mirrors, Windows, and Sliding Doors" by Akhand Dugar TED Talk | Dugar builds on Rudine Sims Bishop's (1990) metaphor to introduce the essential question and discusses how literature impacts identity | What are influential mirrors, windows, and sliding doors in your own life? |

FIGURE 3.20 (continued)

## ENVIRONMENT IMPACTS IDENTITY MULTIMODAL TEXT SET

**Essential Question: How do people's environments impact their identity?**

| Text | Connection to Essential Question | Community-Building Questions |
|---|---|---|
| Excerpt from *The House on Mango Street* by Sandra Cisneros<br>Vignette | Illustrates how physical environment impacts identity | Which physical environments make you feel safe and comfortable? What do these environments have in common? |
| "Fish Cheeks" by Amy Tan<br>Short story | Showcases how cultural environment impacts identity | What are some important aspects of your own culture? How do you celebrate your culture? |
| *We Are the Champions* Episode S1.E4: "Yo Yo"<br>TV episode (TV-MA)<br>or<br>"Fancy Dancer"<br>by Monique Gray Smith<br>Short story from *Ancestor Approved: Intertribal Stories for Kids* | Depicts how social environment and community impact identity | What are your passions? What communities outside of school are you a part of? |

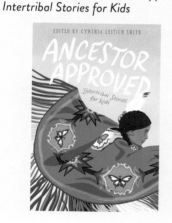

As you've already read, we are fans of in-the-moment assessment tools like anecdotal notes and focused observations. The notes you take while students are engaging with each other about these multimodal texts can inform future literacy experiences and point you toward book recommendations for individual readers.

FIGURE 3.21
*Student Work Sample: TED Talk Reflection*

### WHERE THIS MIGHT LEAD

After students read, listen to, or view a text in the multimodal text set, extend this learning and community building by tying in an authentic task. For instance, after seventh graders watched an episode of *We Are the Champions*, they created flyers advertising their own passions (see Figure 3.22), which resulted in Katie hosting a Rubik's Cube club. Following the viewing of the "Mirrors, Windows, and Sliding Doors" TED Talk, readers presented a quick book talk featuring a book that has acted as a mirror, window, or sliding door for them. Essentially, look for creative ways to invite students to share their identities within the context of the literacy classroom and the texts they are exploring.

FIGURE 3.22
*Students created flyers advertising their unique passions.*

### Keep It Simple: Weave Social Emotional Learning into Literacy Experiences

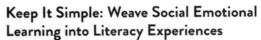 In the "Try This!" sections here and in Chapter 2 on pages 52–57, we featured literacy experiences that seamlessly weave social-emotional learning into literacy instruction. We believe that SEL and literacy go hand in hand and that, when instructional time is in short supply and students' emotional well-being is critical to their success in school, it makes sense to integrate the two. As the semester continues, keep an eye out for other opportunities to merge SEL competencies with literacy standards. To further explore SEL competencies, you will find helpful resources that outline social-emotional learning frameworks and their relationship to culturally responsive teaching practices at LearningforJustice.org and CASEL.org.

### CONFER WITH FAMILIES/CAREGIVERS

In the first few weeks of school, you reached out to students' caregivers to welcome them as partners in their child's in-school literacy life. Keeping them up to date on classroom happenings across the first semester using digital tools like classroom websites, social media accounts, and other applications is an essential aspect of an ongoing partnership. But nothing is more important than meeting face-to-face, either virtually or in person. Every school schedules their family-teacher conferences in a different way. We believe the earlier you can meet with caregivers, the better. Conferences are an excellent time to nurture the home-school connection as you move into a year of learning. Here we offer a few suggestions for creating partnerships and having productive conversations with families/caregivers.

## Try This! Explain the Child's Stage of Reading Development

▶ How do you clearly explain to a family member where their child is on the path to becoming a proficient reader? This is a challenging task, especially in a ten- or twenty-minute conference. A framework that has worked well for us is using a family-friendly explanation of the stages of reading development (see Figure 3.23). This continuum communicates that reading is a developmental process and that every child moves through the stages of development in their own unique fashion. It also steers the conversation away from identifying students by a reading level, centering the discussion on text levels, or comparing the student's progress to that of their same-age peers.

### Why Confer with Families/Caregivers?

■ Our students' learning extends far beyond our classroom walls. We confer with families/caregivers because they are "the essential connective tissue in learning experiences for children; they provide space for curiosity and critical conversation as well as the generational knowledge that is essential to raising a more equitable society" (Qarooni 2022, 35).

■ When we partner with families/caregivers, we get to know the school community and can develop better avenues of communication and support (Pedro Noguera, cited in Bridges 2013, 40).

### GATHER

Print out one copy of the Family-Friendly Explanation of Reading Development (see Appendix A3.7) for each reader. If needed, have the document translated into the languages that your caregivers speak. As you are guiding and assessing your readers, note where they fall in each row of the continuum. To prepare for conferences, circle the descriptors that indicate what behaviors the reader is currently displaying. Note that most readers will not fall neatly into one stage of development—for example, they may be more adept at decoding than comprehension, or they may have strong word knowledge but still be developing fluency. Jot down any anecdotal notes or noticings. Make a copy for families/caregivers to take home.

FIGURE 3.23
*Circle the descriptor that indicates the behaviors readers are currently displaying.*

### GET STARTED

Use the framework as a guide for your conversations with families/caregivers. Show them exactly what you see their child doing, explain the next steps for your in-class instruction, and discuss some ways they can support your work at home. Keep your copy in the child's file to update as the year progresses.

Reader's Name: _____

**Stages of Reading Development**

| Pre-Emergent Reader | Emergent Reader | Early Reader | Transitional Reader | Fluent Reader |
|---|---|---|---|---|
| Enjoys book experiences | Uses repetitive text and familiar patterns to mimic fluent reading | Reads familiar text word by word | Reads familiar text with increasing fluency (rate, accuracy, phrasing, and expression) | Reads independent-level text with fluency (rate, accuracy, phrasing, and expression) |
| Interacts with books | Uses prior knowledge and experiences to make meaning | Uses prior knowledge, clues from text, and experiences to make and predict meaning | Uses prior knowledge, clues from text, text structures, and experiences to make, predict, and infer meaning | Uses prior knowledge, clues from text, text structures, and experiences to make, predict, infer, and synthesize meaning |
| Developing phonemic awareness | Understands the relationship between letters and sounds and begins to apply this knowledge when decoding | Decodes most simple words using sound-spelling relationships and self-monitors using meaning and/or context clues | Decodes multisyllabic words using chunking and word parts and self-monitors by integrating meaning, context clues, and phonics | Uses self-monitoring strategies and self-corrects while reading |
| Recognizes and reads environmental print | Recognizes and reads a few high-frequency words, names, and simple words in context | Recognizes and reads many high-frequency words and simple words in context | Recognizes and reads high-frequency words and an increasing number of difficult words, many of which are content-related | Recognizes and reads most words automatically |

Adapted from *On Solid Ground* (Taberski 2000)

## WHERE THIS MIGHT LEAD

We like this framework because it is an asset-based approach that clearly shows caregivers what their reader is able to do at a particular point in the year. When you meet with families/caregivers again later in the year, you can celebrate areas of growth. This framework is also helpful as a communication tool among teachers who are supporting the same reader. It keeps conversations and instruction focused on the readers' strengths and next steps.

### Try This! Use a List of Talking Points

As educators, we spend so much of our time engaging with children that it can seem daunting to switch gears and spend an entire evening or day meeting with the adults who care for our students. Conferences can be especially intimidating if you teach in a building that holds drop-in-style meetings, where families/caregivers do not have to sign up ahead of time. While this approach offers flexibility and time to see a large number of families/caregivers, the unpredictability can also leave those of us who are planners feeling underprepared. One way to overcome this feeling is to prepare an outline to guide your conversation.

### GATHER

To prepare conference talking points that match your teaching context, identify key topics of conversation. These topics could include school-mandated information, frequently asked questions from families/caregivers, and suggestions from students themselves. Once you have your list of topics, prioritize the most important talking points and create a bullet-point outline to guide each conference (see Figure 3.24). As you create this outline, consider how it will work with the student present and without the student. You may even consider making two separate outlines for these two different conversations.

FIGURE 3.24

**CONFERENCE TALKING POINTS**

- Celebrations
- Areas of growth
- Thoughts on texts read so far
- Action plan/next steps

## GET STARTED

If this is your first time engaging in conferences, consider having a quick practice session with a friend or colleague. Use your template as a guide and give them some questions that you anticipate caregivers might ask, so that you can rehearse answering them on the spot. On the day or evening of conferences, print out copies of your conference talking points and display them in your conference space. Make sure to leave time for questions and other thoughts. It is also wise to have a notebook nearby to jot down any follow-up actions that will need your attention after conferences are over.

## WHERE THIS MIGHT LEAD

You may find that you need to tweak your conference template depending on the time of year or grade level you are teaching. And as the year progresses, consider inviting students to contribute to the conference template. Ask them: "What do you think is important to discuss in tonight's conferences? What would you like your caregivers to know?" You may also find that you no longer need to use the template as you become more comfortable with conference conversations. Just as we scaffold experiences for our students, think of a conference template as a scaffold for yourself.

### Keep It Simple: Listen and Learn

Early in our careers, we approached conferences with the mindset that it was our role to give families/caregivers all the information we had collected about their child. The conference became a telling of observations rather than a two-way conversation. We quickly discovered that we had a lot to learn from our students' caregivers, so we shifted our role to create a partnership approach. Try the ideas that follow to make your conferences more collaborative:

- If you are meeting in person, sit at an angle to the left or right of caregivers, or next to them, rather than across a table. Sitting side by side sets a more collaborative tone.
- Listen first. Start the conference by asking parents/caregivers if they have any questions or concerns. Answer their questions to the best of your ability. If you don't know the answer, write down their question and get back to them when you do. Listen carefully to any concerns.

---

### Back Pocket Wisdom: Prepare Some Go-To Conference Phrases

As much as we prepare, sometimes we are caught off-guard by a family member's unexpected question or heated complaint. In addition to your template, it is helpful to have some go-to phrases that give you time to find answers you may not know in the moment or, if needed, to help bring the conversation to a close. Here are few that have worked for us:

- I appreciate your bringing that to my attention. I will look into it and get back to you.

- I think it's important that we discuss this further, but I have someone waiting right now. I'll email you with some possible times to continue our conversation.

- I know we all want what's best for _____. Let's continue this conversation with other people in our building who also care about _____'s reading progress.

- Ask open-ended questions. For instance, when Maria has first graders who are reading above grade level, she asks families/caregivers, "How did your child learn how to read?" The answers are always fascinating. Another icebreaker question is, "What do you want me to know about your child or your family that I don't already know?" If a student attends the conference, Katie often begins by asking the student questions such as "What is going well in language arts? What are you the most proud of so far this school year?" Then move into "What are some goals you have for your literacy learning for the rest of the year?"

- Avoid educational jargon. We have so many specialized terms and acronyms in education that they seem like everyday language to us. Try to explain ideas to families/caregivers the same way you do to friends and family who work in other professions.

- To support caregivers who speak a language other than English, arrange for an interpreter. Keep in mind that conferences that include an interpreter take longer, so schedule accordingly. During the conference, speak to the caregivers rather than the interpreter. Pause often so that the interpreter can translate manageable amounts of information, and use the student's work or relevant images/infographics to illustrate your points.

If you're leaving this chapter with useful strategies that build on the foundation you set in the first weeks of school and assist you in staying true to your beliefs, we've met our goals. As the first semester stretches on, the daily grind of classroom life can sometimes feel a bit overwhelming. When this happens, remember that you and your students are in it together. Pause to reflect on every small step you've taken toward creating a cohesive literacy community. If this doesn't work, look ahead in your calendar—winter break is just around the corner! When we come back together in Chapter 4, we'll celebrate the new year and think about ways to renew and recharge our reading communities. Until then, be kind to yourself, appreciate your students' unique personalities, and stay the course!

## TIY—Try It Yourself!

| |
|---|
| Are there any ideas from this chapter or PDCast that would be helpful in your classroom? |
| |
| Which ideas would you modify to better fit your teaching context? |
| |
| Did this chapter or PDCast spark any questions, reflections, or new thinking? |
| |

## CHAPTER 4

# Keep the Momentum Going: After Winter Break

*Reignite learners' motivation and commitment to independent reading.*

Love to talk about teaching? Join us to think through the decisions we make after winter break. In Episode Four, we talk about ideas for staying on track with book talks, share innovative ideas for revisiting classroom routines, and discuss practices for involving caregivers in the literacy community. The episode ends with two book suggestions for this time of year.

*Listen to "A Year for the Books" PDCast Episode Four here.*

Whether in your personal life or at school, the dawning of a new calendar year prompts reflection and goal setting. When the month of January appears on your classroom calendar, it creates a sense of enthusiasm and renewal that you can use to propel your reading community forward into the second semester. So, how do we harness students' after-break energy to reignite their motivation and set ourselves up to sustain the momentum we've built thus far? In this chapter, we'll expand on our reflective conversation in the PDCast and share a variety of decisions you can make to begin the second half of the year with intention and purpose.

## REENERGIZE SUPPORTED INDEPENDENT READING

Let's think about the word *reenergize* for a moment. When you pop *reenergize* into an online thesaurus, synonyms like *freshen*, *invigorate*, *recreate*, and *renew* appear. In this section, we'll explore ideas to freshen your classroom book collection and invigorate students' reading plans. We'll give you instructional strategies that you can recreate in your teaching spaces to renew your learners' commitment to independent reading. All it takes is some fine-tuning to reenergize things so that your students can continue to reap the benefits of this essential classroom practice.

### Try This! Refresh the Classroom Library

The goal of a classroom library is to be the hub of a vibrant reading community. With that aim in mind, it's important that the design and contents of your classroom book collection are flexible and responsive to your readers' developing needs and varied interests (Mulligan and Landrigan 2018). Think of your classroom library like a storefront window display, changing regularly to draw customers in. At this point in the year, we're not suggesting a major reorganization, which might unintentionally disrupt the set routines. Rather, we just present a few noticeable updates here and there that can help to renew interest.

### Why Reenergize Supported Independent Reading?

- If students are excited about reading and books, they will be more likely to read. It's our goal as their teachers, and fellow readers, to find "the one good book that changes everything" and put that book in our student's hands (Atwell and Atwell Merkel 2016, 34).

- When students revisit, reorganize, and reinvent the classroom library, it helps them find the books that will lead them to further their love of reading (Miller and Sharp 2018).

### GATHER

Pull together some books that feature the topics or themes you plan to highlight in the coming months, and set them aside to display in a prominent place in the room. Note that the American Library Association Youth Media Awards (including, among others, the Coretta Scott King Award and the Newbery, Caldecott, Belpré, and Sibert Medals) are typically announced at the end of January, so now is an ideal time to reread some past winners or hold a mock Caldecott (or other award) event in your classroom or school. You can find mock award lists on the websites of independent bookstores like Anderson's Bookshop in Illinois or on blogs like that of award-winning nonfiction writer Melissa Stewart, where she hosts a Sibert Smackdown for informational book enthusiasts. Another reliable source is author and children's book champion John Schu's blog *Watch. Connect. Read.* Here he partners with fifth-grade teacher Colby Sharp to post their recommended books along with other helpful resources.

Ask your school or local librarian if your state sponsors any book awards. In some states, the awards are selected by students after reading a certain number of books on the nomination list—another motivator for your readers.

## GET STARTED

Decide on the best way to spotlight and share the books you've selected. Here are a few possible options:

- Create a display entitled "New Year, New Books." Include any titles you discovered over winter break. If you can't get your hands on the physical books, display photos of the book covers. For those books where publishers have created book trailers, add a QR code that leads readers to the book trailer. Ensure that you have a diverse representation of authors, genres, and topics. Keep this display going throughout the second semester by matching the books you display to curricular or seasonal themes. Some seasonal display ideas include: Books You'll Love (February), Spring into a Good Book (March), It's Raining Books (April), and A Garden of Great Books (May).

- Swap out or store the books that your students couldn't put down at the beginning of the year but which are now collecting dust. If you are lucky enough to have storage space, put the books away. In case you are out of space, consider temporarily swapping books with a trusted colleague—a win-win for both classes.

- Swap books in and out to better match your students' current interests and reading abilities. Recall that in Chapter 1 we suggested keeping your classroom library fresh by rotating titles based on curricular topics and/or seasons. This is still a convenient way to update your library from time to time, but now that your readers have experienced half a year's growth, it makes sense to do a quick audit of your shelves to make sure they include or showcase books that your students will find interesting and, if needed, a bit more challenging.

- Check out displays in your school library, in your public library, in local independent bookstores, or on social media for inspiration.

## WHERE THIS MIGHT LEAD

Keeping your classroom book collection fresh and inviting is a career-long task. If you've been teaching for a while, the most difficult aspect of doing a classroom library refresh is weeding out the books that no longer match your students' interests or lived experiences. This is also an issue if you are just starting out and have received book donations from neighbors, friends, or retiring teachers. The landscape of children's literature has changed in recent years with an eye toward making sure that previously underrepresented groups and creators get the spotlight they deserve. Has your classroom library changed to reflect this necessity? If you are having trouble deciding, enlist the help of a knowledgeable colleague in your building or district. Seek out a teacher-librarian, a literacy coach, and/or your district's equity director/officer or team to support you in your work. Don't hesitate to donate or recycle the books that no longer match your students' needs.

### Try This! Recommit to Regularly Scheduled Book Talks

Like many readers, Katie enjoys spending the quiet moments over winter break catching up on as many books in her to-be-read stack as possible. This means that when she gets back to school, she is primed to talk with students about books and reading. We can't assume that all of our students will have spent winter break chipping away at their to-be-read piles. As we come together after break, it is crucial to channel some of our own reading excitement to reignite students' reading lives and support them in continuing to read at high volumes and, in turn, developing their reading proficiency (Allington 2014). One way to do this is by doubling down on regularly scheduled book talks. When we share our enthusiasm about a book by presenting a quick sales pitch in the form of an upbeat and sometimes suspenseful book talk, we are communicating our belief that reading feeds our hearts and minds. We've mentioned book talks a few times in earlier chapters, but let's take a few moments here to chat about this essential component of a reader-focused classroom.

FIGURE 4.1

*Recommit to regularly scheduled book talks.*

### GATHER

When planning your book talks, think about your readers. What kinds of books will appeal to them and reflect their current experiences? Notice the social and emotional changes that occur over winter break. Some students seem to mature by light-years over those few weeks and may be looking for a different type of book. Do you have new students joining the classroom in the second semester? They might want to read about kids who are new to a school. Are a few of your students stuck in a genre reading rut? If so, spotlight high-interest books in lesser-read genres. See Figure 4.2 for a few of our favorite January book talk suggestions.

FIGURE 4.2

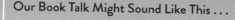

## JANUARY BOOK TALK SUGGESTIONS

| Book | Our Book Talk Might Sound Like This . . . |
|---|---|
|  *Clean Getaway* (Stone 2020) | "Have you ever wanted to go on a road trip? Where would you go? What might you see? The book tells the story of a boy named Scoob and his grandma, who embark on a mysterious road trip through the southern United States. They each have their own secrets and reasons they want to do this road trip and must figure out each other's along the way. If you enjoy learning about history but want some humor and fun mixed in, *Clean Getaway* by Nic Stone is for you!" [We love suggesting this book just after reading aloud the picture book *Ruth and the Green Book* (Calvin 2010).] |
|  *The First Rule of Punk* (Pérez 2017) | "In *The First Rule of Punk*, Malú wants to be punk and dress punk just like her dad, but her mom wants her to act and dress more like a *señorita*. When Malú and her mom move to Chicago, she struggles to fit in at her new school and find her identity. Those of you who like to read about music, middle school, and culture will love this book. Malú is also an artist, making zines, or mini-magazines, whenever she can. Here are a few examples of her zines." [Show some pages of the zines from *The First Rule of Punk*.] |
|  *New Kid* (Craft 2019) | "How many of you have been the new kid in school, on a sports team, or at a gathering? We've welcomed several new students to seventh grade this month. This graphic novel was written for anyone who can relate to being the new kid. Let's listen to the author, Jerry Craft, tell us a little more about the book." [Show beginning of video clip, from 0:00 to 0:57, linked here.]   *Listen to the author, Jerry Craft, talk about his book* New Kid *here.* |

(continued on next page)

FIGURE 4.2 (continued)

## JANUARY BOOK TALK SUGGESTIONS

| Book | Our Book Talk Might Sound Like This . . . |
| --- | --- |
| 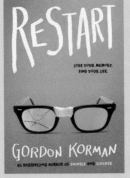<br>*Restart* (Korman 2017) | [Read aloud the first page of *Restart*, up until the word *blank*.] "From there, Chase Ambrose wakes up with total amnesia. He's forgotten his life before the accident, but no one has forgotten him. Why? Because, as he quickly realizes, most people's memories of him are not flattering. Chase must decide whether he wants to go back to his old ways or become a better person." |
| <br>*Rez Dogs* (Bruchac 2021) | "Are you someone who wants to read books about the pandemic, or would you rather read books that do not reference it at all? Depending on your answer, you may or may not be interested in *Rez Dogs* by Joseph Bruchac. Bruchac tells the story of Malian, who lives out the quarantine with her grandparents on the Wabanaki reservation. While there, she experiences many of the same challenges you may have faced during quarantine. You might also choose this book if you're looking to expand the types of genres you read, as this book is written in verse." |

## GET STARTED

After you've generated a list of books, commit to or continue a book talk schedule that you can sustain throughout the rest of the year. Whether your plan is to share one book per day or to target a specific day of the week that will be Book Talk Day, consider posting that schedule so that students can hold you accountable as you get further into what can often be a very busy semester.

As you can see from the sample book talks in Figure 4.2, we try to vary the content of the book talk based on the text. Perhaps you're still getting comfortable doing book talks, or maybe you're looking to refine your technique. To support you, we've included an outline of elements in Figure 4.3. If you start to see your students' interest in your style of book talk wane, or if you want to incorporate more voices into your classroom recommendations, we offer an option of how to involve the community in your book talk experiences in the "Where This Might Lead" section.

FIGURE 4.3

| THE ELEMENTS OF A BOOK TALK | |
| --- | --- |
| **Fiction** | **Nonfiction** |
| ■ Hook<br>  • Quote<br>  • Question<br>  • Introduce main character<br>  • Set the scene<br>■ Snapshot of plot<br>■ Opinion<br>■ Closing<br>  • Question<br>  • Quote<br>  • Cliffhanger | ■ Hook<br>  • Quote<br>  • Question or interesting fact<br>  • Introduce topic<br>■ Snapshot of what the reader will learn<br>■ Opinion<br>■ Closing<br>  • Question<br>  • Quote<br>  • Call to action |

## WHERE THIS MIGHT LEAD

Along with reestablishing book talks as a part of your classroom routine, why not try inviting others to introduce books in your classroom or school? In recent years, Katie's school librarian has invited their public library's teen librarians to give book talks to students. To increase excitement around these visits, they host the book talks in the library space and treat them like a mini-assembly or in-school field trip. During the book talks, not only do students get to add books to their Someday Lists, but also teachers gain a long list of new titles to add to their school or classroom libraries.

To start this process, reach out to your public library and see if they have a children's or young adult librarian who would be willing to come into your school. If coming to your school is not possible, you can see if a virtual presentation is an option. You could also try out other virtual book talk options, such as:

- Invite family members, caregivers, or authors to call in for a live virtual book talk (via an online conferencing platform like Zoom, Google Meet, Microsoft Teams, and so on) or even pre-record a book talk that you can show to students.

- Find and share high-quality book talks from teachers or young adults on platforms such as YouTube, Instagram, TikTok, and/or Twitter.

### Keep It Simple: Let Students Do the Work

Reenergizing supported independent reading is all about facilitating opportunities for students to view books and their reading lives through fresh eyes. Terrific news—you don't have to spend hundreds of dollars at a bookstore to accomplish this goal! It is possible to give learners this new perspective using your existing classroom library by releasing the responsibility of library organization to your students. Ask them to go through parts or all of your classroom library and re-sort books into book baskets that make sense to them, or even to curate book bins that relate to their previous or future learning (see Figure 4.4). As students browse the bookshelves and critically consider how your current books fit into new categories, they might stumble across books that have a newfound appeal or relevance. Task students with labeling the baskets (see Figure 4.5). If you have multilingual learners, invite them to label the baskets in their first language.

FIGURE 4.4

| BOOK BASKET SORTING IDEAS | |
|---|---|
| **If . . .** | **Then . . .** |
| Students are immersed in a character study | Invite readers to find books featuring their favorite types of characters (heroes, villains, friends, detectives, and so on). |
| Readers are learning how to identify themes | Sort and label books by their themes (relationships, courage, compassion, overcoming challenges, hope, taking a stand, and so on). |
| Your instructional focus is nonfiction text structures | Categorize informational books by their primary text structures (description, compare-contrast, question-answer, problem-solution, cause-effect). For additional ideas on categorizing nonfiction texts, we would suggest reading 5 *Kinds of Nonfiction* by Melissa Stewart and Marlene Correia (2021). |
| Learners are preparing to write biographies | Sort biographies into baskets with student-created labels like "Influencers," "Sports Heroes," "Bold Women," and so on. |

FIGURE 4.5
*Invite students to curate and label book bins.*

## REVISIT BELIEFS, ACTIONS, AND GOALS

When Debbie Miller's first book, *Reading with Meaning* (2002), was published, Maria was a midcareer teacher. From that day on, Debbie's thoughtful approach to reader-centered, belief-driven teaching has been something Maria has tried to achieve in her classroom. As we said in earlier chapters, collaborating on shared beliefs and translating those ideals into classroom actions are the foundation for a healthy teaching environment. In *Teaching with Intention* (2008), Debbie reminds us that our beliefs entwine themselves into our classroom culture and that every action, or inaction, communicates what we value to our students. With intention, take advantage of this midyear opportunity to check in with yourself and with your students.

### Why Revisit Beliefs, Actions, and Goals?

■ Taking a moment to reset is important because what we say and do in our classrooms should stem from our research-driven beliefs rather than a publisher's set of directions (Harwayne 2000).

■ When we give students the opportunity to reflect on and share insights into their personal learning and growth, it anchors that newfound knowledge in their long-term memory. This, in turn, helps them create long-lasting habits (Chappuis 2009).

### Try This! Make Resolutions

It seems like elementary school kids grow in surprising ways over winter break. They look so much older when they bustle into your classroom in January, many with new haircuts and several with toothless smiles. This maturity extends beyond their physical growth to how they engage in learning activities, like reading independently for increasingly longer periods of time. One way to revisit your shared classroom beliefs and actions is to lead learners as they set personal literacy goals in the form of a resolution.

### GATHER

We choose to spark this conversation by reading aloud *Squirrel's New Year's Resolution* (Miller 2010), because we appreciate the way the text explains that "a resolution is a promise you make to yourself to be better or help others." This kid-friendly definition is helpful when explaining resolutions to young children. To provide concrete examples of goals or self-promises, pair *Squirrel's New Year's Resolution* with *I Will! A Book of Promises* (Medina 2021).

### GET STARTED

After you've had time to read and discuss the book(s), review the concept of making a resolution. Then ask students to help you brainstorm a list of possible self-promises (see Figure 4.6). Invite learners to write or draw a picture of their resolution on a piece of paper. Stay focused on your end goal—helping students see a direct connection between the shared values they agreed upon at the beginning of the year (see Chapter 2) and the individual resolutions they plan to uphold to make the classroom a pleasant place to read and learn.

FIGURE 4.6
*Brainstorm a list of possible resolutions.*

### WHERE THIS MIGHT LEAD

After a set period of time, confer with individual students to gauge their progress toward keeping their self-promises. Find out if they are facing any challenges or need your support, and discuss actionable next steps. If they're satisfied with their progress toward keeping their promise, establish a new goal.

### Try This! Invite Student Self-Reflection on Shared Values

As you continue to make space in your day for instructional moves that mirror your classroom belief system (see Chapter 3, page 86), it is also important to keep the shared values alive for learners in the community (see Figure 4.7). In Chapter 1, on page 29, we offered feedback phrases to celebrate students' agency when their actions reflect the classroom beliefs. Now is a good time to renew your efforts to use phrases like these to refocus learners' actions. Pausing after winter break to engage in reflection around the shared values you created earlier in the year (see Chapter 2, page 54) brings them back to the forefront of your classroom community. When students take part in self-reflection, they begin to recognize their strengths and consider how they can push past any difficulties they face. Starting the second semester with this intentional reflection reorients classroom community members toward a shared set of values and a positive classroom culture.

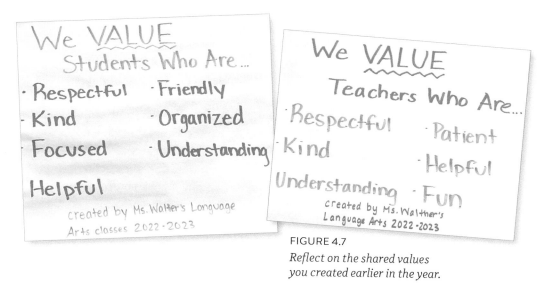

FIGURE 4.7
*Reflect on the shared values
you created earlier in the year.*

## GATHER

To lead students in a self-reflection experience, revisit the shared values you created and brainstorm a few guiding questions like these to jump-start readers' thinking.

"As you reflect on our shared classroom values, think about and answer one or more of these questions":

- Which values do I display each day in class? [Give examples of how you display these values.]

- How has upholding these values contributed to my life as a reader?

- Which values could I work on exhibiting during class? What actions could I strive to do to show these values even more often?

- Why are these values important to our classroom community and to me personally?

- What other shared agreements may we need to add for the second half of our school year?

## GET STARTED

Begin this experience with students by rereading the classroom values anchor chart. Then, using the guiding questions as a starting place, give everyone a few minutes to quietly reflect on the shared values. This could be done through writing, drawing, or mind mapping. At this point, it is helpful to show your own reflection as a demonstration text (see Figure 4.8). Remind students that the guiding questions are only suggestions and that they are welcome to take their self-reflection in a different direction. The main goal of this learning experience is to spend some time considering how the shared principles show up in their literacy lives.

When students are done with their self-reflection, gather them together to share with a partner, a small group, or the entire class. To keep this sharing session brief and focused so that you can hear from as many students as possible, remind learners to summarize their thinking or to read only a portion of what they wrote. As you listen to the different reflections and thoughts from around the room, take notes on interesting insights or ideas that you might want to weave into future literacy experiences, and notice any classroom values that you may need to clarify or reiterate.

**FIGURE 4.8**

*Katie's teacher reflection on shared values.*

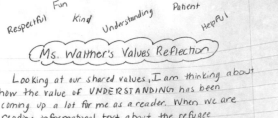

## WHERE THIS MIGHT LEAD

Now is the ideal time to reset reading goals with an eye toward the second half of the school year. So, you could end this experience with learners writing a personal goal of how they will continue to practice the classroom beliefs through the rest of the school year. To guide students' goal setting, refer back to the classroom beliefs and actions we set out in Chapter 3, page 89, and simply add an additional column for goals (see Figure 4.9). We've provided a few sentence stems as examples, but you can revise these to match your own classroom beliefs and actions. Setting their own learning targets will keep readers focused on desired outcomes and chart a clear path for success for the remainder of the year.

You can either have students display their goals somewhere prominent in the classroom or keep them in a specific place in their literacy notebooks. This way, learners can revisit their goals frequently, keeping the classroom belief system up front in their minds.

FIGURE 4.9

## CONNECT GOALS TO BELIEFS AND ACTIONS

| Beliefs | Action | Goals |
|---|---|---|
| We believe everyone is a reader. | We will have ten minutes of reading time each day. | My reading goal is to . . . |
| We believe that reading feeds our hearts and minds. | We will schedule time to talk about the texts we've learned from and enjoyed. | When I'm talking about books I will . . . |
| We believe everyone's voice should be heard. | We will build in time for students to have collaborative conversations during book experiences. | My goal as a conversation partner is . . . |
| We believe that we learn from each other. | We will plan and coordinate student-led learning experiences. | When I'm teaching my classmates, I will remember to . . . |
| We believe talking and writing help us to understand what we've read. | We will provide opportunities for students to reflect on their reading in various ways. | When I reflect on what I've read, I will try to . . . |
| We believe mistakes are learning opportunities. | We will develop a system for revising our classroom work. | When I'm revising my work, my goal is to . . . |

## Keep It Simple: Converse About Shared Values and Classroom Beliefs

As you may have noticed, we believe anchor charts are a powerful classroom tool. However, you do not have to make an elaborate anchor chart or lesson to revisit shared values and your classroom beliefs. One simple way is to have a discussion with students (Fisher and Frey 2015). Display the shared values and classroom beliefs front and center and then talk about them using the following questions:

- Why you think we created these shared values?
- How do our shared values make our classroom a comfortable place to learn?
- How do these values guide our actions?
- Which beliefs does this community show through our actions?
- Which beliefs should we strive harder to uphold through our actions?

As students talk, actively listen. What are their perceptions of the classroom? What might you see differently as the teacher? Can they articulate why shared values are important? You will be amazed at how much information you and the members of your classroom community can glean from a short discussion that centers students' voices.

## REINTRODUCE ROUTINES

When returning to school from an extended break, do you find yourself forgetting some of your daily routines? *What is the password for that account again? Where did I put my classroom keys before I left? How long do I microwave my breakfast?* The same thing happens to students when they come back to school after being away. They may have spent their time at home following different routines and probably enjoying a little less structure. So, just as we give ourselves reminders after an extended break, students need their own classroom routines refresher.

### Why Reintroduce Routines?

■ Over a long break, students may develop new routines or fall back into old habits that they bring into the classroom when they return. Knowing this, it's important to help students reacquaint themselves with community routines in order to return to their typical classroom habits (Duhigg 2012).

■ At this point in the year, you may have new students who were not involved in the initial construction of your classroom culture. Therefore, the beginning of a new semester provides an opportunity to help these students become anchored in the classroom routines (Fisher and Frey 2015).

### Try This! Put Learners in Charge

"How long is independent reading time?" "Where do I put this broken book?" "What do I do when I finish all of my books?" You've probably heard questions like these in your classroom. Before the break, most children had learned to rely on each other to help navigate these routine wonderings, but that agency and independence sometimes fade during the weeks away. To continue communicating to your students that "we are all teachers here," begin the new year by inviting children to be the ones to reintroduce the routines. This is especially helpful if a new student has joined your community.

## GATHER

Make a list of the top five high-priority reading routines you would like to revisit. The list might include the following:

- Find a personal reading spot
- Read the whole time
- Read book after book
- Put books away
- Shop for new books

Invite children to sign up to reintroduce the routine they feel most confident in teaching to others. To do this with efficiency, ask each child to list the three routines they would like to teach, and then strategically place them in groups by giving them one of their three choices.

## GET STARTED

In their small groups, learners collaborate to decide on the best way to reintroduce the routine to their class-mates and gather the supplies they will need to complete the task. Learners may choose to do one of the following or come up with their own idea:

- Act it out (see Figure 4.10)
- Make a short video
- Create a how-to visual
- Take and display photos
- Write a poem or song

Provide time and support for students to complete their product and prepare for their presentation. For the next week or so, ask one group a day to share their routine with the class. Consider starting an anchor chart labeled "Routines We Taught Each Other" to emphasize the fact that helping each other and work-ing together to solve problems are normal and desirable practices in your classroom (Johnston et al. 2020).

FIGURE 4.10
*A kindergartner demonstrates how to read the whole time.*

## WHERE THIS MIGHT LEAD

As the second semester continues, use the same format to reinforce other classroom routines if they go astray. By this time of year, children have heard us explain, prompt, and remind—and sometimes nag—about routines. Releas-ing the responsibility to learners has many benefits. You'll quickly notice that students will develop fresh, innovative ways to teach or carry out routines—some you may never even have imagined! Additionally, when children feel ownership of the routines, they are more diligent in holding themselves and their peers accountable. Finally, putting kids in charge takes one thing off your overfilled plate, freeing up more time for reading-related interactions.

### Try This! Create "Do" and "Don't" Comic Strips

For us, the start of the second semester is usually when we begin to notice that the classroom library is looking a bit disheveled. Students become more lax about adhering to the shared agreements they've set around checking out and returning books, or they've simply forgotten the procedures. While this disorder indicates that students are actively accessing texts, it is still important that your book collection remains an inviting and easy-to-use space for students. So, it is time to refresh this routine! (Actually, this can be true for so many of your classroom routines.)

Starting off the new year with a review of literacy routines is helpful in making sure that students stick to their shared agreements through the rest of the year. But instead of simply discussing the routines or creating a colorful slide deck, consider a more hands-on or interactive way for students to review classroom routines. Katie adapted this comic strip idea from a skit activity one of her colleagues created. As you read on, consider how you could use or adapt this idea for readers in your teaching context.

### GATHER

Hook students into this experience by displaying the first few frames of a popular graphic novel from your classroom (see Figure 4.11 for suggestions). Have a quick discussion about how the creator uses words and images to convey their meaning. Then develop a list of specific literacy routines that could use a refresher as you enter the second semester, like the following:

- Reading independently
- Giving a book talk
- Listening to a book talk
- Checking out a book
- Returning a book
- Participating in book clubs

**POPULAR GRAPHIC NOVELS**

- *Amulet: The Stone Keeper* (Kibuishi 2008)
- *Frizzy* (Ortega 2022)
- *Guts* (Telgemeier 2019)
- *Heartstopper, Vol. 1* (Oseman 2018)
- *Ms. Marvel, Vol. 1: No Normal* (Wilson 2014)
- *Speak Up!* (Burgess 2022)
- *Stuntboy, in the Meantime* (Reynolds 2021)

FIGURE 4.11

## GET STARTED

In pairs or trios, have students pick a specific literacy routine. Each group's task is to collaboratively create two comic strips: the first illustrating what this classroom practice should look like (do), and the second showing what it should *not* look like (don't). Groups can use the graphic novel from your hook as a mentor text for their own comics.

Through their conversations and illustrations, students enjoy thinking of the most outlandish behaviors for the "don't" comic strip while also reminding each other what that routine should look like in the classroom. Once each group completes their comic strips, project their work as they explain it to the class. As groups are sharing, learners have a chance to review all of the routines. Your role is to listen and, if necessary, pause and discuss any misconceptions or misunderstandings.

## WHERE THIS MIGHT LEAD

An effective way to continue the conversations prompted by the student-created comics is to hang them up near the areas of your classroom where they are the most applicable. For instance, if one group made their comic about returning a book, you could place their work near the book return area in your classroom. Then when students are practicing these routines, they can use the comics for reference. If you find that some students show a specific interest in creating comics, consider encouraging their enthusiasm and having them create comics for other areas of the school building as well (hallways, lunchroom, buses, and so on).

### Keep It Simple: Anchor New Routines in Familiar Ones

We often come back from winter break reenergized and ready to try a million new ideas in our classroom. The break offers opportunities for some of us to quietly reflect on a podcast, an inspiring professional book, or a professional learning opportunity that sparked some new thinking. While shifting and adapting your teaching practices is a crucial part of being a reflective practitioner, students thrive when they have routines in place that they can count on (Allyn and Morrell 2016). So if some of your new ideas revolve around classroom routines, think about how you can anchor any new routines in familiar practices. For instance, in the next section, we will discuss releasing responsibility for the book talks to students. We introduce this new routine by having learners reflect on what they've noticed about our teacher book talks. With this vision in their minds, readers are able to ground their understanding of student-led book talk expectations in the established practice of teacher book talks.

## RELEASE RESPONSIBILITY TO COMMUNITY MEMBERS

Over the course of this book and during our reflective PDCast conversations, we've stressed the importance of inviting students into our classroom decision-making. While releasing responsibility begins early in the year, we highlight it again here, discussing specifically how to encourage students to take center stage in their reading community as they enter the second half of their learning year.

### Try This! Launch Reader of the Day

Have you noticed that when your students are reading with a partner or small group, a few will imitate the way you sit or hold a book as you read aloud? After watching you share a wealth of read-aloud experiences, many learners welcome the opportunity to read aloud to the class as the Reader of the Day. Reader of the Day is a simple-to-implement reading event that builds students' fluency, boosts their confidence, and adds to classroom camaraderie. To keep this a novel experience, schedule each interested student, partnership, or group as the Reader of the Day one time between now and the end of the school year. To kick off this event and provide a concrete example, you might invite an upper-grade student (perhaps a former student) to come and read to your kids.

### GATHER

After explaining how this routine will work, ask *interested* students, partnerships, or groups to sign up. In our experience, Reader of the Day is most effective when done no more than once or twice a week, and early in the morning when everyone is fresh. Create a schedule to send home to families with an accompanying family/caregiver letter (see sample in Appendix A4.1). Support students in selecting a *short* poem, picture book, or favorite part of a book to read aloud to the class—the keyword here is *short*!

### GET STARTED

Make your guest reader's big day special in simple ways, such as posting a Reader of the Day banner on your board with their name on it, making a Reader of the Day ribbon for them to wear, or snapping a picture as they read and sending it home to families. Before the reader starts, talk with the class about the importance of being respectful and active listeners. Then let the reading begin!

---

### Why Release Responsibility to Community Members?

■ We want to create a classroom world where children are doing the work so that they learn from their productive effort and take charge of their reading lives (Burkins and Yaris 2016).

■ Students are increasingly motivated to be an active part of their reading community when they have authentic opportunities to teach one another and listen to each other (Keene 2018).

(See Figure 4.12.) Since this is an in-class community-building event, we typically do not invite families to join, but you certainly could do that. Enjoy and celebrate students' read-aloud performances!

## WHERE THIS MIGHT LEAD

Some students are teachers-in-the-making and love the opportunity to read to their own "class." If the Reader of the Day experience sparks this interest, look for easy-to-manage opportunities for students to read to others. If you have students in lower grades at your school, your students could read to a small group of those younger students, or they could record themselves reading aloud and place the recording in a center or station.

FIGURE 4.12
*Students listen to a Reader of the Day share their favorite book.*

### Try This! Encourage Student-Led Book Talks

▶ Similar to Reader of the Day, you can release literacy responsibility to learners through student-led book talks. Now that students have seen you (and perhaps a variety of authors) model book talks for half the school year, they may want to formally take on this role themselves. When readers prepare and share their own book talks, they learn how to summarize, persuade their peers to read the books they love, and connect with others who like similar titles.

## GATHER

Introduce the concept of student-led book talks to your readers and create a paper or virtual sign-up sheet where students can volunteer. Then find a time in your weekly lesson plans to schedule the student-led book talks. Let apprehensive students know this is a rolling invitation and they can sign up at any time. We suggest this because more readers may want to volunteer once they see a few brave peers kick off the series.

## GET STARTED

Once you have a few students signed up, review the elements of a successful book talk (see Figure 4.13 on the following page). From there, give them time to prepare. Since the goal of these book talks is to enhance classroom community, it is important to make sure students feel comfortable. To raise their comfort level, readers may need in-class time to practice with a trusted peer or a chance to share the book talk with you one-on-one before presenting to the group. If a reader would really like the opportunity to share a beloved book but is nervous about speaking in the front of the class, leverage technology and have the student film their book talk.

Now it's time for your students to take the lead and share the enthusiasm that comes from reading and talking about a good book! To help focus listeners' attention, ask them to take out their Someday Lists and jot down appealing titles as their peers present. Invite them to ask questions of the book talk presenters.

FIGURE 4.13

## ELEMENTS OF STUDENT-LED BOOK TALKS

- Say the title and introduce the author (learn how to pronounce their name).
- Show the actual book or a visual of the cover.
- Share an original summary (fiction) or main topics covered (nonfiction)—but no spoilers!
- Read a tiny bit from the book to share a scene, a few facts, or an interesting quote.
- Recommend the book to readers who might like it.
- Keep the book talk short in length (one to three minutes).

### WHERE THIS MIGHT LEAD

As your students talk about books, use this as an opportunity to notice and note underrepresented genres, authors, and titles. Refer to these notes as you gather books for your teacher-led book talks. Taking notes on individual readers' text selections also gives you a chance to challenge readers to step outside of their comfort zone. Be up front with students about genres and authors that you notice are missing from their reading diet. Encourage them to broaden their reading horizons for personal reasons and so that they can introduce their peers to a more diverse range of titles, which will enhance the entire community's collective knowledge about creators and books.

### Keep It Simple: Welcome New Community Members

The beginning of the second semester is often a time when new students join our classrooms. Our aim is to make these students feel welcome and support them as they find their place in the reading community as quickly as possible. In a learner-centered classroom it makes sense to put students in charge of acclimating new students. Ask a welcoming student or two if they will be the new student's classroom host for the day, talking with them about classroom procedures and helping them navigate classroom routines. When looking for hosts for multilingual learners, work to find another student who speaks the same first language. If time allows, collaborate as a class to create a list of welcoming procedures or perhaps a slide deck to support the classroom hosts. Once this routine is established, you'll be able to quickly pair a new student with a classroom buddy—someone they can go to with any wonderings or concerns.

## CREATE FAMILY/CAREGIVER ENGAGEMENT OPPORTUNITIES

At this point in the school year, you've regularly communicated with families. Depending on your schedule, they may have been invited into your classroom or visited with you virtually for curriculum night, open house, and perhaps parent-teacher conferences. Therefore, they most likely have a basic understanding of the curriculum and a general sense of the instruction happening every day. Why not invite them to experience a bit more of classroom life and actively participate in the reading community? In this section, we provide suggestions for how you might invite families into your classroom in low-stress yet productive ways.

### Try This! Set Up a Read to Me! Program

With class sizes growing and support staff being stretched thin, we are often at a loss as to how to give our emergent and early readers the vast amount of individualized attention they need to gain competence and confidence. It was out of this need that the Read to Me! program was born. This program offers family members and caregivers the opportunity to visit the classroom either in person or via a virtual platform like Zoom or Google Meet and listen to a few children (including their own) reread a familiar book. Since students are always rereading a book they've already read, the listeners are not *teaching*. Instead, the focus for caregivers is providing a listening ear and a bit of individual attention.

### Why Invite Families/Caregivers into the Classroom?

■ Family/caregiver engagement activities that focus on building caregivers' abilities to support their child's education can improve students' performance in school. One way to strengthen the home-school bond is to engage caregivers *at school* in order for them to experience what children are learning (Henderson and Mapp 2002).

■ When caregivers talk with their children about school, it positively impacts student achievement, leading to higher grades and test scores (Ho Sui-Chu and Willms 1996). Therefore, we look for innovative ways to give families an inside look into our classrooms so that they have the knowledge and the lingo to have these essential conversations.

### GATHER

With input from family members and caregivers, create a mutually agreeable yet flexible schedule. We've found that the best times to host Read to Me! volunteers are during independent reading, when you're conferring or meeting with small groups. To introduce this program to adults, Maria makes a video to demonstrate the process. In addition, she creates an infographic reminder to guide volunteers when they listen to readers (see Appendix A4.2). Coach and practice with students so that they know where to find the books they will read and how the program will work in your classroom. You can use or modify the sample student introduction in the "Get Started" section.

## GET STARTED

Before the first volunteer is scheduled to listen to a reader, prepare your students by explaining the goal and process of the Read to Me! program. A student introduction might sound something like this:

- **Share the goal.** "We are going to welcome some grown-ups into our classroom, either in person or virtually. They are excited to listen to you reread an 'old favorite' book. When we reread familiar books, we get even better at reading."

- **Explain the process.**
  - **Before reading:** "Whether the guest is here in person or on the computer screen, you will pick a book to read to them. Choose a book that you know well. [Share where they can find those books in your classroom—book box, special basket, and so on.] If it's a longer book, pick a favorite part."
  - **During Reading:** "If you've never met the grown-up, tell them your name. Then read to them! Remember to read in a voice that is loud enough for them to hear."
  - **After Reading:** "After you're done reading, you can talk with them about your book. Remember to thank the grown-up for listening."

- **Discuss next steps.** "When you're done, it will be time for the grown-up to listen to another reader. You can help them do this by walking over to the next reader and quietly telling them it is their turn to read with our guest."

Once the family members/caregivers are scheduled and students know what to do, this program takes very little work on your part.

## WHERE THIS MIGHT LEAD

If you found this program successful, think about expanding it to vetted community members. Over the years, we've had our students read to senior citizens (Rockin' Readers), therapy dogs (Furry Friends), and high school students who are interested in a career in education. We've even held single-day Read to Me! events with high school sports team members, local business leaders, politicians, and folks from the school board or district office.

### Try This! Host a Gallery Walk

In middle school, we often invite families into the classroom during student presentations or speeches. While this is an amazing opportunity for students to have an authentic audience for formal presentations, the amount of time it takes to plan a presentation schedule and slot families to the right days and times can be overwhelming. Instead, you could try inviting families into the classroom for a less formal gallery walk of student work. Katie has received positive feedback from families after hosting a gallery walk of student infographics, but the format we're going to detail can be used to showcase a variety of student work.

### GATHER

Look at your upcoming units and see if there is a product that might lend itself to a gallery-style presentation. Some possibilities might include infographics, magazine articles, or photo essays. Then decide on one product that students will present to the community. As you plan for this gallery walk, consider the timing of the event. We've found that attendance is higher when we aim for having it close to lunchtime or near the end of the day. In the "Get Started" section, we provide some modifications to help make sure all caregivers have access to this event.

**Back Pocket Wisdom: Read to Me! Tips**

■ Designate a space either in your classroom or close to it so that both volunteers and students know where to go. Make sure it has enough room to house all of the equipment you will need for virtual guests.

■ Try to have someone special to each child participate once during the second half of the year. This might mean inviting a sibling, or perhaps a former teacher if a family member or caregiver is unable to make it.

### GET STARTED

Planning and working out the logistics are the keys to hosting a successful family/caregiver literacy experience. While you certainly can't anticipate every scenario, the more prepared you are, the better. With that goal in mind, we outline our process for preparing for and hosting an event for families and caregivers below.

| Timeline | For Students | For Families and Caregivers |
| --- | --- | --- |
| At beginning of unit | ■ Introduce work students will showcase.<br>■ Inform students that they will be showcasing this work to families, caregivers, and community members. | ■ Send an electronic invitation to families with a form for collecting RSVPs. |

(continued on next page)

GET STARTED (continued)

| Timeline | For Students | For Families and Caregivers |
|---|---|---|
| A few days before gallery walk | ■ Provide time for students to practice a thirty-second elevator pitch explaining their work for people when they visit their table.<br>■ Discuss, model, and role-play how to show professionalism in a gallery walk setting (see Figure 4.14) for tips to share with students. | ■ Compile a list of families who will be attending.<br>■ Remind staff members about the event.<br><br>**For families unable to join in person:** Enlist the help of staff members to video-record or photograph students' thirty-second elevator pitch. |
| Day of gallery walk | ■ Work with students to set everyone up on the perimeter of the gallery walk space.<br>■ Walk around and check in with students.<br>■ Take photographs to share as examples with future students, for a celebration display, or to send home to family members and caregivers who were unable to attend. | ■ Hang up signs directing caregivers to the proper location.<br>■ Provide a visitor's guide with directions and questions for families (see Appendix A4.3).<br><br>**For families unable to join in person:** Provide a virtual station for caregivers who would like to attend the event virtually and have students rotate through this station. |
| Day after gallery walk | ■ Reflect with students about successes and areas for growth. | ■ Send a thank-you to all caregivers. |

FIGURE 4.14

### TIPS FOR STUDENTS ABOUT PROFESSIONALISM DURING A GALLERY WALK

- Welcome visitors with a verbal or visual greeting.
- Make visitors feel welcome by smiling or asking them questions.
- Avoid using filler words like "um" or "like."
- Check that your body language shows you are being attentive.
- Thank visitors for viewing your work.

## WHERE THIS MIGHT LEAD

The day after the gallery walk is an excellent time for reflection and gratitude. Plan a specific time for students to reflect upon their successes and identify areas of growth related to both the product they presented and the gallery walk itself. Depending on the amount of time you have and the personality of your class, their self-analysis could start in their notebooks and flow into a conversation with a partner, a small group, or the whole class. Ask them to think about what was challenging for them, what they would do differently, and what they would keep the same the next time they present their work to a group.

After completing their reflection, create a class-wide thank-you email or video that you can send to all families to thank them for their support. This thank-you message can encompass appreciation to caregivers for helping the student create the product (if they worked on it at home) and/or for attending the gallery walk. Once you've sent this home, celebrate a successful event with the students!

### Keep It Simple:
### Provide Specific Questions to Caregivers

Both the Read to Me! program and the gallery walk event provide families a peek into the inner workings of the classroom. Family members and caregivers get to meet children they may have only heard about, and they have the opportunity to listen to conversations between the teacher and students and among peers. This helps to spark more in-depth conversations about school at home. (We often hear caregivers lament that when they ask their child, "What did you do in school today?" the child quickly responds, "Nothing!")

In addition to inviting caregivers into the classroom, another effective technique we've found to help families have a more in-depth conversation about school involves providing a daily schedule and definitions of terms they may encounter, along with specific questions to ask. (See a snippet in Figure 4.15 for elementary-grade families and the entire document in Appendix A4.4. You will also find a middle school version in Appendix A4.5.) It's the specific questions that make the difference. We sometimes forget how much educational jargon we use in our classrooms. Terms like *morning message*, *literacy notebook*, and even *book talk* might be new to families. This document demystifies some of these classroom practices and provides family members and caregivers insights into the specific kinds of questions they might ask to encourage their kids to reflect on their learning day.

**Back Pocket Wisdom: Hosting a Gallery Walk**

- Before sending out invitations, check with your school about established safety procedures for having families in the building.

- Prior to scheduling the event, check in with building stakeholders such as the front office staff, custodians, and other grade-level teachers.

- If needed, arrange for interpreters.

- On the invitation email, provide a clear deadline for RSVPing. Send a reminder email one day before the RSVP deadline.

- On your write-up and during the gallery walk, encourage guests to visit all students, not just their own. This allows all students to have visitors whether or not their family member or caregiver can attend.

- Invite staff members from within your building to attend the gallery walk as well.

FIGURE 4.15

## A DAY IN OUR CLASSROOM—ELEMENTARY SCHOOL

| Subject/Activity | What Your Child Is Doing | Specific Questions You Can Ask About This Part of Our Day |
|---|---|---|
| Independent reading time | After doing their "morning jobs" (attendance, lunch count, turning in items, and hanging up coat/backpack), children read their own "just-right" books, which are stored in a book box, or other books that match their interests, which they select from the various shelves in our room. Sometimes we read with a friend! | What books did you read this morning?<br><br>Which book is your favorite? Why? |
| Morning message, poem, read-aloud | Students meet in their "place for learning" on the carpet to read, write, revise, and edit the morning message. We chant and sing poems and songs together (poems are stored in your child's own song and poem book). Next, we read aloud a book or two. | Did you help with the morning message today?<br><br>What poem are you singing in the morning?<br><br>What book(s) did your teacher read to you today? |

The second half of the school year is a time for looking back and forging ahead. Pause and congratulate yourself on how far your community of learners has come. Think about all of the ways you've worked diligently to create supported opportunities for reading, hold fast to your beliefs, practice positive literacy routines, cultivate a strong community, and invite families into the learning. This is the time of year when you see all of the small teaching decisions you've made pay off! With some small readjustments you can quickly get back in a groove and capitalize on the time you have left with your readers as you inch closer to the end of the school year.

## TIY—Try It Yourself!

Are there any ideas from this chapter or PDCast
that would be helpful in your classroom?

Which ideas would you modify to better fit your
teaching context?

Did this chapter or PDCast spark any questions,
reflections, or new thinking?

## CHAPTER 5

# Think Outside the Box: Spring Toward the Finish Line

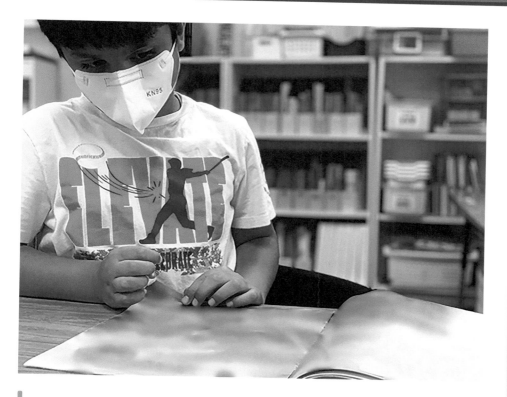

*Wrap up, reflect on, and celebrate a year of literacy experiences.*

Love to talk about teaching? Join us to think through the decisions we make during the last few months of the school year. In Episode Five, we discuss strategies to set readers up for success for the upcoming summer months, brainstorm how to highlight different types of texts, and map out ways to celebrate the amazing literacy community you've created during the school year.

*Listen to "A Year for the Books" PDCast Episode Five here.*

Is it possible that we're preparing to wrap up, reflect on, and celebrate a jam-packed year of literacy experiences? One of Maria's colleagues dubbed the spring season "MarchAprilMay" (say it quickly!) because the final few months seem to fly by. Like each distinct part of the year, this season offer unique joys and challenges. One of our greatest joys comes from sitting back and watching our students go about their learning without even noticing we are in the room—reading, thinking, chatting, and problem-solving. In terms of challenges, spring is typically the testing season, so we'll talk a bit about making decisions regarding test preparation and navigating testing days. In addition, we've noticed that when the weather changes, spring fever sets in, and kids who have been together for eight months or so either fall in love or snap at each other like siblings. It is helpful to keep the evolving social dynamics in mind when you are designing year-end learning experiences. In this chapter, we'll nudge you to think outside the box as you make curricular choices that will help bring your learners full circle and set them up to continue their reading habits and behaviors into the summer and beyond.

## BROADEN SUPPORTED INDEPENDENT READING

At this point, we shift our attention toward broadening supported independent reading, for two reasons. First, when you invite students to reflect on what they've learned during the year about their unique reading identities, you are closing the loop while at the same time nudging them to carry this self-awareness into their literacy life outside of school. Layered on top of this is a push to get as many different types of texts as possible into readers' hands and hearts, especially those students who still haven't shown an interest in reading. With these dual purposes guiding the support we put in place to nurture independent readers, we'll redouble our efforts to expand students' awareness of the wide variety of available texts and the ways in which they might access these texts to enrich their lives.

### Why Broaden Supported Independent Reading?

■ Broadening supported independent reading helps learners develop textual dexterity, or the ability to actively orchestrate the full repertoire of competencies to decode, comprehend, use, and analyze as they read and engage with others around texts that matter to them (Aukerman and Schuldt 2021).

■ As the year draws to a close, it is helpful to repeatedly and explicitly connect the routines you've engaged in during the school year to summer reading habits and behaviors. Clearly connecting the two gives students a vision of what summer reading might look like and communicates the expectation that it will happen (Cahill et al. 2013).

### Try This! Get Readers Hooked on a Series

Reflect on your own reading life. Do you recall being hooked on a series? As a teen reader, Maria couldn't get enough of the series that began with *Flowers in the Attic* (Andrews 1979) (yes, she was a teen in the 1970s!). Katie flew through the unique scrapbook-like series created by the two-sister team of Kate and M. Sarah Klise. After reading the first book, *Regarding the Fountain* (1998), she was a fan. What is it about series books that appeal to and captivate readers? To begin with, researchers have found that series books offer all learners, but specifically multilingual learners, the following benefits:

- Are highly motivating because they contain these elements:
  - Interesting content
  - Comprehensible language
  - Easy-to-follow storylines
  - Relatable characters
- Facilitate language development because the books offer multiple exposures to similar vocabulary and grammatical structures.
- Offer an easier and more enjoyable reading experience as readers make their way through each book in the series (Renandya, Krashen, and Jacobs 2018).

Along with these proven benefits, if we can persuade readers to read the first few books in a series before summer break, they just might seek out the next book after they leave our classroom.

## GATHER

When you are selecting appealing and approachable series books to put in the hands of your primary and middle-grade readers, look for early readers, transitional chapter books, and graphic-format books.

- **Early readers.** There is a wide range of text difficulty in what publishers categorize as early readers. Now that you know your readers well, a quick scan of the pages can help you determine whether a series would be a good fit for a reader. To ensure that the reader gets off on the right foot, confer with them as they familiarize themselves with the book. Offer any tips or strategies that will support them as they continue to read the book on their own. When looking for early reader series, one resource that we've found helpful is the Association for Library Service to Children (ALSC) Geisel Award list. The Geisel Award recognizes authors and illustrators of books who use creative and imaginative techniques to engage children in reading. Some award-winning series books that would be ideal for emergent and early readers include:

  - *The Adventures of Otto: See Pip Flap* (Milgrim 2018)
  - *Fox + Chick: The Party and Other Stories* (Ruzzier 2020)
  - *Hi! Fly Guy* (Arnold 2005)
  - *A Big Guy Took My Ball* (An Elephant and Piggie Book) (Willems 2013)
  - *Ty's Travels: Zip, Zoom!* (Lyons 2020)

- **Transitional chapter books.** As their name implies, transitional chapter books help readers make the leap from picture books and easy readers to longer novels. Transitional chapter books have these common text features:

  - Table of contents

  - Larger font size

  - Brief chapters

  - Supportive illustrations interspersed throughout

  - Around a hundred pages of text

  A few transitional chapter book series that would be ideal for readers at this stage include series that begin with the following books:

  - *Astrid and Apollo and the Starry Campout* (Bidania 2021)

  - *Charlie and Mouse* (Snyder 2017)

  - *Juana and Lucas* (Medina 2016)

  - *King and Kayla and the Case of the Missing Dog Treats* (Butler 2017)

  - *Meet Yasmin!* (Faruqi 2019)

- **Graphic-format books.** Whether in elementary school or middle school, graphic-format books, also known as comics or graphic novels, are perennial favorites with readers. In our experience, it is pretty easy to get students hooked on books in these series, but it is sometimes challenging to convince adults of their value. In her guide to teaching with graphic texts, Dr. Laura Jiménez underscores the value of sharing and teaching with graphic-format texts because they "require active, engaged, and recursive reading to make meaning from the layers of written text, images, and sequence" (2022, 3). Readers predict, infer, and question in order to peel back the layers of meaning on each page of a graphic novel. This layered path to understanding makes what some may view as "easy" reading much more complex than it appears. To that end, as you're introducing series books with a graphic format, take time to demonstrate how readers use the various features like panels, gutters (spaces between the panels), speech and thought bubbles, and other visual information to make meaning. A few graphic novel series for elementary school readers include:

  - *Arlo and Pips: King of the Birds* (Gravel 2020)

  - *The Cardboard Kingdom* (Sell 2018)

  - *Beak and Ally: Unlikely Friends* (Feuti 2021)

  - *Nathan Hale's Hazardous Tales: One Dead Spy* (Hale 2012)

  - *Wings of Fire—The Dragonet Prophecy: A Graphic Novel* (Sutherland 2018)

## GET STARTED

One of the best ways to get your students hooked on a series is to read aloud the first book or first chapter of a book in that particular series. Introduce readers to the characters, notice their unique traits, and discuss any other elements of the series that will be helpful if they choose to continue reading the rest of the books. If it is a nonfiction series, study the text structure and recurring text features. Then, if possible, display the rest of the books in the series. Periodically check the author or publisher's website to see when the next book in the series will be released. Post that date along with a copy of the book cover so that children can anticipate its arrival.

## WHERE THIS MIGHT LEAD

In addition to introducing readers to series books that span a variety of genres, it is also helpful to zero in on and feature the various genres that have grabbed your students' attention thus far. Like series books, each genre has unique characteristics that readers can rely on as they explore books in their preferred genre.

You might be thinking, *I see the importance of reviewing genres that might appeal to my readers, but I don't have time to spotlight all of them before the end of the year.* Great news—you have a whole class of experts to help you out! Consider setting aside forty-five minutes to an hour a day for five days to support learners as they take the lead and present a genre fair. You could do this during small-group time with your existing small groups, with the whole class, or with a few interested independent workers.

The value of this learning event is that it helps readers to synthesize their understanding of the various genres they've studied throughout the year. To do this, select the genres based on your curriculum. They might include the following:

- Biography
- Poetry
- Nonfiction
- Realistic stories
- Make-believe stories

### Back Pocket Wisdom: Books in a Series

If you have multiple children who want to read the first book in a series, place a sticky note on the inside cover and ask them to sign up (see Figure 5.1). Once the first reader finishes, it is their job to cross off their name and hand the book off to the next reader. The beauty of this simple strategy is that the students who are waiting for the book will prompt the reader to finish. Also, there is a record of all of the children who have read the series, so they could form an impromptu series book club or even get together to write some fan fiction.

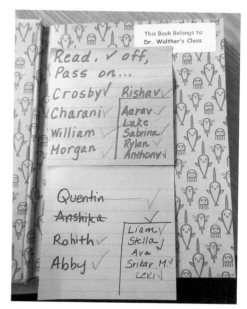

FIGURE 5.1
*Invite students to sign up to be the next reader.*

A five-day genre fair plan might look something like this:

**Day 1:** Share learning goals, demonstrate conducting research and creating your own product (poster, Google Slide, short video, and so on). Create student genre research teams.

**Day 2:** Research teams conduct genre research by reviewing familiar books from that genre and referring back to any anchor charts or other learning tools you created when studying that specific genre. Use the following sentence stems to guide their research and collect findings:

| | |
|---|---|
| We know it's a [biography] because . . . <br> ■ It tells about a person's life <br> ■ It is true <br> ■ Some have extra facts in the back | If we wanted to write a [biography], we would have to . . . <br> ■ Learn about a person <br> ■ Organize the information <br> ■ Write it like a story <br> ■ Write it in time order |
| Biographies are fun to read because . . . <br> ■ You learn about interesting people <br> ■ Sometimes you learn about life long ago | Our favorite biographies are . . . <br> ■ *Bessie the Motorcycle Queen* (Smith 2022) <br> ■ *How to Hear the Universe* (Valdez 2022) <br> ■ *The Rise (and Falls) of Jackie Chan* (Giang 2022) |

**Day 3:** Research teams create their product.

**Day 4:** Research teams create their product and practice their presentation.

**Day 5:** Genre fair. Students share the products they created to highlight the genre.

### Try This! Extend Reading Practices Beyond the Classroom

Don't you just love walking into a classroom during independent reading in the spring? By this point, most readers have found a book or series they can't put down, students are sharing titles with one another, and, overall, learners are in a groove. Acknowledge all of the small steps that were put into place to help students get to this point, and then reflect on how to help learners extend these habits outside of the classroom and into their future reading journeys. We believe it is important to guide students through this process because the end goal is to not only cultivate reading habits and behaviors in our own classrooms, but to also help learners broaden these routines so they carry them wherever they may go.

## GATHER

Begin this process by listing the different reading experiences you've had with learners throughout this year, such as read-aloud, book clubs, book talks, independent reading, and more. As students continue to take part in these practices during the last few months of the school year, plan to spend a bit of time together contemplating how these classroom reading practices will support them as they venture into a reading-filled summer and beyond. If the reading routine you want to revisit and highlight isn't currently a part of your daily schedule, you only need to find a small amount of time to remind readers of this practice. For instance, if you want learners to reflect on the power of your read-aloud experiences but don't have time left to enjoy a whole novel, read aloud a favorite picture book or short story. Alternatively, if you want students to remember what they learned from participating in a book club earlier in the year, create a scaled-down version by having groups meet to discuss a series of poems or an informational article related to something you're currently studying or a current event.

## GET STARTED

Once you've identified the reading behaviors you want to highlight, intentionally build a bridge between your classroom practices and students' future reading lives by discussing how they can reimagine these experiences in ways that might happen in their personal lives. In Chapter 2, we made the opposite connection by offering an opportunity for learners to conduct a Community Literacy Survey to discover how family and community members use literacy outside of school. Therefore, you might be thinking, *I already did this at the beginning of the year. Why do it again now?* Now is the time to cement the opposing understanding so that readers can clearly see the value of reading beyond the classroom environment.

Capture students' thinking on an anchor chart or shared document (see Figure 5.2 on the following page) to be displayed in your classroom and sent home as a summer reading resource for students and families/caregivers. In addition, work with your colleagues and administration to make sure students have access to books to read while they're away from school. Partner with your public library and offer opportunities for students and their caregivers to sign up for library cards. If your public library has a bookmobile, request that they schedule stops at your school. Consider opening your school library a few times over the summer for book checkout. If your district subscribes to an online database of books, make sure students have their passwords, access to devices, and Internet service so that they can keep reading during the summer months.

FIGURE 5.2

| READING BEYOND THE CLASSROOM | |
|---|---|
| **Classroom Reading Practices** | **Ways to Extend Practices Beyond the Classroom** |
| Read-alouds | ■ Check out and listen to audiobooks from the public library or using library apps.<br>■ Read aloud a page or section of your text when you find you're having difficulty understanding.<br>■ Record a read-aloud of a poem or other treasured text to send as a gift to a family member.<br>■ Seek out opportunities to read texts aloud, like poetry slams, theater camps, worship services, family events, and so on.<br>■ Read aloud to younger family members, trusted neighbors, or kids you're babysitting. |
| Book clubs | ■ Join a book club at a local library, at a local bookstore, or through a reliable online organization.<br>■ Organize your own book club with friends or family members (in person or virtual). Penguin Random House's Brightly website has a wealth of book suggestions and book club guides for readers ages nine to twelve to get you started.<br>■ Discuss what you're reading with others to hear various opinions and perspectives.<br><br>*Explore Penguin Random House's Brightly website here.* |
| Multimodal text sets | ■ Seek out multiple sources when trying to figure out how to make or do something.<br>■ Use multiple forms of texts to learn more about a person, current event, or topic of interest.<br>■ Teach an older family member how to access information in various ways. |
| Genre studies | ■ Notice the format or structure of the books you're reading. Use the genre-specific features (timelines, glossary, maps, and so on) to help you better understand the text.<br>■ Ask friends and family members for genre-specific recommendations.<br>■ Read outside of your "genre comfort zone."<br>■ Read books in different subgenres of your preferred genre in order to compare and contrast. |
| Writing about reading | ■ Keep a record of the books you've read, either in a journal or online, to record your ratings and notice your preferences (see Figure 5.3).<br>■ Create your own table of contents to track your learning while reading informational texts (see Figure 5.4). |

FIGURE 5.3

*Katie has kept a record of the books she's read since fourth grade.*

Summer 2011

340. The Second Summer of the Sisterhood —————— 4½
    Ann Brashares
    realistic fiction
    Bridget, Carmen, Tibby, and Lena all set off on new
    adventures while wearing the Pants

341. The Hunger Games —————— 5
    Suzanne Collins
    science fiction
    In the world of Panem, the Capitol controls everything, and
    every year they showcase their power through the Hunger Games.
    The Hunger Games are an intense fight to the death that
    24 randomly chosen 12-18 year olds must participate in.
    This novel chronicles one of these competitors, Katniss, as
    she competes in the Games.

FIGURE 5.4

*Maria's table of contents while reading* Shifting the Balance K-2 *(Burkins and Yates 2021).*

p. 3-4 Guiding Questions
p. 9 Great opening paragraph to set stage
SHIFT 1 → Rethinking How Comprehension Begins → Treat oral language development as an essential ingredient for comprehension.
p. 11 Listening comprehension
p. 13 Listening comprehension → Processing Systems
p. 16 Reading comprehension is basically the same work as Listening Comprehension
p. 17 Opportunities to grow oral language develop the comprehension mechanisms of reading
p. 18 Simple View of Reading
p. 21 Oral Language Development + Knowledge Building
p. 27 Use strong vocabulary
p. 28 Read Aloud Tips
p. 30 Dialogic Conversations Engage → Repeat → Expand
SHIFT 2 → Recommit to Phonemic Awareness Instruction
p. 41 Phonics + Phonemic Awareness
p. 43 Phonemic Awareness Consistency is more important than quantity
SHIFT 3 Reimagining the Way We Teach Phonics →
p. 65 Purpose of phonics instruction
p. 66 3-Dimensional letters to manipulate
p. 73 Assess phonics through writing
Explicitly & systematically teach the secrets of how to crack the written code.

Take these discussions a step beyond the hypothetical by asking readers to make a direct connection between what they've learned from their in-class reading experiences and how they might use these lessons in the future. Figure 5.5 provides a sample graphic organizer learners can use to map out this thinking. In the first column of the graphic organizer, ask students to list the classroom reading practice you're highlighting that particular day. In the middle column, have them jot down what they've learned personally from participating in that reading practice. In the last column, nudge students to ponder how they might use what they learned in class to guide their future reading experiences. Once students have their reading course laid out, prompt them to share their thinking with other classmates in order to give readers different ideas and perspectives on the various pathways they might follow when they leave your classroom.

FIGURE 5.5

| Reading Beyond the Classroom Graphic Organizer | | |
|---|---|---|
| Reading Experience | When We Did This in School, I Learned . . . | I Can Use What I've Learned Beyond the Classroom by . . . |
| Read-aloud | | |
| Book clubs | | |
| Multimodal text sets | | |

## WHERE THIS MIGHT LEAD

At the beginning of the next school year, invite a few of your former students who have gone through this process back to the classroom to share their on-going reading journey with your new learners. In our experience, students are much more likely to take advice from their peers than from their teachers! The intentional work you've done to connect classroom practices to out-of-school literacy experiences can lead to an opportunity for readers to hear from someone who is closer to their age.

In order to get your new students thinking about reading beyond the classroom right away, host a live or recorded interview with former learners about their reading journeys and how they use reading in their everyday lives. Some questions you might ask include:

- Tell us a little bit about yourself as a reader.
- What kinds of books or other texts do you like to read?
- What have you learned about yourself as a reader?
- How does reading show up for you outside of the classroom?
- What types of reading do you do daily?
- What are you still working on as a reader?
- What advice would you give to my students about reading?

If possible, and with permission, record the interviews so that you can show them in future years or so that your teammates' classes can benefit from the ideas that are shared. When your visitors leave, give students an opportunity to debrief and discuss what they learned and how the insights that were shared might affect their reading life.

### Keep It Simple:
### Invite Current Readers to Inspire Future Readers

As readers reflect on their personal progress, invite them to create resources for the learners who will be joining your reading community next year. This is a meaningful way for readers to pay their knowledge forward while, at the same time, celebrating their accomplishments. In Figure 5.7, you'll find a few ideas about how readers' self-reflection can lead to the creation of valuable tools for next year's class.

Student Reading
Tips + Tricks

- read before bed
- find an engaging book
- read in a comfy space
- have a reading "spot"
- make sure you understand what you are reading
- listen to audiobooks
- visualize while reading
- avoid distractions, phone on silent
- talk to people about your book
- go to the library
- find authors + genres you enjoy
- ask family + friends for recs
- break it up/read in chunks
- use social media for recs
- make predictions
- read in accents in your head

FIGURE 5.6
*Students' advice to next year's readers.*

FIGURE 5.7

| WHERE MIGHT STUDENTS' REFLECTIONS LEAD? | |
| --- | --- |
| **When Students' Reflection Leads Them to . . .** | **They Can . . .** |
| Discuss the most memorable books they read this school year | Write book recommendations for next year's readers. Provide each student with a 3-by-5-inch index card. Ask them to sell the book to future readers by writing a short blurb on an index card. You can either store these cards in a library pocket affixed to the inside front cover of the book or display the card near the book on your bookshelf, like you see in many independent bookshops. To personalize, add the student's photo, with their permission, to the corner of the card. |
| List books they still want to read | Compile a shopping list of suggested books for you to add to your classroom library. Keep this list on hand as you write book grants, walk through garage sales, or peruse the shelves of used-book stores over the summer. |
| Count the books they've read this year | Offer a challenge to next year's readers. Gather a group of math-minded students to calculate the class total and create a sign that reads something like this: "In 2023, this class period read _____ books. How many books will you read this year?" |
| Notice their genre preferences | Collaborate in small groups or as a class to curate a "Top Ten List of [insert genre here] Books" they recommend for readers in next year's class. Post these genre-based recommendations in your classroom library near the shelves that house that particular genre. |
| Evaluate their personal growth toward applying reading habits and behaviors | Offer advice to next year's readers. Write, create a slide, or video-record one piece of advice for next year's class. Share these at the beginning of the year as you are setting up routines and creating shared beliefs (see Figure 5.6). |
| Categorize the different types of books they read | Design a better system for organizing books on the bookshelves. Give interested learners time to draw a classroom map or blueprint to suggest ways to reorganize your classroom library to be more user-friendly. |

## HOLD TRUE TO YOUR BELIEFS

Because you've engaged in an ongoing cycle of modeling, practicing, and revisiting your shared beliefs throughout the school year, your literacy instruction is on stable footing. With the end of the year inching closer, it's time to anchor into those beliefs, as many things may try to steer you off course. The wind from the north could bring in a chilly gust of standardized testing, while the southerly breezes blow in feelings of restlessness and anticipation of summer break. Here we've brainstormed a few suggestions for how to continue to steer in the direction of reader-centered decisions.

### Try This! Plan Belief-Driven Events and Celebrations

▶ All the special events and celebrations happening at the end of the year can sneak in and derail belief-driven teaching. Typically, they start to occur during the last few months of school and, depending on how many your school has planned, can take time away from literacy learning. While we firmly believe in joy and celebration, we've also been able to make small shifts to keep the focus on readers and reading. Whether this particular scenario is an issue for you or not, it is a solid educational practice to continue to weigh your planned learning experiences against your beliefs to see how they stand up.

## Why Hold True to Your Beliefs?

■ As the end of school nears, beliefs help us to answer the age-old teaching question "Is this worth the time?" (Gallagher and Kittle 2018).

■ When we hold true to our beliefs, we can prioritize the essential understandings that are most important during the last months with our learners. This helps us to focus on "moving students dynamically through the curriculum" rather than on spending precious instructional minutes reviewing with the whole class (Parker 2022).

### GATHER

Look ahead in your team's or school's calendar and note the various activities and celebrations your grade level or school community engages in during the final months of school. Consider options for making small changes or additions to the existing event to keep instruction focused on readers and reading.

### GET STARTED

One example of a common activity in primary-grade classrooms is an A–Z countdown to end the year. For example, on "A day" students bring a stuffed animal to school, and on "B day" they pretend their classroom is a beach. While stuffed animals and sunglasses are certainly fun, they can often distract from achieving your learning goals. On top of that, it's a lot to expect families/caregivers to keep track of what to send on a particular day at an already busy time of year, and sending in items may be a financial burden. If you have a celebration similar to this in your school or grade level, you could work with your teammates or PLC to shift this celebration toward being a more reading-focused event. For instance, consider keeping it an in-class celebration centered on books. Each day, read aloud a picture book whose title contains the featured letter of the alphabet (see Figure 5.8 for some book suggestions). To sneak in a little writing, you could even have students record the books they heard, like Katherine Phillips-Toms's kindergarten students did (see Figure 5.9).

FIGURE 5.8

## A–Z BOOK CELEBRATION SUGGESTED TITLES

| A | B | C | D | E |
|---|---|---|---|---|
| *Abdul's Story* (Thompkins-Bigelow 2022) | *Blue Bison Needs a Haircut* (Rothman 2022) | *Creepy Crayon* (Reynolds 2022) | *Dress-Up Day* (Gómez 2022) | *Ear Worm* (Knowles 2022) |
| **F** | **G** | **H** | **I** | **J** |
| *Fly* (Thurman, 2022) | *Gibberish* (Vo 2022) | *The Hair Book* (Yvette 2022) | *I Am!* (Medina 2022) | *Joy* (Ismail 2019) |
| **K** | **L** | **M** | **N** | **O** |
| *Kicks* (Garrett 2022) | *Lift* (Lê 2020) | *Maybe* (Haughton 2021) | *Not That Pet!* (Prasadam-Halls 2022) | *Out!* (Chung 2017) |
| **P** | **Q** | **R** | **S** | **T** |
| *Paletero Man* (Diaz 2021) | *Be Quiet!* (Higgins 2017) | *Ride, Roll, Run: Time for Fun* (Bolling 2022) | *Seaside Stroll* (Trevino 2021) | *Turtle in a Tree* (Hudson 2021) |
| **U** | **V** | **W** | **X** | **Y/Z** |
| *Underwear!* (Harney 2019) | *¡Vamos! Let's Go Read* (Raúl the Third 2023) | *Wonder Walkers* (Archer 2021) | *What About X? An Alphabet Adventure* (Houppert 2021) | *You Can!* (Strick 2022) *Zonia's Rain Forest* (Martinez-Neal 2021) |

Use this same thinking as you consider other celebrations that exist in your classroom and work with your colleagues to create more belief-driven celebratory moments. Be sure to keep a record of the shifts you make. We got the record started in Figure 5.10 on the following page with some of the shifts we've made over the years. Add to it as you find new ways to rethink celebrations to better match your beliefs and meet the needs of your students.

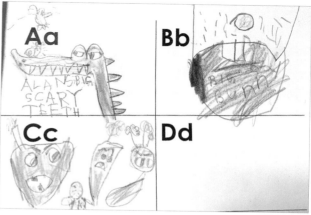

FIGURE 5.9

*Student Work Sample: A-Z Read-Aloud Celebration*

FIGURE 5.10

## RECORD OF CELEBRATION SHIFTS

| Current Celebration | Belief-Driven Celebration |
|---|---|
| A-Z countdown | A-Z read-aloud celebration |
| Chalk the Walk | Chalk the Walk with book talks: Students decorate sidewalks or the playground by drawing book characters or covers from their favorite books. Take photos to share or invite other classes to view them on a book talk walk (before it rains and washes them away!). |
| Fundraising run or walk | Post a StoryWalk® for participants to enjoy as they walk or after the finish line of a running race. A StoryWalk® is simply a way to post the pages of a picture book for people to enjoy as they stroll past them. It was developed by Anne Ferguson of Montpelier, Vermont.    *Find more information about copyright-friendly ways to host a StoryWalk® here.* |

## WHERE THIS MIGHT LEAD

Taking time to carefully examine the celebrations and activities that are part of your team's or school's traditions paves the way for continued conversations about how you choose to spend instructional time. Just as you weed your classroom library from time to time, it is equally important to critically examine how you are spending instructional minutes and, if necessary, trim and discard practices that no longer match your beliefs. The end of the year is ideal for this type of reflection because what you did this past year is still fresh in your mind. As a team or with a thinking partner, look back over the year and target an event/activity or two that you want to improve. Brainstorm ideas and jot them down in a place you'll remember to access and refer to when the time comes. That way when the event comes up in the middle of a busy year, you are not starting from scratch and have seed ideas to make it even better.

### Try This! Treat Test Preparation Like a Genre or Unit

In many parts of the country, spring not only ushers in warmer weather but also kicks off standardized testing season. Testing season can add a layer of stress to your joyful literacy community and challenge some of your deeply rooted beliefs. While, as a teacher, you generally cannot control the number of tests students take or when these tests will occur, you can make decisions related to how you go about preparing learners for the exams. First and foremost, we take Regie Routman's words to heart and try to remember that "the best test prep is expert teaching in whole, real-world, meaningful contexts" (Routman 2018, 320). With her wisdom guiding our way, we hold tight to our convictions and student-focused practices. However, it is also important to help students feel prepared for the standardized testing context in order to alleviate any anxiety and help ready them for the inevitable future testing scenarios. Therefore, we follow Regie's lead and suggest treating test preparation like any other genre that you might introduce to learners.

**Back-Pocket Wisdom: Plan Belief-Driven Events and Celebrations**

Conversations about long-held traditions must be navigated with care, especially if you are new to the team or the school. Keep in mind someone has likely put a lot of time and energy into developing the activity, so you want to be sure to honor that work while at the same time collaboratively problem-solving ways to make sure it meets the needs of your current students and enhances their learning.

## GATHER

If you commit to trusting that what you've taught students has adequately prepared them to take the test, then the one missing piece is teaching the ins and outs of taking a standardized test. Prepare to introduce this reading genre as you would any other, by gathering mentor texts and experiences. To do this, access a few practice tests or sample questions that have the same format as the ones students will see on the actual text. Most standardized tests provide practice options for classroom use. To increase engagement, select the highest-interest reading passages and/or writing prompts that you can find. Also, plan to do the practice items in a format similar to how they will be administered. For instance, if your learners will be taking the assessment on a computer, see if you can find online practice options.

## GET STARTED

Once you have your materials gathered, reground yourself in your classroom beliefs. Even though standardized testing tends to run counter to many of our shared literacy principles, you can still challenge yourself to stay true to your classroom beliefs even when preparing for these assessments. In Figure 5.11 on the following page, we provide a sampling of how our own beliefs guide our instructional decisions as we plan how to prepare students for the testing season.

FIGURE 5.11

| HOW OUR BELIEFS GUIDE INSTRUCTIONAL DECISIONS DURING TESTING SEASON | |
|---|---|
| **Our Belief** | **Instructional Decision** |
| We believe everyone is a reader. | We teach all learners how to access the genre of standardized testing passages, just as we teach the other genres. |
| We believe that reading feeds our hearts and minds. | As much as possible, we balance standardized testing with time to read for pleasure. |
| We believe everyone's voice should be heard. | We offer a variety of options for students to ask test-related questions. |
| We believe that we learn from each other. | We create opportunities for students to collaborate and learn tips from their peers during test preparation experiences. |
| We believe talking and writing help us to understand what we've read. | We share the importance of self-talk and note taking (if the test allows) as ways to think through answers. |
| We believe mistakes are learning opportunities. | We provide time, space, and scaffolding for students to learn standardized testing conventions in a low-stakes environment. |

Now that you are firmly grounded in your beliefs, begin by introducing the genre of standardized test reading to learners. Invite students to share what they've already learned or experienced during previous standardized testing situations. Discuss how the type of reading they will be doing during a standardized test is different and, therefore, requires a unique set of skills and strategies. To help them see the transfer to real-life testing scenarios, share that these test-taking skills may come in handy in the future when they take a similar kind of test to get their driver's license, to enter many trades or professions, or to continue with their schooling. Mention how, for the next few days, you will work together to compile a list of strategies that will help prepare them for the upcoming test.

As with other learning experiences, use the gradual-release-of-responsibility model to walk students through the standardized testing genre. First, explain how you approach a test and model a few questions as a whole class. Next, support learners as they process through a few questions with a partner. Finally, give them time to try a few questions on their own.

Using what they've learned from studying the genre of test taking, co-create an anchor chart of test-taking strategies that learners discovered and found useful during their practice (see Figure 5.12). Reference and add to these tips as you continue to do practice tests or questions. Students will remember this list and call back to it during future literacy assessments, whether they are standardized or not.

## WHERE THIS MIGHT LEAD

The process we suggested for teaching the genre of standardized test taking is a research-proven instructional sequence for introducing any genre to readers. We'll quickly recap the steps here:

- Immerse readers in the genre by sharing and studying a stack of mentor texts.

- Demonstrate and practice genre-specific reading strategies or writer's-craft moves.

- Record thinking and learning for future use.

- Apply new understandings to personal reading and writing.

Ultimately, the goal of treating test preparation as its own unit or genre is to allow students not only to feel confident when taking the test but also to be able to move on from this unit and forward into learning that matches your classroom beliefs. So, congratulate students on using their standardized test taking skills and then move on to a new unit . . . until next year.

### Keep It Simple: Break Up Testing and Instruction in Creative Ways

If your schools are similar to those in our experiences, you may have a modified schedule during the standardized testing window. This disjointed schedule often leads to having breaks between tests that need to be filled. When "normal" instruction seems unrealistic because students have spent hours in a testing environment and they just need some guided free time to let off some steam, we suggest breaking up testing in these creative ways:

#### No Prep

After hours of sitting silently for an extended amount of time, giving students a chance to play and converse with their peers may be the most valuable learning they can do at this point in their day. Remember, play + conversation = learning! Hand out some blank paper and encourage students to teach each other how to play paper-and-pencil

**Test-Taking Tips**

- Skip challenging questions + go back later
- Use online tools (annotation, calculator, glossary, etc.)
- Get a good night's sleep
- Take deep breaths
- Use process of elimination
- Make an outline for writing
- Be aware of how much time you have
- Summarize the passage after reading

FIGURE 5.12
*Anchor Chart: Test-Taking Tips*

games like Tic-Tac-Toe or Dots and Boxes, how to create your own Wordle, and so on. Or, if possible, grab some sidewalk chalk and do the same thing outside.

### Low Prep

Engage learners in critical thinking and wordplay with a list of brain teasers. Challenge learners to solve the brain teasers in partners or small groups. Give hints as they work through them. To prepare, print a list of brain teasers and let the students puzzle through them together.

### Some Prep

Create a classroom Olympic Games experience that spans each break in your testing window. First, split students into teams and have them collaborate to make a team flag. Then play music and have students process around the room for the opening ceremonies. Now it is time for the games to begin. We suggest creating different Olympic events based solely on things you already have lying around your classroom (watch *The Office* episode "Office Olympics" for inspiration). Events in Katie's classroom include a race around the room balancing books on heads, a paper outfit-making contest, and a sticky-note scavenger hunt. Keep track of which teams win each event and end your Olympics with a closing ceremony to celebrate being done with testing. Bonus points if you create medals out of yogurt lids like they did in *The Office*!

## INNOVATE ON ROUTINES

In Chapter 4, we explored ideas for reenergizing literacy routines after winter break. You might be thinking, *If I continue to reenergize and innovate on my everyday classroom practices, they will no longer be routine.* If your students' literacy learning is going well and the majority of them continue to be engaged, then there is no need to modify things again. But in our experience, the last few months call for increased creativity on our part to stave off boredom and continue to keep even the most resistant learners involved in the classroom rituals.

From a professional learning perspective, we've found that the end of the school year is an ideal time to dabble with ideas that you've learned or want to try next year. Because you've built strong relationships and, in general, students know what to expect, it is easier to try new things now than it is at the beginning of the school year. Simply say something like, "I learned a new way of doing _____ and want to try it out. I'd love to know what you think." Inviting kids to weigh in may give you some insights to carry into next year.

Explore the ideas we offer for innovating on routines and consider how they might be helpful for your learners.

## Why Innovate on Routines?

■ Students' needs at the beginning of the school year may be different from those at the end. We strive to be responsive to those changes (Fountas and Pinnell Literacy Team 2016).

■ We innovate on routines so that we continue to move forward. True learning happens for our students and for ourselves when we ask questions and push the boundaries of what is possible (Couros 2015).

### Try This! Integrate Poetry and the Arts

▶ Think about the type of texts students are consuming and the responses or reactions to the texts they are producing. Do you notice them losing interest in the texts they're reading and the literacy-related work you're asking them to do? Springtime offers an opportunity to look for ways to incorporate poetry into your reading fare and infuse the arts into the choices that students have when they are responding or reacting to their reading.

Let's start with poetry. Poetic texts come in many shapes and sizes, including anthologies, poetic picture books, and, for upper elementary and middle-school readers, verse novels. From a teaching perspective, poetry is versatile because it is easily woven into any unit, used as a way to introduce or review a content area concept, or read and performed for pure enjoyment.

As far as the arts go, finding occasions to weave in music, movement, or visual arts can tap into students' creative sides and liven up an otherwise routine task. Keep reading and we'll show you what we mean.

### GATHER

When you are selecting poetic texts to share with students, look for those that could serve as a mentor text to illuminate a reading skill or strategy or lead to a thoughtful response. Along with poetic mentor texts, seek out anthologies about topics like animals, bugs, or school, and those that contain rib-tickling poems. To infuse the arts, put together a collection of low-effort, high-engagement creative tasks to mix and match while doing your plans for the last few months. In Figure 5.14 (on the next page), we've started you out with some alternatives to standards-based responses that have worked well in our classrooms.

## GET STARTED

As you plan your literacy instruction, look for occasions to slip in a poem (Figure 5.13) or to try your own artsy alternative (Figure 5.14). Observe readers' engagement level and ask them their opinion. Jot down notes and/or take a few pictures so that you can remember their reactions and, if needed, make a few adjustments so that it goes even more smoothly in the future.

FIGURE 5.13

| INCORPORATING POETRY | |
|---|---|
| **When?** | **How?** |
| Reinforcing foundational skills | Whether you're tuning your students' ears to rhyming words or teaching them how to orthographically map, or make letter-sound connections, to decode a high-frequency word, project a poem and dig right in. |
| Read-aloud | Spice up your read-aloud experiences by reaching for a poetic picture book like *Happy Sloth Day!* (Sayre and Sayre 2022) or *Hustle Bustle Bugs* (Bailey 2022). Pair the poetic book with a descriptive informational text on the same topic to compare and contrast whether readers prefer learning from books written in poetry or those written in prose. |
| Shared reading | Engage in a short burst of shared reading (Walther 2022) with a poem. Focus on a foundational skill or strategy in a "my turn, our turn, your turn" format. Begin by pointing out and demonstrating how readers use the foundational skill or strategy. Next, invite students to join their voices with yours as they reread, to practice noticing or applying what you've modeled. Finally, nudge students to incorporate what they've learned as they read the text on their own. |
| Guiding readers in small groups | If you are focusing on using text clues to infer, select a poem that describes a person, place, animal, or event. Share the poem without showing the title. Invite readers to use text clues to infer the topic of the poem. |
| Independent reading | Once students are familiar with a poem or song, make a copy for them to keep in a three-ring binder. Readers love rereading or singing these with a partner or on their own. |

FIGURE 5.14

| ARTSY ALTERNATIVES TO STANDARDS-BASED RESPONSES | |
|---|---|
| **Standards-Based Learning Target** | **Artsy Alternative** |
| Retell stories | Teach students how to make a paper bag theater to use when retelling. To do this, students draw and cut out the main character(s) of the story. If available, tape each character to a straw or craft stick. To serve as a backdrop for the action, learners illustrate the setting of the story on a paper lunch bag oriented the landscape way. If the story has two main settings, they will draw one on each side of the bag. Once the theater is ready, learners use the characters and setting to retell the story. Students could also use a paper bag theater to compose and tell their own version of a familiar tale (see Figure 5.15). |

FIGURE 5.14 (continued)

## ARTSY ALTERNATIVES TO STANDARDS-BASED RESPONSES

| Standards-Based Learning Target | Artsy Alternative |
| --- | --- |
| Demonstrate understanding of key details in an informational text | Create an infographic, diagram, or other visual representation of the key details found in informational selections. Begin familiarizing students with infographics by sharing and studying some mentor graphics, like those found in Steve Jenkins's books *Animals by the Numbers* (2016) and *Disasters by the Numbers* (2021). Work with students to notice the symbols and structures used in the mentor infographics. To create their own, students determine the topic and goal of their visual. Then they plan the flow and organization. Once they have a plan, they can design their infographic either on paper or using a digital tool. |
| Use words and phrases for effect | Write a poem or song about a text or topic. We've found success with teaching children how to write a list poem that details places, people, sounds, emotions, and other aspects related to the topic. You can find a collection of mentor poems in the book *Underneath My Bed: List Poems* (Cleary 2016). For songs, we show writers how to use their knowledge of familiar tunes like "Twinkle, Twinkle, Little Star" or "Happy Birthday" to write a piggyback song with their own lyrics (see Figures 5.16 and 5.17 for examples). |
| Infer the theme, moral, or lesson | Use loose parts (a random collection of items found in nature or around your classroom—think twigs, pebbles, straws, cotton balls, craft sticks) to visually represent the character(s), setting, plot, conflict, or theme of the text. Take a photo of the visual representation and then explain with written and/or recorded words (see Figure 5.18). |

FIGURE 5.15
*Student Work Sample:*
*Paper Bag Theater*

FIGURE 5.17
*Demonstration Text:*
*Piggyback Song*

FIGURE 5.16
*Demonstration Text:*
*List Poem*

FIGURE 5.18
*Student Work Sample:*
*Loose Parts*

## WHERE THIS MIGHT LEAD

Getting in the habit of integrating as much as possible into one lesson is a smart way to streamline your instruction. Along with infusing poetry and the arts, look for opportunities to blend big ideas or content-area topics into your literacy instruction. Think of it as multitasking while also expanding the role reading plays in other areas of your curriculum. Remember back in Chapter 2 when we had students write identity equations? That is a perfect example of integrating math and literacy.

### Try This! Remix Routines to Increase Engagement

Both of us thrive on routine and structure. Because of this, we sometimes get stuck in a rut. After many months of reviewing and practicing routines, it is only natural for these routines to begin to feel a bit mundane or rote. As we've established in the previous section, there is no need to change up your entire classroom or belief system. However, you can still hold true to your beliefs while making a few slight modifications to further students' engagement in the literacy practices of the community.

### GATHER

Through informal observations, take some time to notice and evaluate daily classroom practices in order to determine which routines could use a bit of a shake-up. Have you observed students getting restless during supported independent reading? Are readers spending most of their time in book clubs talking about their summer plans? Do learners seem less engaged during book talks than even a few weeks ago? Pick one or two routines that might need a refresh, and read on.

### GET STARTED

Based on your observations, find a learning activity that you've done before but now have noticed is not generating the type of engagement or understanding that you had hoped. Ask yourself if there's a way to swap out some aspect of this experience in order to liven it up. As you think about what adjustment you want to make, keep in mind the end goal of these experiences and make sure your modifications are still aligning with those goals. In Figure 5.19 we share some possibilities for remixing different routines depending on what you are noticing in your classroom and the goals of your reading community. Our hope is that this will spark some of your own thinking about the small changes that will work best for your readers.

FIGURE 5.19

| A FEW IDEAS FOR REMIXING ROUTINES | |
|---|---|
| **Routine** | **If-Then** |
| Whole-class read-aloud | If learners struggle to stay engaged while you are reading aloud, **then** invite them to perform short texts using a reader's theater approach. To prepare for reader's theater, students practice reading aloud a script based on a poem, story, or nonfiction text. When their performance is polished, they present it to their peers, usually without costumes or props. |
| | If readers have only heard you read aloud throughout the year, **then** introduce a guest reader or listen to an audiobook. |
| | If you've focused on novels during read-aloud time, **then** use a different type of text—perhaps an audiobook, video clip, image, short story, poem, picture book, and so on. |
| Supported independent reading | If students are getting a bit of spring fever, **then** take them outside for reading time. |
| | If learners are struggling to stay "in" a book, **then** bring in newspapers to read and discuss for a day or week. |
| | If readers are focused on peer relationships, **then** introduce partner reading options or transition into book clubs. |
| Book talks | If students seem drawn to devices, **then** find a few YouTube, TikTok, or Instagram book talks to share. |
| | If learners are getting antsy during book talks, **then** change the setting by going to another location in your building (perhaps the library). |
| | If readers are wanting to share with peers, **then** do student-led book talks in small groups so that each person can share what they are reading. |

Don't feel the need to try everything at once. We've found that holding ourselves accountable to innovate on *one* aspect of our instruction each week helps to keep things fresh. More than that can become overwhelming for both you and the students.

## WHERE THIS MIGHT LEAD

If you've observed the benefits of small changes to students' literacy routines, try releasing some of this responsibility and include them in the decision-making. See if there are other routines that could use some livening up. Work together to brainstorm ideas of how they would go about modifying this practice. Get them started by using "if" scenarios like the ones found in Figure 5.19. Once learners are done brainstorming, give them time to experiment with the remixed routine. Then discuss whether this change increased their overall engagement, and make adjustments from there. This process could help enhance a variety of classroom procedures as you move toward the end of the year.

### Keep It Simple: Try New Grouping Structures and Supplies

Students are familiar with working in groups to collaborate with their peers, and so a quick shift in grouping structure or change in tools can be just enough to energize students. Plus, it takes minimal effort on your part. Consider the following:

- **Change the grouping arrangement.** Think about pairs, triads, small groups, and cross-grade-level partners (this last one takes a bit more planning).

- **Increase the movement level.** Try one of the following ideas:
  - *Gallery walk.* Create six to eight different gallery walk stations. The contents of those stations can be anything related to your literacy curriculum that might elicit multiple responses, like a question, prompt, quote, image, and so on. Divide students into six to eight groups. As groups rotate, they record a response. To keep track of their responses, you have each group use a different-color marker or have individuals write their initials below their response. After students have visited multiple stations (or all of them, if you have time), debrief and discuss.
  - *Scoot.* Similar to a gallery walk but more geared to elementary-grade learners. Small groups of learners scoot around the room from one literacy-related activity to the next. We used activities like putting the letters of the alphabet in order, singing the alphabet song, and matching rhyming pictures.
  - *Walk-and-talk.* Similar to turn-and-talk, but students stroll around the room with a partner to ponder a question you've posed.
  - *Matching cards.* Use a set of matching cards (like those found in the game Memory) or make your own. Give half of the cards to half of the class and the matching cards to the other half of the class. Students find the person with the matching card and pair up with them as thinking partners.

- **Offer some new materials.** In Maria's experience, kids will write anything with a scented marker! If students usually use lined paper, try blank paper. Or change the paper size or shape—give them poster-size paper or a teeny little booklet. Use loose parts or building blocks to portray a character or setting. Introduce a new online platform for creating work, such as Canva or Google Drawings.

## REFRESH POSITIVE COMMUNITY

You and your learners have spent countless hours, days, and weeks learning, reading, and growing together. With the end of the year in sight, students (and teachers) can grow a bit restless, and sometimes this prolonged togetherness can lead to tension or frustration. So how do you continue to foster the positive relationships you've established so far this year? Try out or adjust the ideas that follow to continue to maintain a productive learning environment as your time with these particular literacy learners comes to an end.

### Try This! Sprinkle in Kindness

Where do kindness and literacy intersect? Kindness can take center stage in a read-aloud, and that same book can offer an opportunity for readers to track a character's feelings over the course of the story. Clearly, kindness plays a key role in the conversations learners have with each other about the books they're reading. Students who can empathize with their peers are better able to understand their perspectives. A concern for others bubbles up as readers meet characters and learn about situations that call them to action. Bringing kindness back to the forefront not only makes your days more joyful, but it also strengthens students' literacy learning. Let's think about a few ways to sprinkle more kindness into students' literacy experiences during the final months of the school year.

### Why Refresh Positive Community?

- Developing a caring and healthy learning space led by readers is crucial to the success of a classroom. However, it is just as important to continue reflecting on and reworking processes so that the community can thrive through the end of the year (Johnston 2012).

- Returning to ideas of spreading kindness can help to revive a positive literacy community (Currie 2015).

### GATHER

Curate a kindness text set to integrate into your current literacy lessons and feature in your classroom library. Ask your students to suggest any titles they've read that helped them learn more about being kind. A few books you might add include:

- *Finding Kindness* (Underwood 2019)
  Summary: Simple acts of kindness throughout a community are portrayed in this rhyming book. Notice that each page connects to the next one through someone or something in the illustrations. Readers will have to infer the act of kindness by combining the clues from the text with the clues in the illustrations.

- *KINDergarten: Where Kindness Matters Every Day* (Ahiyya 2022)
  Summary: Ms. Perry and her kindergartners work together to create a kindness pledge.

- *The Power of One* (Ludwig 2020)
  Summary: A chain reaction sparked by one kind act results in a community coming together to plant a garden and harvest the seeds of kindness. Pair and compare with *If You Plant a Seed* (Nelson 2015).

- *When We Are Kind* (Smith 2020)
  Summary: Highlights the reciprocal relationships between performing kind acts and the satisfaction one gains from being kind.

## GET STARTED

While reading books with the theme of kindness, work with your students to analyze how the actions of the characters can apply to the way learners in the classroom talk and act during your literacy block. Add these to an on-going anchor chart like the one you see in Figure 5.20. If time and interest permit, extend the learning into your school community. Readers can use themes from the books you've read aloud to create kindness table tents to display on lunch tables, signs to post above the drinking fountains, or posters to hang on the back of bathroom stall doors. Gather a small group of students and show them how to select kindness quotes from the books you're reading. Ask your administrator if they could share some of the quotes during the announcements or add them to a school e-newsletter. If you are on a campus where students will be leaving to head off to middle school or high school, make a wall of wishes for them to read before they leave.

FIGURE 5.20

*Anchor Chart:
Readers Use Kind
Words and Actions*

## WHERE THIS MIGHT LEAD

Reach out even further by stressing the importance of kindness beyond your school and into the neighborhood. For instance, in April, target ideas for being kind to the earth. Approach any activities you are doing around Earth Day from a kindness lens. Ponder how being kind to the earth impacts your learners' local environment. Collaborate with your students to brainstorm other places in their community where some words of kindness might brighten someone's day. Over the years, we've sent cheerful, uplifting pictures and notes to members of the military, families dealing with loss, children's hospitals, shelters for people without housing, retirement communities, and nursing homes.

### Try This! Look Back to Move Forward

Remember the beginning of the school year when you and your learners walked into the classroom bright-eyed, curious, and full of new ideas?

At this point in the year, it might feel like you've lost some of that spark. So how do you get it back? We suggest allocating time at the end of the year to revisit some of the most impactful learning events. These shared moments can create a sense of completion and remind students of the growth and joy they've experienced throughout the school year.

## GATHER

Go back to your plans from the first few weeks of school and scan through to find the different experiences that you felt were most impactful in bringing your group of readers together. Then look ahead at your final months' plans and decide when you could close out these moments in order to honor the growth students have achieved. This initial plan will help you to determine which experiences you want to invest a bit more time revisiting and which you can review a bit more quickly.

## GET STARTED

Contemplate how to meaningfully close out different practices that are on your list. Think about how you can leverage these experiences to further students' sense of ownership in their learning. Here we offer a few suggestions based on the ideas we shared in previous chapters; be sure to add your own to the list.

| Look Back | Move Forward |
|---|---|
| Community Literacy Survey | Reanalyze the results of the Community Literacy Survey. Ask students to ponder how they've grown in the different aspects of language arts (reading, writing, speaking, listening, researching) and which they feel like they've used the most this school year. Take a moment to celebrate the areas in which learners have seen personal growth and those where they put forth the most effort. |
| Book Speed Dating | Plan one final round of Book Speed Dating or Scan the Stacks with any new books that you've added to the classroom library or books you think students would enjoy reading over the summer. Invite readers to suggest a few of their favorite lesser-read titles to add to the mix. Enjoy every minute of the last Book Speed Dating round. View it as a culmination and celebration of a year of joyful reading. Join in, video-record, or take photos as students chat about books and reading. |
| Someday Lists | Make time for readers to look back over their Someday Lists before sending them home. Students can mark which books they read and which they still want to read in the summer or fall. Show learners ways they can access these books, so that they keep up their reading pace during the summer. These ideas might include trading books with friends from class, going to the public library, using the public library bookmobile, consulting the online district library, accessing online district book subscriptions, and so on. |

(continued on next page)

GET STARTED (continued)

| Look Back | Move Forward |
|---|---|
| Read-alouds | Ask students to share their favorite read-aloud experience (whole books, short stories, poems, and so on) and reread those texts during your last few days or class periods as a way to wrap up your whole-class readings. For longer texts, read excerpts based on what readers remember most about the books. |

## WHERE THIS MIGHT LEAD

As you look back on these practices with your learners in order to culminate a year of cultivating a reader-centered classroom, ask yourself how you can use these end-of-the-year moments to grow your teaching practice for the forth-coming years.

| Revisit | Reflect |
|---|---|
| Community Literacy Survey | Consider learners' responses about which literacy practice they feel they used most this school year. Was this your intention? How can you create more balance among literacy practices in future years? |
| Book Speed Dating | Take the books that stand out most to students and put those in a pile for your beginning-of-the-year Book Speed Dating. |
| Someday Lists | Make a list of the most popular books students are planning to read and hand it off to their future teachers. That way the teachers have a sense of the kinds of books they might want to add to their classroom libraries or to their first book talk stack. |
| Read-alouds | Reflect on which reading experiences stuck with students. Ask them why these stand out, and use that feedback to plan engaging lessons and practices for the next school year. |

### Keep It Simple: Express Gratitude

A social-emotional skill that goes hand in hand with kindness is expressing gratitude. Personally, we find that focusing on gratitude not only gives students a positive boost but also helps us to approach our day with a healthier mindset. Harness the power of gratitude by taking time for students to express gratitude to people who have helped them on their reading journey throughout the school year.

Begin by making a list of possible recipients. To generate this list, ask students, "Who has helped you to grow as a reader this year?" and make note of their ideas (family members, caregivers, specialists and support teachers, peers, school librarian, authors, guest readers, and so on.). Then, collaborate to determine how they want to express their gratitude. The most common way is simply a note. Notes may vary depending on the age of your students and the materials available in your school building. Younger learners can draw a picture of the person for whom they are grateful; with older students, create a class outline of a more formal letter. Alternatively, learners could record voice memos or video clips, or they could create word clouds with various phrases that describe the recipient. There are endless ways to show gratitude, so this is an excellent chance to offer students choice in how they want to express their thankfulness. Once the notes are completed, either students can hand-deliver them or you can hang on to them and deliver them throughout the week. Raising students' awareness of the impact others have had on their reading life will help them realize the importance of reaching out when they need support and taking the time to thank people who help them along the way.

## PROMOTE STUDENT-TO-CAREGIVER COMMUNICATION

Throughout the book, we've puzzled through the ways to invite families and caregivers to be a part of the school community by honoring all they have to offer. In this chapter we've made an intentional shift to focus on supporting students in carrying reading routines forward. The same is true here. We think about what readers can create or experience to help them reflect upon the learning that shaped the reader they are right now. If we offer students opportunities to reflect on their growth by creating concrete artifacts, we provide the foundation for a conversation that will support their families/caregivers in fueling their reading lives beyond the context of our literacy classrooms.

### Why Promote Student-to-Caregiver Communication?

- We've spent the year nurturing an affirming learning environment in the classroom. Now we work to extend this guidance throughout the summer and into the following school year so that each reader can enjoy the benefits of an integrated support system even when they leave their current classroom (Dwyer, Kern, and Williams 2019).

- A student-to-family reading connection helps caregivers and students look forward in order to "create hopes and dreams" about their reading lives (Allyn and Morrell 2016).

### Try This! Curate a Collection of Reading Memories

What are the items you keep and look back on? Are there memories from your childhood that stick? If you have had the experience of parenting, what artifacts do you hold on to as mementos of your child's school life? The answers to these questions are as different as we are, but we all have our own ways of preserving our treasured memories. As the year comes to a close, we consider how we can help students capture a year's worth of learning in a meaningful way. Depending on the students' imaginations, this could look like anything from a portfolio to a time capsule. Here we ground this work in picture books and then offer choice in how readers might archive their learning.

### GATHER

Select a book to start a conversation about gathering memories like:

- *In a Jar* (Marcero 2020)
  Summary: Llewellyn and Evelyn collect everything imaginable. Throughout the seasons, they fill their jars with memorable moments and much more. When Evelyn tells Llewellyn she is moving away, his jar feels empty. Fortunately, the two collectors figure out a way to share their new experiences across the miles.

- *Time Capsule* (Redniss 2022)
  Summary: A girl finds an empty jar and glues the date on the bottom. She fills it with memorable items, a nightmare, and a dream. After labeling it "Open in 100 Years," she buries it and wonders where it will end up. The lengthy backmatter includes information about the various ways mementos have been stored and saved throughout the years, along with ideas for children to create their own time capsule.

After reading your chosen book aloud, discuss the reading-related experiences that students have had during the school year. Collaborate to determine how they will capture their own unique journey using objects, images, text, and other artifacts. Provide time for students to collect objects from around their homes and school. Some items students might include:

- A few book cover images that represent their reading timeline—perhaps specific books they enjoyed at the beginning, middle, and end of the year.

- A photo of them with their favorite books or stack of books they read during the school year.

- An object or item that represents a memorable character, book, nonfiction topic, or other reading-related experience.

- A quote from a favorite poem or song during the year.

- A headline about a memorable event that happened during the school year.

## GET STARTED

Once students have curated their artifact collection, provide an opportunity for them to annotate the items they've chosen. Their annotation could be written or an audio or video recording. The items and annotation provide a meaningful way to represent the growth that happens in one short year, and serve as a way for students to communicate this to their family and caregivers.

## WHERE THIS MIGHT LEAD

Although we are writing about this at the end of the year, this is certainly something you could start at the beginning of the year and make a year-long project. Adding or collecting a few items at the end of each month and recording the reasons behind the choices would be a powerful ongoing way for students to reflect on their growth as readers.

### Try This! Engage in Community Book Matching

National Public Radio (2022) produces an annual web feature titled "Books We Love" (formerly "The Book Concierge"). "Books We Love" takes thousands of book reviews and sorts them with different tags based on reading interest. You can then find a "just-right" book for you (or for a gift) by winnowing down the recommendations using tags such as "Eye-Opening Reads," "Tales from Around the World," and "For Sports Lovers." Here we use "Books We Love" as inspiration to facilitate ongoing conversations between readers and the people in their communities outside of the school building.

## GATHER

Begin community book matching by inviting learners to create two lists. First, have them compile a list of books and texts they read this school year. This might be something students already have in their literacy notebooks, or you could get the class started with a list of whole-group texts and students can add their independent reading from there. Either way, encourage readers to think of a variety of texts (poems, short stories, magazine articles, picture books, plays, and so on) rather than only listing novels they've finished.

Once the text lists are done, students can move on to making a list of family and friends outside of the classroom to whom they would like to recommend a text. The number of people on this list may vary by student, or it may depend on how much time you have for this task.

With these two lists handy, tell readers that it's time to play matchmaker! Ask them to contemplate which text they think each person on their list would most enjoy. Modeling this thinking out loud might sound like, "I'm thinking my mom would really enjoy the graphic novel *Heartstopper* by Alice Oseman (2018) because we loved watching romantic comedies together when

I was younger" or "I want to recommend a spoken word poem to my friend Moriah because she's always loved music and I think she would enjoy the musical nature of this type of poetry. Does anyone have ideas of good spoken word poems to introduce someone to the format?" As students brainstorm, encourage them to make note of their matches and rationales, as this will be helpful when creating their products.

## GET STARTED

After the initial brainstorming and matching process, inform students that it is time to share their recommendations. Be transparent in letting learners know that book matching is a way for them to establish or broaden their reading community outside of the classroom. Once your purpose is set, provide students with choice in the products they can make to share their recommendations. Here are a few ideas:

- Website (similar to "Books We Love")
- Email
- Voice note
- Handwritten letter
- Infographic (we like using Piktochart)
- Video

As you think about which products will work best for your classroom, consider the time frame and sharing capabilities. For instance, if you are somewhat short on time but students have access to a computer, perhaps everyone can write a quick email or record a voice memo.

When students are creating their community book-matching products, demonstrate how to include the following elements:

- Brief (spoiler-free) summary of the text
- Why they believe this person would enjoy the text
- Query to encourage the recipient to reach out after they've finished the text or with their own book suggestions

Once everyone has completed their product, provide time for students to share their recommendations with their family and friends. If possible, regroup to discuss how their recipient reacted, and congratulate them on promoting the joy of reading in the wider community.

## WHERE THIS MIGHT LEAD

As the goal of community book matching is to connect students with folks outside the school, you may not see the effects of these products. However, the hope is that they will lead to ongoing reading suggestions and conversations over the summer. If you would like to provide further support to families/caregivers as they receive the matches, you could send home questions that can encourage conversation around the recommendations. Here are a few possible questions:

- What types of texts were you looking for as you determined recommendations for me as a reader?

- Thinking about the text you matched me with, what stood out most to you or what did you enjoy most?

- Would you want to read this text with me so that we can discuss it along the way?

- Were there any other texts that you thought would be a good fit for me as a reader? Why?

- What type of text suggestions would you like from me? What types of reading are you planning to do over the summer?

### Keep It Simple: Encourage Summer Experiences

Near the end of the year caregivers often request suggestions for summer learning opportunities and enrichment. When curating ideas, keep in mind the realities of summer and remember that summer learning should look different from learning during the school year. Something Maria learned from her mom and has passed down to Katie is the power of experiential learning, and summer is the perfect time to learn from interacting with the world around us. Therefore, when providing summer suggestions, think about how families/caregivers can incorporate meaningful learning events into their summer lives. Consider what hidden gems are in your neighborhood that families/caregivers may not know about. Suggest walking around a city block, fixing a family dinner together, or observing animals in a nearby park. Then, remind families/caregivers it is the conversation that turns an outing into an opportunity for learning and growth. Encourage them to add talk to any activity in order to help their learner make the most of each experience. See Appendix A5.1 for a family/caregiver letter that encourages experiences.

**Back Pocket Wisdom: Create an End-of-Year Checklist**

As you spring toward the finish line, consider setting yourself up for success by creating an end-of-year checklist. The checklist that follows includes many of the ideas we shared in this chapter. Sprinkling these tasks into your year-end plans a few at a time will make it easier to get them done and help you prepare for the upcoming school year before you leave for summer. With these tasks complete, you'll be able to jump into creating a vibrant reading community more quickly and seamlessly.

## END-OF-YEAR CHECKLIST

| Grounding Principle | Teacher Action |
|---|---|
| **Prepare for Supported Independent Summer Reading** | ☐ Invite students to help you clean and weed the classroom library, adding to their Someday Lists as they find books that interest them. <br> ☐ Ask learners to set aside or take photographs of their favorite books so that you can create a display of engaging recommendations for next year's readers. <br> ☐ Guide students in setting summer reading goals. <br> ☐ If possible, gift or loan books to students to take home for summer reading. |
| **Reflect on Beliefs** | ☐ Make notes about things you want to keep or change for the following school year. <br> ☐ Find a professional development session or book that aligns with a belief you want to carry into the following school year. |
| **Establish Personal Reading Routines** | ☐ Scour your local bookstores and online websites to find summer reads that align with the types of books you want to add to your classroom library. <br> ☐ Create a summer reading goal that will push your own reading skills or habits. <br> ☐ Join a local library's summer reading challenge. |
| **Give Closure to the Community** | ☐ Have a reading celebration in the last weeks of school. <br> ☐ Revisit favorite texts from the school year. <br> ☐ Have students write a list of Top Ten Tips for you to display the following year for incoming students. |
| **Provide Resources to Caregivers** | ☐ Send home information about summer reading opportunities, book lists, book mobile, etc. <br> ☐ Email home asking for classroom library books to be returned (give option to return the following school year if found over the summer). <br> ☐ Send home summer reading lists from local libraries or your school. |

## END-OF-YEAR CHECKLIST

| Keep It Simple | Teacher Action |
|---|---|
|  | ☐ If you receive funds from your school, create a list of supplies needed for next year so you can replenish before the year begins.<br><br>☐ Maintain a folder/notebook titled "Ideas for Next Year" to capture ideas as they come to you.<br><br>☐ Set clear boundaries for if and/or when you will plan and prepare over the summer in order to take a true mental break from school work. |

✿ ✿ ✿

Whew! You've made it to the end of the year. It's time to say goodbye to your wonderful group(s) of readers. We hope the ideas in this chapter sparked thinking that helps you and the learners in your literacy community enjoy a successful end to the school year. Remember, within the spring fever chaos, the end of the year is a time for celebration, joy, and reflection. Sit back and reflect on the incredible work the readers in your classroom have accomplished. Be proud that you've committed to supporting independent readers, anchoring in your beliefs, developing strong literacy routines, creating positive communities, and partnering with families/caregivers. That is a lot to accomplish in one school year! Soak it all in and, hopefully, you'll have a bit of time to rest and recharge because . . . it's SUMMER!

## TIY—Try It Yourself!

> **Are there any ideas from this chapter or PDCast that would be helpful in your classroom?**

> **Which ideas would you modify to better fit your teaching context?**

> **Did this chapter or PDCast spark any questions, reflections, or new thinking?**

# Someday List

**Reader:** _____

| Book Title | Author |
|---|---|
| | |
| | |
| | |
| | |
| | |
| | |
| | |
| | |
| | |
| | |

Researcher's Name: _____ Researcher's Class Period: _____

# Community Literacy Survey

**Directions:** Survey five different student-age children and five different adults about their daily literacy habits using the Survey Question below. Briefly record your research findings in the charts provided. Once your individual research is complete, we will compile and analyze everyone's data during class.

> **SURVEY QUESTION:**
> On a daily basis, which one of the following literacy skills do you use most often: reading, writing, listening, speaking, or researching?

**STUDENT SURVEY:**

| Person's Name | Response | Explanation/Notes (Did they explain WHY?) |
|---|---|---|
| | ☐ Reading<br>☐ Writing<br>☐ Listening<br>☐ Speaking<br>☐ Researching | |
| | ☐ Reading<br>☐ Writing<br>☐ Listening<br>☐ Speaking<br>☐ Researching | |
| | ☐ Reading<br>☐ Writing<br>☐ Listening<br>☐ Speaking<br>☐ Researching | |
| | ☐ Reading<br>☐ Writing<br>☐ Listening<br>☐ Speaking<br>☐ Researching | |
| | ☐ Reading<br>☐ Writing<br>☐ Listening<br>☐ Speaking<br>☐ Researching | |

\* MORE ON BACK \*

## SURVEY QUESTION:
On a daily basis, which one of the following literacy skills do you use most often: reading, writing, listening, speaking, or researching?

**ADULT SURVEY:**

| Person's Name | Response | Explanation/Notes (Did they explain WHY?) |
|---|---|---|
| | ☐ Reading<br>☐ Writing<br>☐ Listening<br>☐ Speaking<br>☐ Researching | |
| | ☐ Reading<br>☐ Writing<br>☐ Listening<br>☐ Speaking<br>☐ Researching | |
| | ☐ Reading<br>☐ Writing<br>☐ Listening<br>☐ Speaking<br>☐ Researching | |
| | ☐ Reading<br>☐ Writing<br>☐ Listening<br>☐ Speaking<br>☐ Researching | |
| | ☐ Reading<br>☐ Writing<br>☐ Listening<br>☐ Speaking<br>☐ Researching | |

## Photograph Request Letter

Dear Families,

I am so excited to spend this year learning alongside your child. I have worked hard to make our classroom a safe and comfortable place to learn. Now I need your help to make it feel a bit more like home.

If possible, please send in a photograph of a person, place, or item that is special to your child. You can either send me a print or share via email. Talk with your child about why they chose this particular photo so that they can share their reasons with their new classmates.

Thanks for your support. I'm looking forward to a fantastic year of learning!

Warmly,
Your Child's Teacher

Name: _____     Class Period: _____

# Thinking About My Reading

- **Purpose:** To reflect on your reading and provide ideas for conversations with teachers and classmates.
- **Directions:** Place a sticky note in any box. Write the name of the text you're reading and a short response to the question. As the weeks continue, simply place new sticky notes on top of the old ones. The goal is to complete at least one sticky-note response per week, but feel free to complete more.

| | |
|---|---|
| **ENGAGEMENT:** Rate your engagement with the text from 1–10. Explain your rating. | **CONNECTION:** Share something in the text that connects to your learning, your life, or what is going on in the world. |
| **EMOTIONS:** Jot down any emotions that came up while you were reading this text. What happened in the text to cause these emotions? | **ROADBLOCKS:** Did you run into any roadblocks while you were reading? What did you try? Is there anything I can do to help? |

# READ-O: Primary Grades

Name: _____

| | | |
|---|---|---|
| **NONFICTION BOOK**<br><br>Title: _____<br><br>Author: _____ | **FUNNY BOOK**<br><br>Title: _____<br><br>Author: _____ | **ANIMAL BOOK**<br><br>Title: _____<br><br>Author: _____ |
| **BIOGRAPHY**<br><br>Title: _____<br><br>Author: _____ | **YOUR CHOICE!**<br><br>Title: _____<br><br>Author: _____ | **GRAPHIC NOVEL**<br><br>Title: _____<br><br>Author: _____ |
| **MAKE-BELIEVE BOOK**<br><br>Title: _____<br><br>Author: _____ | **POETRY BOOK**<br><br>Title: _____<br><br>Author: _____ | **CHAPTER BOOK**<br><br>Title: _____<br><br>Author: _____ |

# READ-O: Middle Grades

_____'s READ-O Challenge

**Directions:** Pick two genres that interest you and write them here:

Genre #1: _____  Genre #2: _____

Challenge yourself to get READ-O (5 across, down, or diagonal) by this date: _____.

| GENRE #1—SHORT STORY | AUDIOBOOK | NEWS ARTICLE | VERSE NOVEL | GENRE #1—SHORT STORY |
|---|---|---|---|---|
| Title:<br>Author: | Title:<br>Author: | Title:<br>Author: | Title:<br>Author: | Title:<br>Author: |
| **NEWS ARTICLE** | **GENRE #1—BOOK** | **GENRE #1—BOOK** | **GENRE #2—BOOK** | **VERSE NOVEL** |
| Title:<br>Author: | Title:<br>Author: | Title:<br>Author: | Title:<br>Author: | Title:<br>Author: |
| **GENRE #2—MOVIE** | **YOUR CHOICE!** | **YOUR CHOICE!** | **GENRE #1—SHORT STORY** | **NEWS ARTICLE** |
| Title:<br>Director:<br>Initials of Adult who watched with you: | Title:<br>Author: | Title:<br>Author: | Title:<br>Author: | Title:<br>Author: |
| **GENRE #1—SHORT STORY** | **AUDIO BOOK** | **AUDIO BOOK** | **GENRE #2—MOVIE** | **GENRE #2—BOOK** |
| Title:<br>Author: | Title:<br>Author: | Title:<br>Author: | Title:<br>Director:<br>Initials of Adult who watched with you: | Title:<br>Author: |
| **GENRE #2—BOOK** | **NEWS ARTICLE** | **GENRE #1—SHORT STORY** | **ANY BOOK** | **GENRE #1—MOVIE** |
| Title:<br>Author: | Title:<br>Author: | Title:<br>Author: | Title:<br>Author: | Title:<br>Author: |

# Reading Bucket List: Primary Grades

Name: _____

| FILL YOUR BUCKET WITH BOOKS | | |
|---|---|---|
| **I will read a book . . .** | **Book Title/Author** | **✓ Finished** |
| In a series that I've never read | | |
| That won an award | | |
| With a number in the title | | |
| Based on a true story | | |
| Written and illustrated by the same person | | |
| Written and illustrated by two different people | | |
| Set somewhere far away | | |
| With a color in the title | | |
| About an animal | | |
| About a person | | |

Name: _____

# Reading Bucket List: Middle Grades

**Directions:** Pick __·___ items off the reading bucket list. Write down the title and author. Once you have finished the text, put a checkmark in the "Finished" column. When you've completed the challenge, ask your parent/caregiver to sign the paper.

|  | **Book Title and Author** | ✓ **Finished** |
|---|---|---|
| A book in a series you have never read |  |  |
| A book published this year |  |  |
| A book with a number in the title |  |  |
| A book written by someone under age thirty |  |  |
| A book of short stories |  |  |
| A chapter book that won the Sibert Medal |  |  |
| A chapter book that won the Newbery Medal |  |  |
| A book based on a true event |  |  |
| A book your parent/caregiver loves |  |  |
| A book published in the year you were born |  |  |
| A book set somewhere you want to visit |  |  |
| A book with a color in the title |  |  |
| A book by an author whose lived experiences are different from yours |  |  |
| A play |  |  |
| A novel in verse |  |  |
| A nonfiction book |  |  |
| An autobiography, biography, or memoir |  |  |
| Other (get this option approved by your teacher) |  |  |

**Due Date:** _____   **Caregiver Signature:** _____

# Collaborative Conversation Anecdotal Note Sheet

Date(s) _____     Text _____

| Readers | Active Listening | Linking Thinking | Defining Vocabulary Words | High-Level Comprehension | Additional Notes |
|---------|------------------|------------------|---------------------------|--------------------------|------------------|
|  |  |  |  |  |  |
|  |  |  |  |  |  |
|  |  |  |  |  |  |
|  |  |  |  |  |  |
|  |  |  |  |  |  |
|  |  |  |  |  |  |

Reader's Name: _____

# Stages of Reading Development

| Pre-Emergent Reader | Emergent Reader | Early Reader | Transitional Reader | Fluent Reader |
|---|---|---|---|---|
| Enjoys book experiences | Uses repetitive text and familiar patterns to mimic fluent reading | Reads familiar text word by word | Reads familiar text with increasing fluency (rate, accuracy, phrasing, and expression) | Reads independent-level text with fluency (rate, accuracy, phrasing, and expression) |
| Interacts with books | Uses prior knowledge and experiences to make meaning | Uses prior knowledge, clues from text, and experiences to make and predict meaning | Uses prior knowledge, clues from text, text structures, and experiences to make, predict, and infer meaning | Uses prior knowledge, clues from text, text structures, and experiences to make, predict, infer, and synthesize meaning |
| Developing phonemic awareness | Understands the relationship between letters and sounds and begins to apply this knowledge when decoding | Decodes most simple words using sound-spelling relationships and self-monitors using meaning and/or context clues | Decodes multisyllabic words using chunking and word parts and self-monitors by integrating meaning, context clues, and phonics | Uses self-monitoring strategies and self-corrects while reading |
| Recognizes and reads environmental print | Recognizes and reads a few high-frequency words, names, and simple words in context | Recognizes and reads many high-frequency words and simple words in context | Recognizes and reads high-frequency words and an increasing number of difficult words, many of which are content-related | Recognizes and reads most words automatically |

Adapted from *On Solid Ground* (Taberski 2000)

# Reader of the Day Family/Caregiver Letter

Dear Families,

Throughout this school year, I have shared many books with your child during our read-aloud time. Now it's your child's turn to read aloud to the class! Below you will find their scheduled date. You can support them at home by:

- Helping them pick a short text to read aloud
  (I can also help them with this)
- Listening to them read the text aloud

Thank you for helping your child spread the read-aloud joy!

Warmly,
Your Child's Teacher

[Insert schedule here]

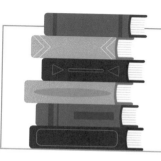

## GOALS:

■ **Enjoy** the children.

■ **Help** them read with fluency (like they talk).

■ **Listen** to them tell you about the book.

**You should be spending about 5–7 minutes with each child.**

■ If a child is reading short books, they may read more than one.

■ If a child is reading longer books, have them pick a favorite part or page(s).

■ If the book is too difficult, read along with them or ask them to choose a "just-right" book from their box.

# Read to Me!

*Thanks for volunteering to listen to readers today!*

### Step 1

■ Begin with your own child.

■ Invite your child to bring their "old favorite" books over and select a book to read to you.

■ After they are finished reading, say, "Tell me about the book in your own words."

### Step 2

■ Record the following information:
  • **Whole-Class Grid**—today's date
  • **Individual Student Log Sheet**—today's date, book title, your initials

### Step 3

■ Select the next student on the whole-class grid who has not read lately. (I will usually provide a list.)

■ Enjoy listening to and talking about books!

### To help with retelling, ask these questions:

 **Questions About Stories**
  ■ Who was in the story?
  ■ What happened in the story?
  ■ How did the story end?
  ■ What was your favorite part?

 **Questions About Nonfiction Books**
  ■ What did you learn from reading this book?
  ■ What was this book mainly about?
  ■ Can you tell me an interesting fact?

# Gallery Walk Visitor's Guide

**Gallery Walk Format:** Students will be set up on the edges of the room. You are welcome to visit as many tables as you wish in whatever order you want. Please listen to as many students as possible, so they all get practice sharing their information.

Each student has prepared a short (thirty-second) "elevator pitch" explaining their infographic. Once they have shared this information, feel free to ask any of your own follow-up questions or a few questions from the list below.

If you are attending virtually, students will rotate through and share their "elevator pitch." Feel free to unmute or type your questions in the chat. Enjoy!

- Explain your research process. Where did you find your information? How did you determine which sources were reliable?
- What was the most interesting piece of information you learned? Why did you find this interesting?
- What other questions do you still have about your topic?
- Tell me about a few of the images on your infographic. How do they relate to your topic?
- Tell me about how you designed your infographic. How does your design help people better understand your topic?

Thank you so much for supporting our work!

# A Day in Our Classroom: Elementary

| Learning Experience | What Your Child Is Doing | Specific Questions You Can Ask About This Part of Our Day |
|---|---|---|
| **Independent reading time** | After doing their "morning jobs" (attendance, lunch count, turning in items, and hanging up coat/backpack), children read their own "just-right" books, which are stored in a book box, or other books that match their interests, which they select from the various shelves in our room. Sometimes we read with a friend! | What books did you read this morning? Which book is your favorite? Why? |
| **Morning message, poem, read-aloud** | Students meet in their "place for learning" on the carpet to read, write, revise, and edit the morning message. We chant and sing poems and songs together (poems are stored in your child's own song and poem book). Next, we read aloud a book or two. | Did you help with the morning message today? What poem are you singing in the morning? What book(s) did your teacher read to you today? |
| **Reading workshop** | During our whole-group lesson we focus on a reading strategy or skill. We learn strategies for decoding and comprehension. In addition, we learn about different genres of literature. | What did you learn about being a reader? What strategies do readers use? |
| **Guiding readers** | During this time, I guide readers in small groups as they read books and apply decoding and comprehension strategies they are learning during our whole-group lesson. While I'm meeting with groups, students visit multilevel literacy centers or read independently. | What literacy center did you visit today? Do you check out library books? Did you read with a teacher? |
| **Word study** Spelling Grammar Vocabulary | During word study, we work on a phonic element or pattern. This year we will systematically study how to read and spell words using consonants (review), short vowels, long vowels, digraphs, blends, and more. We will also focus on building your child's vocabulary. | What kinds of words did you spell on your whiteboard or in your practice book? |
| **Lunch/ recess** | We eat lunch first, and then we go outside for recess. | Did you eat your lunch today? Who did you play with during recess today? What games did you play? Did you make any new friends? |
| **Mini-lesson and independent reading** | Before we read, we do a quick mini-lesson on a reading skill or strategy. Then students independently read books while I confer with readers. | Did you use your independent reading time wisely? Are you building your reading stamina? |
| **Writing workshop** | Each workshop begins with a mini-lesson focused on a writing genre, strategy, or skill. I model my own writing, and then students write in their "little books" about various topics or create books in various genres including personal narrative, biography, poetry, and nonfiction. | What did you do as a writer today? What genre are you studying? What did you learn about being a writer? |
| **Special classes** | P.E.: Monday, Tuesday, Friday Music: Wednesday, Friday Art: Thursday | What game did you play in gym? What project are you creating in art? What songs did you sing in music? |
| **Math workshop** | The lesson consists of mental math practice, a teacher-directed lesson, and then independent practice in a math thinking journal or in a game format. | What kind of problems did you solve today? Did you share your thinking with the class? |
| **Science or social studies** | Social studies topics: [List your topics here] Science topics: [List your topics here] | What/who are you learning about in science/ social studies? Did your teacher read you a book? Did you do any experiments? |

# A Reading Day in Our Classroom: Middle School

| Learning Experience | What Your Child Is Doing | Specific Questions You Can Ask About This Part of Our Day |
|---|---|---|
| **Independent reading time** | After entering the classroom and grabbing their materials, students begin the class period with ten minutes of independent reading time. This is your child's opportunity to read a self-selected text that matches their current reading interests and goals. Students may also be looking for new books to read in the classroom library or conferring with their teacher. | What book are you currently reading? What is happening in the book right now? What are you learning about as you read? What connections can you make between the book and your own life? |
| **Read-aloud** | To enhance their listening comprehension and build our classroom community, the teacher will read aloud a variety of texts throughout the year. Read-aloud is a whole-class learning event where students listen to the same text and develop understanding together by talking with their peers and participating in whole-class discussions. | Did you listen to your teacher read aloud today? What stood out to you about the text? What did the class talk about as you read? |
| **Book talks** | At least once a week, the teacher or students will talk about new and notable books that your child might be interested in reading. Listeners use this time to add books to their Someday List (a list of books they may want to read someday). | What books did you hear about today that sounded interesting? What piqued your interest? How can you get access to these books? |
| **Reading mini-lesson** | During our whole-group lesson we focus on a reading strategy or skill that moves your child toward their learning target(s). The teacher demonstrates how to apply the strategy or skill, and then students practice in pairs or small groups. | What did you learn about being a reader? What strategies do readers use? |
| **Practice time** | We end the class period with time for students to practice the reading skill or strategy from the mini-lesson. This time can look very different depending on the day. Students might be revisiting the text their teacher is reading aloud, analyzing their self-selected text, creating a product, or discussing in a small group. | How did you practice the reading skill or strategy? How might you use what you practiced today to help you as a reader tomorrow? |

APPENDIX 4.5 • **190** •

# Summer Family/Caregiver Letter
## EXPERIENCE SUMMER!

**READ!** Join your public library. Ask if they have a summer reading program.

**WRITE!** Write in a journal, write an email to a relative, write a story or nonfiction book with your family, write, write, write!

**EXPERIENCE!** Experience all the wonderful free activities your neighborhood has to offer, like walking to parks or going on nature trails, star watching, bug catching, picnicking, and much more!

**IMAGINE!** Turn off your devices and use your imagination. Put on a skit or fashion show, make something out of an old cardboard box, set up an obstacle course. Imagine ideas of your very own!

**CREATE!** Use what you have around your home or in your neighborhood to create a piece of art.

**PLAY!** Be active either indoors or outdoors—have a dance party, play catch, run, jump, and just have **FUN!**

## CHILDREN'S LITERATURE AND MULTIMODAL TEXTS CITED

Ahiyya, Vera. 2022. *KINDdergarten: Where Kindness Matters Every Day.* Illustrated by J. Chou. New York: Random House.

Alessandri, Alexandra. 2021. *Isabel and Her Colores Go to School.* Illustrated by C. Dawson. Ann Arbor, MI: Sleeping Bear Press.

Andrews, V. C. 1979. *Flowers in the Attic.* New York: HarperCollins.

Archer, Micha. 2021. *Wonder Walkers.* New York: Nancy Paulsen/Penguin Random House.

Arnold, Tedd. 2005. *Hi! Fly Guy.* New York: Scholastic.

Bailey, Catherine. 2022. *Hustle Bustle Bugs.* Illustrated by L. Eldridge. New York: Little, Brown.

Beaty, Andrea. 2022. *I Love You Like Yellow.* Illustrated by V. Harrison. New York: Abrams.

Bidania, V. T. 2021. *Astrid and Apollo and the Starry Campout.* Illustrated by D. L. Lee. North Mankato, MN: Picture Window/Capstone.

Bolling, Valerie. 2022. *Ride, Roll, Run: Time for Fun!* Illustrated by Sabrena Khadija. New York: Abrams.

Bowles. David. 2021. *Two Border Towns.* Illustrated by E. Meza. New York: Kokila/Penguin.

Brantley-Newton, Vanessa. 2021. *Becoming Vanessa.* New York: Knopf.

Bruchac, Joseph. 2021. *Rez Dogs.* New York: Dial.

Butler, Dori Hillestad. 2017. *King and Kayla and the Case of the Missing Dog Treats.* Illustrated by N. Myers. Atlanta, GA: Peachtree.

Burgess, Rebecca. 2022. *Speak Up!* New York: HarperCollins.

Byrne, Richard. 2014. *This Book Just Ate My Dog.* New York: Holt.

———. 2015. *We're in the Wrong Book.* New York: Holt.

Calvin, Alexander Ramsey. 2010. *Ruth and the Green Book.* Illustrated by F. Cooper. Minneapolis, MN: Carolrhoda.

Chung, Arree. 2017. *Out!* New York: Holt.

Cisneros, Sandra. 1983. *The House on Mango Street.* New York: Knopf/Doubleday.

Cleary, Brian P. 2016. *Underneath My Bed: List Poems.* Illustrated by R. Watson. Minneapolis, MN: Millbrook.

Craft, Jerry. 2019. *New Kid.* New York: HarperCollins.

Davis, Brian, dir. 2020. *We Are the Champions*. Season 1, episode 4, "Yo-Yo." Aired November 17 on Netflix.

Diaz, Lucky. 2021. *Paletero Man.* Illustrated by M. Player. New York: Harper-Collins.

Dugar, Akhand. 2020. "Mirrors, Windows, and Sliding Doors." TEDxMountainViewHighSchool. https://www.ted.com/talks/akhand _dugar_mirrors_windows_sliding_doors.

Faruqi, Saadia. 2019. *Meet Yasmine!* Illustrated by H. Ali. North Mankato, MN: Picture Window/Capstone.

Feuti, Norm. 2021. *Beak and Ally: Unlikely Friends.* New York: HarperCollins.

Finison, Carrie. 2022. *Hurry, Little Tortoise, Time for School!* Illustrated by E. Kraan. New York: Random House.

Gardner, Whitney. 2021. *Long Distance.* New York: Simon and Schuster.

Garrett, Van G. 2022. *Kicks.* Illustrated by R. Brown. New York: HarperCollins.

Giang, Kristen Mai. 2022. *The Rise (and Falls) of Jackie Chan.* Illustrated by A. Chau. New York: Crown Books/Penguin Random House.

Gómez, Blanca. 2022. *Dress-Up Day.* New York: Abrams.

Gravel, Elise. 2020. *Arlo and Pips: King of the Birds.* New York: HarperCollins.

Hale, Nathan. 2012. *Nathan Hale's Hazardous Tales: One Dead Spy.* New York: Abrams.

Harney, Jenn. 2019. *Underwear!* New York: Disney/Hyperion.

Haughton, Chris. 2021. *Maybe.* Somerville, MA: Candlewick.

Healy, Christopher. 2019. *This Is Not That Kind of Book.* Illustrated by B. Mantle. New York: Random House.

Higgins, Ryan T. 2017. *Be Quiet!* New York: Disney/Hyperion.

Houppert, Anne Marie. 2021. *What About X? An Alphabet Adventure.* Illustrated by D. Wiseman. New York: Abrams.

Hudson, Neesha. 2021. *Turtle in a Tree.* New York: Dial.

Ismail, Yasmeen. 2019. *Joy.* Illustrated by J. Desmond. Somerville, MA: Candlewick.

Jenkins, Steve. 2016. *Animals by the Numbers: A Book of Infographics.* New York: Houghton Mifflin Harcourt.

———. 2021. *Disasters by the Numbers: A Book of Infographics.* New York: Houghton Mifflin Harcourt.

Kelkar, Supriya. 2019. *The Many Colors of Harpreet Singh.* Illustrated by A. Marley. New York: Sterling.

Khalil, Aya. 2020. *The Arabic Quilt: An Immigrant Story.* Illustrated by A. Semirdzhyan. Thomaston, ME: Tilbury.

Kibuishi, Kazu. 2008. *Amulet: The Stone Keeper.* New York: Graphix.

King, Thomas. 1993/2021. *Borders*. Illustrated by N. Donovan. New York: Little, Brown.

Klise, Kate. 1998. *Regarding the Fountain*. Illustrated by M. Klise. New York: HarperCollins.

Korman, Gordon. 2017. *Restart*. New York: Scholastic.

Knowles, Jo. 2022. *Ear Worm!* Illustrated by G. Bernstein. Somerville, MA: Candlewick.

Lê, Minh. 2020. *Lift*. Illustrated by D. Santat. New York: Disney/Hyperion.

Ludwig, Trudy. 2020. *The Power of One: Every Act of Kindness Counts*. Illustrated by M. Curato. New York: Knopf.

Lyons, Kelly Starling. 2020. *Ty's Travels: Zip, Zoom!* Illustrated by N. Mata. New York: HarperCollins.

Marcero, Deborah. 2020. *In a Jar*. New York: G.P. Putnam's Sons.

———. 2022. *Out of a Jar*. New York: G.P. Putnam's Sons.

Martinez-Neal, Juana. 2021. *Zonia's Rain Forest*. Somerville, MA: Candlewick.

Medina, Juana. 2016. *Juana and Lucas*. Somerville, MA: Candlewick.

———. 2021. *I Will! A Book of Promises*. New York: HarperCollins.

———. 2022. *I Am! A Book of Reminders*. New York: HarperCollins.

———. 2022. *I Feel! A Book of Emotions*. New York: HarperCollins.

Meganck, Margaux. 2022. *People Are Wild*. New York: Knopf.

Miller, Pat. 2010. *Squirrel's New Year's Resolution*. Illustrated by K. Ember. Chicago: Albert Whitman.

Milgrim, David. 2018. *The Adventures of Otto: See Pip Flap*. New York: Simon and Schuster.

Mitchell, Malcolm. 2021. *My Very Favorite Book in the Whole Wide World*. Illustrated by M. Robertson. New York: Scholastic.

Nelson, Kadir. 2015. *If You Plant a Seed*. Balzer and Bray/HarperCollins.

Ortega, Claribel. 2022. *Frizzy*. Illustrated by R. Bousamra. New York: First Second.

Oseman, Alice. 2018. *Heartstopper, Volume 1*. New York: Scholastic.

Pérez, Cecilia C. 2017. *The First Rule of Punk*. New York: Viking.

Prasadam-Halls, Smriti. 2022. *Not That Pet!* Illustrated by R. Beardshaw. Somerville, MA: Candlewick.

Raúl the Third. 2023. *¡Vamos! Let's Go Read*. New York: Houghton Mifflin Harcourt.

Rector, Rebecca Kraft. 2022. *Little Red and the Big Bad Editor*. Illustrated by S. McCloskey. New York: Simon and Schuster.

Redniss, Lauren. 2022. *Time Capsule*. New York: Penguin Random House.

Reynolds, Aaron. 2022. *Creepy Crayon!* Illustrated by P. Brown. New York: Simon and Schuster.

Reynolds, Jason. 2021. *Stuntboy, in the Meantime.* Illustrated by Raúl the Third. New York: Simon and Schuster.

Rosenthal, Amy Krouse. 2011. *This Plus That: Life's Little Equations.* Illustrated by J. Corace. New York: HarperCollins.

Rothman, Scott. 2022. *Blue Bison Needs a Haircut.* Illustrated by P. Oswald. New York: Random House.

Ruzzier, Sergio. 2020. *Fox + Chick: The Party and Other Stories.* San Francisco: Chronicle.

Salas, Laura Purdie. 2019. *Snowman – Cold = Puddle: Spring Equations.* Illustrated by M. Archer. Watertown, MA: Charlesbridge.

Sayre, April Pulley, with Jeff Sayre. 2022. *Happy Sloth Day!* New York: Beach Lane/Simon and Schuster.

Scanlon, Liz Garton, and Audrey Vernick. 2018. *Dear Substitute.* Illustrated by C. Raschka. New York: Disney/Hyperion.

Schu, John. 2022. *We Are a School.* Illustrated by V. M. Jamison. Somerville, MA: Candlewick.

Sell, Chad. 2018. *The Cardboard Kingdom.* New York: Knopf.

Silvestro, Annie. 2019. *Butterflies on the First Day of School.* Illustrated by D. Chen. New York: Sterling.

Smith, Charles R., Jr. 2022. *Bessie the Motorcycle Queen.* Illustrated by C. Kristensen. New York: Scholastic.

Smith, Monique Gray. 2020. *When We Are Kind.* Illustrated by N. Neidhardt. Victoria, BC: Orca.

———. 2022. "Fancy Dancer." In *Ancestor Approved: Intertribal Stories for Kids,* edited by Cynthia Leitich Smith, 4-19. New York: Heartdrum/HarperCollins.

Sosa, Daniela. 2022. *Friends.* New York: Paula Wiseman/Simon and Schuster.

Stone, Nic. 2020. *Clean Getaway.* New York: Random House.

Strick, Alexandra. 2022. *You Can! Kids Empowering Kids.* Illustrated by S. Antony. Somerville, MA: Candlewick.

Snyder, Laurel. 2017. *Charlie and Mouse.* Illustrated by E. Hughes. San Francisco: Chronicle.

Sutherland, Tui T. 2018. *Wings of Fire—The Dragonet Prophecy: A Graphic Novel.* Illustrated by M. Holmes. New York: Scholastic.

Tan, Amy. 1987. "Fish Cheeks." Reprinted in *Opposite of Fate: A Book of Musings* (2003), 125-127. New York: Putnam.

Tarshis, Lauren. (2020-). *I Survived: Graphic Novel.* (book series). Various illustrators. New York: Scholastic.

Telgemeier, Raina. 2019. *Guts*. New York: Graphix.

Thompkins-Bigelow, Jamilah. 2022. *Abdul's Story*. Illustrated by T. Rose. New York: Simon and Schuster.

Thurman, Brittany. 2022. *Fly*. Illustrated by A. Cunha. New York: Atheneum.

Trevino, Charles. 2021. *Seaside Stroll*. Illustrated by M. Lechuga. Watertown, MA: Charlesbridge.

Underwood, Deborah. (2019). *Finding Kindness*. Illustrated by I. Chan. New York: Holt.

Valdez, Patricia. (2022). *How to Hear the Universe: Gaby González and the Search for Einstein's Ripples in Space-Time*. Illustrated by S. Palacios. New York: Knopf.

Vo, Young. 2022. *Gibberish*. Hoboken, NJ: Levine Querido/Chronicle.

Warga, Jasmine. 2019. *Other Words for Home*. New York: HarperCollins.

Willems, Mo. 2013. *A Big Guy Took My Ball*. New York: Hyperion.

Wilson, G. W. 2014. *Ms. Marvel, Vol. 1: No Normal*. New York: Marvel.

Woodson, Jacqueline. 2022. *The Year We Learned to Fly*. Illustrated by R. López. Nancy Paulsen/Penguin Random House.

Yvette, LaTonya. 2022. *The Hair Book*. Illustrated by A. J. Jones. New York: Sterling.

## PROFESSIONAL RESOURCES

Allington, Richard. 2014. "How Reading Volume Affects Both Reading Fluency and Reading Achievement." *International Electronic Journal of Elementary Education* 7 (1): 13-26.

Allington, Richard, and Anne M. McGill-Franzen. 2021. "Reading Volume and Reading Achievement: A Review of Recent Research." *Reading Research Quarterly* 56 (S1): 1-8.

Allyn, Pam, and Ernest Morrell. 2016. *Every Child a Super Reader: 7 Strengths to Open a World of Possible*. New York: Scholastic.

———. 2022. *Every Child a Super Reader: 7 Strengths for a Lifetime of Independence, Purpose, and Joy*. 2nd ed. New York: Scholastic.

Atwell, Nancie. 2007. *The Reading Zone: How to Help Kids Become Passionate, Skilled, Habitual, Critical Readers*. New York: Scholastic.

Atwell, Nancie, and Anne Atwell Merkel. 2016. *The Reading Zone: How to Help Kids Become Passionate, Skilled, Habitual, Critical Readers*. 2nd ed. New York: Scholastic.

Aukerman, Maren, and Lorien Chambers Schuldt. 2021. "What Matters Most? Toward a Robust and Socially Just Science of Reading." *Reading Research Quarterly* 56 (S1): S85-S103.

Beechum, Nicole Williams. 2020. "What Happens When Students Have Ownership over Their Success." *Education Week*, September 9. https://www.edweek.org/leadership/opinion-what-happens-when-students-have-ownership-over-their-success/2020/09.

Bridges, Lois. 2013. "Make Every Student Count: How Collaboration Among Families, Schools, and Communities Ensure Student Success." Family and Community Engagement Research Compendium. Scholastic. http://teacher.scholastic.com/products/face/pdf/research-compendium/Compendium.pdf.

Burkins, Jan, and Kim Yaris. 2016. *Who's Doing the Work? How to Say Less So Readers Can Do More.* Portland, ME: Stenhouse.

Burkins, Jan, and Kari Yates. 2021. *Shifting the Balance: 6 Ways to Bring the Science of Reading into the Balanced Literacy Classroom K–2.* Portsmouth, NH: Stenhouse.

Cahill, Carrie, Kathy Horvath, Anne McGill-Franzen, and Richard L. Allington. 2013. *No More Summer-Reading Loss.* Portsmouth, NH: Heinemann.

CASEL. 2023. "SEL in the Classroom." Collaborative for Academic, Social, and Emotional Learning. https://casel.org/systemic-implementation/sel-in-the-classroom/.

Chappuis, Jan. 2009. *Seven Strategies of Assessment for Learning.* Boston: Pearson.

Cherry-Paul, Sonja, and Dana Johansen. 2019. *Breathing New Life into Book Clubs: A Practical Guide for Teachers.* Portsmouth, NH: Heinemann.

Currie, Lisa. 2015. "Why Teaching Kindness in Schools Is Essential to Reduce Bullying." Edutopia. Last modified August 10, 2015. https://www.edutopia.org/blog/teaching-kindness-essential-reduce-bullying-lisa-currie.

Couros, George. 2015. *The Innovator's Mindset: Empower Learning, Unleash Talent, and Lead a Culture of Creativity.* San Diego: Dave Burgess Consulting.

Dotson, Ronnie. 2016. "Goal Setting to Increase Student Academic Performance." *Journal of School Administration Research and Development* 1 (1): 44–46.

Duhigg, Charles. 2012. *The Power of Habit: Why We Do What We Do in Life and Business.* New York: Random House

Duke, Nell K. 2020. "When Young Readers Get Stuck." Association for Supervision and Curriculum Development, Alexandria, VA. https://www.ascd.org/el/articles/when-young-readers-get-stuck.

Duke, Nell K., and Laura Varlas. 2019. "Turn Small Reading Groups into Big Wins." Association for Supervision and Curriculum Development, Alexandria, VA. https://www.ascd.org/el/articles/turn-small-reading-groups-into-big-wins.

Duke, Nell K., Alessandra E. Ward, and P. David Pearson. 2021. "The Science of Reading Comprehension Instruction." *The Reading Teacher* 74 (6): 663–672.

Dwyer, Bernadette, Diane Kern, and Jennifer Williams. 2019. "Children's Rights to Excellent Literacy Instruction." International Literacy Association. https://www.literacyworldwide.org/docs/default-source/where-we-stand/ila-childrens-rights-to-excellent-literacy-instruction.pdf.

Feig, Paul, dir. 2005. *The Office*, season 2, episode 3, "Office Olympics." Written by Greg Daniels, Michael Schur, and Ricky Gervais. Aired October 4 on NBC.

Fisher, Douglas, and Nancy Frey. 2015. *Unstoppable Learning: Seven Essential Elements to Unleash Student Potential.* Bloomington, IN: Solution Tree Press.

Fisher, Douglas, Nancy Frey, and John Hattie. 2021. *The Distance Learning Playbook: Teaching for Engagement and Impact in Any Setting.* Thousand Oaks, CA: Corwin.

Fountas and Pinnell Literacy Team. 2016. "What Is Responsive Teaching?" November 6. https://fpblog.fountasandpinnell.com/what-is-responsive-teaching.

Francois, Chantal. 2015. "An Urban School Shapes Young Adolescents' Motivation to Read." *Voices from the Middle* 23 (1): 68–72.

Gallagher, Kelly. 2009. *Readicide: How Schools Are Killing Reading and What You Can Do About It.* Portland, ME: Stenhouse.

Gallagher, Kelly, and Penny Kittle. 2018. *180 Days: Two Teachers and the Quest to Engage and Empower Adolescents.* Portsmouth, NH: Heinemann.

Goldberg, Gravity. 2016. *Mindsets and Moves.* Thousand Oaks, CA: Corwin.

Graham, Steve. 2022. "Creating a Classroom Vision for Teaching Writing." *The Reading Teacher* 75 (4): 475–484.

Hammond, Zaretta. 2015. *Culturally Responsive Teaching and the Brain: Promoting Authentic Engagement and Rigor Among Culturally and Linguistically Diverse Students.* Thousand Oaks, CA: Corwin.

Harwayne, Shelley. 2000. *Lifetime Guarantees: Toward Ambitious Literacy Teaching.* Portsmouth, NH: Heinemann.

Henderson, Anne T., and Karen L. Mapp. 2002. *A New Wave of Evidence: The Impact of School, Family, and Community Connections on Student Achievement Annual Synthesis.* Austin, TX: Southwest Educational Development Laboratory.

Hiebert, Elfrieda H. 2014. *The Forgotten Reading Proficiency: Stamina in Silent Reading.* Santa Cruz, CA: Text Project.

Ho Sui-Chu, Esther, and J. Douglas Willms. 1996. "Effects of Parental Involvement on Eighth Grade Achievement." *Sociology of Education* 69 (2): 126–141.

Hunter, Phyllis C. 2012. *It's Not Complicated: What I Know for Sure About Helping Our Students of Color Become Successful Readers.* New York: Scholastic.

Irwin, Véronique, et al. 2022. "Characteristics of Public School Teachers." National Center for Education Statistics, US Department of Education. https://nces.ed.gov/pubs2022/2022144.pdf.

Jiménez, Laura M. 2022. "Thematic Guide: Teaching with Graphic Fiction and Nonfiction." Penguin Random House Elementary Education. https://penguinrandomhouseelementaryeducation.com/wp-content/uploads/2022/02/4861_Thematic-Guide_Graphic-Novel-Elementary_Final.pdf.

Johnston, Peter H. 2004. *Choice Words: How Our Language Affects Children's Learning.* Portland, ME: Stenhouse.

———. 2012. *Opening Minds: Using Language to Change Lives.* Portland, ME: Stenhouse.

Johnston, Peter, Kathy Champeau, Andrea Harwig, Sarah Helmer, Merry Komar, Tara Krueger, and Laurie McCarthy. 2020. *Engaging Literate Minds: Developing Children's Social, Emotional, and Intellectual Lives, K–3.* Portland, ME: Stenhouse.

Keene, Ellin Oliver. 2018. *Engaging Children: Igniting a Drive for Deeper Learning K–8.* Portsmouth, NH: Heinemann.

Kittle, Penny. 2012. *Book Love: Developing Depth, Stamina, and Passion in Adolescent Readers.* Portsmouth, NH: Heinemann.

Kugler, Sara. 2022. *Better Book Clubs: Deepening Comprehension and Elevating Conversation.* Portsmouth, NH: Stenhouse.

Lacina, Jan, and Robin Griffith. 2021. "Hope for the Future: An Interview with Linda Darling-Hammond." *The Reading Teacher* 74 (6): 673–676.

Ladson-Billings, Gloria. 2021. *Culturally Relevant Pedagogy: Asking a Different Question.* New York: Teachers College Press.

Mapp, Karen L., Ilene Carver, and Jessica Lander. 2017. *Powerful Partnerships: A Teacher's Guide to Engaging Families for Student Success.* New York: Scholastic.

Miller, Debbie. 2002. *Reading with Meaning: Teaching Comprehension in the Primary Grades.* Portland, ME: Stenhouse.

———. 2008. *Teaching with Intention: Defining Beliefs, Aligning Practice, Taking Action.* Portland, ME: Stenhouse.

Miller, Debbie, and Barbara Moss. 2013. *No More Independent Reading Without Support.* Portsmouth, NH: Heinemann.

Miller, Donalyn. 2009. *The Book Whisperer: Awakening the Inner Reader in Every Child.* San Francisco: Jossey-Bass.

———. 2014. *Reading in the Wild: The Book Whisperer's Keys to Cultivating Lifelong Reading Habits.* San Francisco: Jossey-Bass.

Miller, Donalyn, and Colby Sharp. 2018. *Game Changer: Book Access for All Kids.* New York: Scholastic.

Miller, Donalyn, and Teri S. Lesesne. 2022. *The Joy of Reading.* Portsmouth, NH: Heinemann.

Moll, Luis C., Cathy Amanti, Deborah Neff, and Norma Gonzalez. 1992. "Funds of Knowledge for Teaching: Using a Qualitative Approach to Connect Homes and Classrooms." *Theory into Practice* 31 (2): 132-141.

Muhammad, Gholdy. 2020. *Cultivating Genius: An Equity Framework for Culturally and Historically Responsive Literacy.* New York: Scholastic.

Mulligan, Tammy, and Clare Landigran. 2018. *It's All About the Books.* Portsmouth, NH: Heinemann.

National Public Radio. 2022. "Books We Love." https://apps.npr.org/best-books/#tags=staff+picks&view=covers&year=2022.

NCTE. 2019. "Statement on Independent Reading." National Council of Teachers of English. https://ncte.org/statement/independent-reading/.

NCTE Committee Against Racism and Bias in the Teaching of English. 2018. "First-Day Actions for a Culturally Sustaining Classroom Environment." National Council of Teachers of English. https://ncte.org/blog/2018/08/first-day-actions-for-a-culturally-sustaining-classroom-environment.

Parker, Kimberly N. 2022. "Ending the School Year Strong." Association for Supervision and Curriculum Development, Alexandria, VA. https://www.ascd.org/blogs/ending-the-school-year-strong.

Qarooni, Nawal. 2022. "Seeing Families as Partners in Literacy Growth." *Educational Leadership* 80 (1): 34-41.

Renandya, Willy A., Stephen Krashen, and George M. Jacobs. 2018. "The Potential of Series Books: How Narrow Reading Leads to Advanced L2 Proficiency." *LEARN Journal: Language Acquisition Research Network Journal* 11 (2): 148-154.

Richardson, Jan. 2016. *The Next Step Forward in Guided Reading: An Assess-Decide-Guide Framework for Supporting Every Reader.* New York: Scholastic.

Robb, Laura. 2010. *Teaching Reading in Middle School: A Strategic Approach to Teaching Reading That Improves Comprehension and Thinking.* 2nd ed. New York: Scholastic.

Routman, Regie. 2008. *Teaching Essentials: Expecting the Most and Getting the Best from Every Learner, K-8.* Portsmouth, NH: Heinemann.

———. 2018. *Literacy Essentials: Engagement, Excellence, and Equity for All Learners.* Portsmouth, NH: Stenhouse.

———. 2019. "10 Lessons Learned from Being (Mostly) Happily Married 50 Years +: Apply to Teaching, Learning, and Living." Presentation at CCIRA 2019, Denver, CO, February 8.

Scharf, Amy. 2018. "Critical Practices for Anti-Bias Education." Learning for Justice, a project of the Southern Poverty Law Center, Montgomery, AL. https://www.learningforjustice.org/sites/default/files/2021-11/LFJ-2111 -Critical-Practices-for-Anti-bias-Ed-November-2021-11172021.pdf.

Serravallo, Jennifer. 2020. *Connecting with Students Online: Strategies for Remote Teaching and Learning.* Portsmouth, NH: Heinemann.

Sims Bishop, Rudine. 1990. "Mirrors, Windows, and Sliding Glass Doors." *Perspectives: Choosing and Using Books for the Classroom* 1 (3): ix-xi.

Souers, Kristin, and Pete Hall. 2016. *Fostering Resilient Learners: Strategies for Creating a Trauma-Sensitive Classroom.* Alexandria, VA: ASCD.

Souto-Manning, Mariana, Carmen Lugo Llerena, Jessica Martell, Abigail Salas Maguire, and Alicia Arce-Boardman. 2018. *No More Culturally Irrelevant Teaching.* Portsmouth, NH: Heinemann.

Stewart, Melissa, and Marlene Correia. 2021. *5 Kinds of Nonfiction.* Portsmouth, NH: Stenhouse.

Taberski, Sharon. 2000. *On Solid Ground: Strategies for Teaching Reading K-3.* Portsmouth, NH: Heinemann.

Walther, Maria. 2019. *The Ramped-Up Read Aloud: What to Notice as You Turn the Page.* Thousand Oaks, CA: Corwin.

———. 2022. *Shake Up Shared Reading: Expanding on Read Alouds to Encourage Student Independence.* Thousand Oaks, CA: Corwin.

Walther, Maria, and Karen Biggs-Tucker. 2020. *The Literacy Workshop: Where Reading and Writing Converge.* Portsmouth, NH: Stenhouse.

Wiggins, Grant, and Jay McTighe. 2011. *The Understanding by Design Guide to Creating High Quality Units.* Alexandria, VA: ASCD.

# CREDITS

## Chapter 1

Cover of *Gibberish* by Young Vo. © 2022 Levine Querido. Used with permission of the publisher.

Cover of *Hurry, Little Tortoise, Time for School!* by Carrie Finison. Illustrated by Erin Kraan. © 2022 Penguin Random House. Used with permission of the publisher.

Cover of *Isabel and Her Colores Go to School* by Alexandra Alessandri. Illustrated by Courtney Dawson. © 2021 Sleeping Bear Press. Used with permission of the publisher.

Cover of *This Is a School*. Text copyright © 2022 by John Schu. Illustrations copyright © 2022 by Veronica Miller Jamison. Reproduced by permission of the publisher, Candlewick Press, Somerville, MA.

## Chapter 2

Cover of *Out of a Jar* by Deborah Marcero. © 2022 G.P. Putnam's Sons Books for Young Readers. Used with permission of the publisher.

Cover of *The Arabic Quilt: An Immigrant Story* by Aya Khalil. Illustrated by Anait Semirdzhyan. © 2022 Tilbury House. Used with permission of the publisher.

Cover of *My Very Favorite Book in the Whole Wide World* by Malcolm Mitchell, illustrated by Michael Robertson. Cover art copyright © 2020 by Michael Robertson. Reprinted by permission of Scholastic, Inc.

Cover of *Dress-Up Day* by Blanca Gómez. Text and illustrations © 2022 Blanca Gómez. Used by permission of Abrams Books for Young Readers, an imprint, New York. All rights reserved.

Cover of *People Are Wild* by Margaux Meganck. © 2022 Knopf Books for Young Readers. Used with permission of the publisher.

## Chapter 3

Cover of *The Year We Learned to Fly* by Jacqueline Woodson. Illustrated by Rafael López. © 2022 Nancy Paulsen Books. Used with permission of the publisher.

Cover of *Ancestor Approved: Intertribal Stories for Kids* edited by Cynthia Leitich Smith. © 2022 Heartdrum/HarperCollins. Used by permission of Heartdrum/HarperCollins.

## Chapter 4

Cover of *Clean Getaway* by Nic Stone. © 2021 Yearling Books. Used with permission of the publisher.

Cover of *The First Rule of Punk* by Celia C. Pérez. © 2018 Puffin Books. Used with permission of the publisher.

Cover only from *New Kid* by Jerry Craft. Illustrated by Jerry Craft. Text copyright 2019 by Jerry Craft. Used by permission of HarperCollins Publishers.

Cover of *Restart* by Gordon Korman, cover art by Mary Claire Cruz. Cover art copyright 2017 by Scholastic, Inc. Reprinted by permission of Scholastic Inc.

Cover of *Rez Dogs* by Joseph Bruchac. © 2022 Dial Books. Used with permission of the publisher.

## Chapter 5

Cover of *Ty's Travels: Zip Zoom!* by Kelly Starling Lyons. Illustrated by Nina Mata. © 2020. Used with permission of HarperCollins Publishers.

Cover of *The Cardboard Kingdom* by Chad Sell. © 2018 Knopf Books for Young Readers. Used with permission of the publisher.

Cover of *KINDergarten: Where Kindness Matters Every Day* by Vera Ahiyya. Illustrated by Joey Chou. © 2022 Penguin Random House. Used with permission of the publisher.

Cover of *Time Capsule* by Lauren Redniss. © 2022 Penguin Random House. Used with permission of the publisher.

Cover of *Fatima's Great Outdoors* by Ambreen Tariq. Illustrated by Stevie Lewis. © 2021 Kokila. Used with permission of the publisher.

# INDEX

*Abdul's Story* (Thompkins-Bigelow), 151

Actions
   connect goals to, 123-124
   revisit, after winter break, 119-124

Advance reader copies (ARCs), 20

*Adventures of Otto: See Pip Flap* (Milgrim), 141

Ahiyya, Vera, 163

Alessandri, Alexandra, 34

Allington, Richard, 88, 114

Allyn, Pam, 3, 32, 127, 167

American Library Association Youth Media Awards, 112

*Amulet: The Stone Keeper* (Kibuishi), 126

*Ancestor Approved: Intertribal Stories for Kids* (Smith), 103

Anchor charts
   Co-created Values, 56-57
   How We Want Our Classroom to Feel, 53
   Independent Reading, 46
   Previewing a Book, 50
   Readers Use Kind Words and Actions, 164
   Test-Taking Tips, 155

Andrews, V. C., 140

Anecdotal note sheet
   collaborative conversation, 184
   document observations with, 37

*Animals by the Numbers* (Jenkins), 159

*Arabic Quilt, The: An Immigrant Story* (Khalil), 55

Archer, Micah, 151

ARCs. See Advance reader copies (ARCs)

*Arlo and Pips: King of the Birds* (Gravel), 142

Arnold, Tedd, 141

Article of the Week (Gallagher), 51, 91

Arts, integrate into literacy routines, 157-160

Association for Library Service to Children (ALSC), 141

*Astrid and Apollo and the Starry Campout* (Bidania), 142

Atwell, Nancie, 3, 79, 112

Atwell Merkel, Anne, 112

Audio recording, document observations with, 37

Auditory signals, literacy routines and, 32

Aukerman, Maren, 140

A-Z Read-Aloud Celebration, 150-152

Back Pocket Wisdom
   belief-driven celebrations, 153
   book bins, 17
   calm reading environment, 97
   conference phrases, 107
   end-of-year checklist, 171
   gallery walk, 135
   honor language preferences, 74
   prepare for day one, 11
   Read to Me! tips, 133
   series books, 143
   showcasing books, 23
   values charts, 57

Bailey, Catherine, 158

*Beak and Ally: Unlikely Friends* (Feuti), 142

*Beauty and the Beast*, 49

Beechum, Nicole Williams, 52
Belief-driven teaching, 3-4
    events and celebrations, 150-153
    *See also* Beliefs
Beliefs
    classroom layout and, 21-25
    connect goals to actions and,
        123-124
    converse about, 123-124
    define and communicate, 3-4, 10
    hold true to, 149-156
    revisit, after winter break,
        119-124
    student agency and, 29-30
    translate to action, 86-92
    use of term, 4, 21
Belpré Medal, 112
*Be Quiet!* (Higgins), 151
*Bessie the Motorcycle Queen* (Smith),
    144
*Better Book Clubs: Deepening Compre-
    hension and Elevating Conversa-
    tion* (Kugler), 101
Bidania, V. T., 142
*Big Guy Took My Ball, A* (Willems),
    141
Biggs-Tucker, Karen, 50, 88
*Blue Bison Needs a Haircut* (Rothman),
    151
Bolling, Valerie, 151
Book bins
    small-group, 14-17
    sorting ideas, 118
    student-curated, 118-119
Book clubs
    beyond the classroom, 146
    impromptu series, 143
    setting up, 101
    student-led, checking on, 85
Book genres. *See* Genres and specific
    entries for particular genres
*Book Love* (Kittle), 3
Book matching. *See* Community
    Book Matching

Book Speed Dating, 49-50
    choose popular books for next
        year, 166
    final round, 165
Book swap, 20
Book talks
    elements of, 117
    ideas for remixing, 161
    January suggestions, 115-116
    other options, 117-118
    regularly scheduled, 114-118
    student-led, 129-130
Book Title Challenge, 17-19
*Book Whisperer, The* (Miller), 3
"Books We Love" (National Public
    Radio), 169
Borders (King), 95
*Breathing New Life into Book Clubs*
    (Cherry-Paul and Johansen), 101
Bridges, Lois, 105
Brightly website, 146
Bruchac, Joseph, 116
Bucket list, reading, 98-99
Burgess, Rebecca, 126
Burkins, Jan, 128
Butler, Dori Hillestad, 142
*Butterflies on the First Day of School*
    (Silvestro), 38
Byrne, Richard, 47

Cahill, Carrie, 140
Caldecott Medal, 112
Calvin, Alexander Ramsey, 115
Canva platform, 162
*Cardboard Kingdom, The* (Sell), 142
Carver, Ilene, 38
CASEL, 52, 104
Celebrations, belief-driven, 150-152
Cereal boxes, 51
Chalk the Walk, 152
Chappuis, Jan, 119
Chapter book series, 142
*Charlie and Mouse* (Snyder), 142
Cherry-Paul, Sonja, 101

Children's magazines, 51
Chung, Arree, 151
Cisneros, Sandra, 103
Class reading challenges, 98
Classroom beliefs. *See* Beliefs
Classroom diagram, 37
Classroom environment
 calm, for reading, 97
 student preferences, 52-54
Classroom library
 adding books to, 19-20
 book genres for, 47-48
 familiarizing students with,
  46-51
 first day of school and, 22-24
 furniture and supplies for, 22
 ILA equity audit, 20
 preparation for, 10
 refresh, 112-114
 seasonal display ideas, 113
 sources of books for, 20
 variety of books in, 46-49
*Clean Getaway* (Stone), 115
Cleary, Brian P., 159
Collaboration on shared values. *See*
  Shared values, collaborate on
Collaborative conferences, 107-108
Collaborative conversations
 Anecdotal Note Sheet, 184
 small-group, 100-102
Collaborative learning, multimodal
  text sets and, 102-104
Comics
 "do" and "don't," 126-127
 as graphic-format books, 142
 *See also* Graphic novels
Communication with families/care-
  givers, 41-42. *See also* Families/
  caregivers *entries*
Community, literacy. *See* Literacy
  community *entries*
Community Book Matching, 169-171
Community Literacy Survey
 reanalyze results of, 165

review learners' responses to, 166
 template, 176-177
Coretta Scott King Award, 112
Correia, Marlene, 15, 118
Couros, George, 157
Craft, Jerry, 115
*Creepy Crayon* (Reynolds), 151
*Cultivating Genius* (Muhammad), 3,
  66
Currie, Lisa, 163

Darling-Hammond, Linda, 46
Day in Our Classroom, A (elemen-
  tary), 189
*Dear Substitute* (Scanlon and
  Vernick), 71
Details
 informational text, demonstrating
  knowledge of, 159
 nonfiction book, paying attention
  to, 61
Diaz, Lucky, 151
*Disasters by the Numbers* (Jenkins),
  159
Displays
 book, seasonal ideas, 113
 family photographs, 70-71
 "New Year, New Books," 113
 thought leader quotations, 24-25
"Do" and "don't" comic strips,
  126-127
Dorling Kindersley (DK) Eyewitness
  series, 15
Dotson, Ronnie, 97
*Dress-Up Day* (Gómez), 59, 151
Dugar, Akhand, 102
Duhigg, Charles, 124
Duke, Nell K., 46, 81
Dwyer, Bernadette, 167

Early readers
 reading development stage, 185
 series books for, 141
*Ear Worm* (Knowles), 151

Educational jargon, avoiding, 41, 108
Elephant and Piggie Book, 141
Emergent reader, 185
End-of-year checklist, 171-173
Engagement
    family/caregiver, 5, 131-136
    gathering data about, 79
    observe readers' reactions, 158
    students' rating of their, 84, 179
    remix routines to increase, 160-162
Events, belief-driven, 150-152
*Every Child a Super Reader* (Allyn and
        Morrell), 3
Experience Summer! letter, 191

Families/caregivers
    Day in Our Classroom questions,
        189-190
    encourage summer experiences,
        171
    Experience Summer! letter, 191
    introduction directions, 41-42
    partnerships with, 5-6, 11
    promote student communication
        with, 167-171
    Read to Me! instructions, 187
    Reader of the Day letter, 186
Families/caregivers, confer with,
        104-108
    go-to phrases, 107
    listen and learn, 107-108
    reading development stages,
        105-107
    research into, 105
    talking points, 106-107
Families/caregivers, connect with,
        69-74
    compose family letters. *See* Family
        letters
    display photographs, 70-71
    ways to remember, 74
Families/caregivers, engagement
        opportunities, 131-136
    gallery walk, 133-135

questions caregivers can ask,
        135-136
    Read to Me! program, 131-133
Families/caregivers, launch partner-
        ships with
    clear communication, 41-42
    family questionnaire, 38-39
    video introduction, 39-41
Family-Friendly Explanation of
        Reading Development, 105
Family letters, 71-74
    checklist for students, 72
    delivery options, 73
    prompts for, 73
Family questionnaire, 38-39
"Fancy Dancer" (Smith), 103
Faruqi, Saadia, 142
Feedback phrases, for student
        agency, 29-31
Ferguson, Anne, 152
Feuti, Norm, 142
*Finding Kindness* (Underwood), 163
Finison, Carrie, 33
First day of school, 12-44
    add books to classroom library,
        19-20
    beliefs about classroom layout,
        21-25
    book title challenge, 17-19
    develop relationships with stu-
        dents, 32-37
    first-grade schedule, 26
    kick off routines, 26-32
    launch partnerships with families/
        caregivers, 38-42
    motto for, 42
    overplan, prioritize, stay flexible,
        25
    picture books stack, 33-34
    seventh-grade agenda, 27
    showcasing books on, 22-24
    small-group book bins, 14-17
    thought leader quote displays,
        24-25

*First Rule of Punk* (Pérez), 115
First semester, 77-109
  confer with families/caregivers, 104-108
  demonstrate and practice routines, 92-99
  elevate community through literacy, 99-104
  supported independent reading, 78-85
  translate beliefs into action, 86-92
"Fish Cheeks" (Tan), 103
Fisher, Douglas, 52, 123, 124
*5 Kinds of Nonfiction* (Stewart and Correia), 118
*Flowers in the Attic* (Andrews), 140
Fluent reader, 185
*Fly* (Thurman), 100, 151
Foundational skills, reinforce, with poetry, 158
Fountas and Pinnell Literacy Team, 157
*Fox + Chick: The Party and Other Stories* (Ruzzier), 141
Francois, Chantal, 14
Frey, Nancy, 52, 123, 124
*Friends* (Sosa), 59
*Frizzy* (Ortega), 126

Gallagher, Kelly, 3, 21, 27, 51, 78, 91, 150
Gallery walk, 133-135
  to increase movement level, 162
  professionalism during, 134
  Visitor's Guide, 188
Gardner, Whitney, 95
Garrett, Van G., 151
Geisel Award, 141
Genre fair, 143-144
Genre studies, beyond the classroom, 146
Genres
  for classroom library, 47-48
  selecting, 143-144

Giang, Kristen Mai, 144
*Gibberish* (Vo), 33, 34, 151
Goals
  connect to beliefs and actions, 123-124
  revisit, after winter break, 119-124
Gómez, Blanca, 151
Goodreads website, 24
Google Drawings, 162
Graham, Steve, 86
Graphic novels
  popular, 126
  in small-group book bins, 16
  series, 142
  for supported independent reading, 95
Graphic organizer, reading beyond the classroom, 147
Graphic-format books, 142. *See also* Graphic novels
Gravel, Elise, 142
Griffith, Robin, 46
Grounding principles, 1-6
  belief-driven teaching, 3-4. *See also* Beliefs
  end-of-year checklist, 172-173
  family/caregiver partnerships, 5-6. *See also* Families/caregivers *entries*
  literacy community, 5. *See also* Literacy community *entries*
  literacy routines, 4-5. *See also* Literacy routines *entries*
  preparation for school year and, 10-11
  supported independent reading, 2-3. *See also* Supported independent reading *entries*
*Guts* (Telgemeier), 126

*Hair Book, The* (Yvette), 151
Hale, Nathan, 142
Hall, Pete, 27
*Hamilton*, 25

Hammond, Zaretta, 92
*Happy Sloth Day!* (Sayre and Sayre), 158
Harney, Jenn, 151
Harwayne, Shelley, 119
Hattie, John, 52
Haughton, Chris, 151
Healy, Christopher, 47
*Heartstopper* (Oseman), 126, 169
Henderson, Anne T., 70, 131
Hiebert, Elfrieda, 58, 78
*Hi! Fly Guy* (Arnold), 141
Higgins, Ryan T., 151
Ho Sui-Chu, Esther, 131
Houppert, Anne Marie, 151
*House on Mango Street, The* (Cisneros), 103
*How to Hear the Universe* (Valdez), 144
Hudson, Neesha, 151
Hunter, Phyllis C., 14, 46
*Hurry, Little Tortoise, Time for School!* (Finison), 33
*Hustle Bustle Bugs* (Bailey), 158

*I Am!* (Medina), 151
Identity equations, 65–66
*I Feel! A Book of Emotions* (Medina), 52
If-then questions, 4
*If You Plant a Seed* (Nelson), 164
*In a Jar* (Marcero), 168
Independent reading
    poetry, 158
    supported, 2–3
Infographics
    for family/caregiver conferences, 108
    for gallery walk, 133
    for key details in informational text, 159
International Literacy Association (ILA)
    classroom library equity audit, 20
Introduction circle, 35–37

Irwin, Véronique, 24
*Isabel and Her Colores Go to School* (Alessandri), 34
Ismail, Yasmeen, 151
I Survived series (Tarshis), 95
*I Will! A Book of Promises* (Medina), 120

Jacobs, George M., 141
Jenkins, Steve, 159
Jiménez, Laura, 142
Johansen, Dana, 101
Johnston, Peter H., 29, 125, 163
*Joy* (Ismail), 151
*Juana and Lucas* (Medina), 142

Keene, Ellin Oliver, 128
Kelkar, Supriya, 53
Kern, Diane, 167
Khalil, Aya, 55
Kibuishi, Kazu, 126
Kick off routines, 26–32
    proximity, music, visual signals, 31–32
    student agency and independence and, 28–31
    visual schedule, 27–28
*Kicks* (Garrett), 151
*KINDergarten: Where Kindness Matters Every Day* (Ahiyya), 163
Kindness, 163–164
King, Thomas, 95
*King and Kayla and the Case of the Missing Dog Treats* (Butler), 142
Kittle, Penny, 3, 21, 27, 150
Klise, Kate, 140
Klise, M. Sarah, 140
Knowles, Jo, 151
Korman, Gordon, 116
Krashen, Stephen, 141
Kugler, Sara, 101

Lacina, Jan, 46
Ladson-Billings, Gloria, 100

Lander, Jessica, 38
Landrigan, Clare, 112
Lê, Minh, 151
Learning for Justice, 104
Lesesne, Teri S., 32
*Lift* (Lê), 151
Lighting, for reading environment, 97
List poem, 159
Literacy community, cultivate, 5, 11,
 64-69
 chat with students, 69
 community literacy survey, 66-69
 identity equations, 65-66
Literacy community, elevate, 99-104
 multimodal text sets, 102-104
 small-group collaborative conversations, 100-101
 social-emotional learning, 104
Literacy community, member
 responsibilities, 128-131
 reader of the day, 128-129
 student-led book talks, 129-130
 welcome new members, 130-131
Literacy community, refresh, 163-167
 express gratitude, 166-167
 look back to move forward,
  164-166
 sprinkle in kindness, 163-164
Literacy routines, 4-5
 kick off, 26-32
 preparation for, 10
 reasons for developing, 58
 social-emotional learning (SEL)
  activities, 26
Literacy routines, demonstrate and
 practice
 daily reading routine, 94-98
 play happy tunes, 98-99
 supporting skills and strategies,
  93
 teach-demonstrate-practice-
  reflect cycle, 92-94
Literacy routines, develop, 58-64
 reflect on known routines, 62-64

stop, reflect, regroup, 64
 text-focused conversations during
  read-aloud, 58-62
Literacy routines, innovate on,
 156-162
 integrate poetry and the arts,
  157-160
 new grouping structures and supplies, 162
 remix routines to increase
  engagement, 160-162
Literacy routines, reintroduce, after
 winter break, 124-127
 "do" and "don't" comic strips,
  126-127
 anchor new routines in familiar
  ones, 127-128
 put learners in charge, 124-126
Literacy survey, community, 66-69
*Literacy Workshop, The* (Walther and
 Biggs-Tucker), 88
*Little Red and the Big Bad Editor*
 (Rector), 72
*Long Distance* (Gardner), 95
Looks Like, Sounds Like, Feels Like,
 and Why protocols, 62
Loose parts, 159
Ludwig, Trudy, 164
Lyons, Kelly Starling, 141

*Many Colors of Harpreet Singh, The*
 (Kelkar), 53
Mapp, Karen L., 38, 70, 131
Marcero, Deborah, 53, 168
Martinez-Neal, Juana, 151
Matching cards, 162
Materials, offer new, 162
*Maybe* (Haughton), 151
McGill-Franzen, Anne M., 88
McTighe, Jay, 86
Medina, Juana, 52, 120, 142, 151
*Meet Yasmin!* (Faruqi), 142
Meeting notes, organizing, 11
Meganck, Margaux, 59

Mentor poems, 159
Mentor text, dual-purpose picture books, 47
Middle-grade readers, small-group book bins for, 15-16
Milgrim, David, 141
Miller, Debbie, 3, 14
Miller, Donalyn, 3, 23, 32, 49, 65, 112
Miller, Pat, 120
Miranda, Lin-Manuel, 25
"Mirrors, Windows, and Sliding Doors" (Dugar), 102
Mitchell, Malcolm, 55
Moll, Luis, 6, 70
Mood lighting, 97
Moral, inferring, 159
Morrell, Ernest, 3, 32, 127, 167
Moss, Barbara, 3
*Ms. Marvel, Vol. 1: No Normal* (Wilson), 126
Muhammad, Gholdy, 3, 24, 66
Mulligan, Tammy, 112
Multilingual learners
    benefits of book series to, 141
    classroom hosts for, 131
    labeling book baskets, 118
    language preferences of, 74
Multimodal text sets, 102-104, 146
Music
    for calm reading environment, 97
    literacy routines and, 32, 98-99
*My Very Favorite Book in the Whole Wide World* (Mitchell), 55

*Nathan Hale's Hazardous Tales: One Dead Spy* (Hale), 142
National Center for Education Statistics, 24-25
*National Geographic Kids*, 51
National Public Radio, "Books We Love," 169
NCTE, 21, 58
Nelson, Kadir, 164
Newbery Medal, 112

*New Kid* (Craft), 115
Newslea.com, 51
Noguera, Pedro, 105
*No More Independent Reading Without Support* (Miller and Moss), 3
*Not That Pet!* (Prasadam-Halls), 151

Observations, documenting, 37
Olympic Games experience, 156
Online platforms
    classroom visits via, 131
    conferencing, 117
    for ongoing communication, 11
    professional group meeting via, 84
    school's learning, 40
    for student work creation, 162
Open-ended questions, in collaborative conferences, 108
Ortega, Claribel, 126
Oseman, Alice, 126, 169
*Other Words for Home* (Warga), 83
*Out!* (Chung), 151
*Out of a Jar* (Marcero), 53

*Paletero Man* (Diaz), 151
Paper Bag Theater, 159
Parker, Kimberly N., 150
PDCast 6, 13, 45, 77, 111, 139
Pérez, Cecelia C., 115
Pearson, P. David, 46
Penguin Random House, Brightly website, 146
*People Are Wild* (Meganck), 59
Phillips-Toms, Katherine, 150
Photograph Request Letter, 178
Photographs
    display students', 70-71
    document observations with, 37
    of families/caregivers, 74
Picture books
    conversation-provoking, 58-59
    demonstrating values, 55
    dual-purpose, 47
    for first day of school, 33-34

Piggyback song, 159
Poetry
    integrate into literacy routines, 157-160
    for kids, 51
    list poem, 159
*Power of One, The* (Ludwig), 164
Prasadam-Halls, Smriti, 151
Pre-emergent reader, 185
Primary-grade readers, book bins for, 15-16
Proximity, literacy routines and, 32

Qarooni, Nawal, 105
Quotations, thought leader, 24-25

*Ramped-Up Read Aloud, The* (Walther), 62
Raschka, Chris, 71
Raúl the Third, 151
Read-alouds
    beyond the classroom, 146
    modeling text-focused conversations during, 58-62
    poetry, 158
    students' favorite, 166
    watch and listen during, 32-35
    whole-class, 161
READ-O, 98-99
    Middle grades template, 181
    Primary grades template, 180
Reader of the Day, 128-129
    family/caregiver letter, 186
*Readicide* (Gallagher), 3
Reading beyond the classroom, 144-148
Reading Bucket List, 98-99
    Middle grades template, 183
    Primary grades template, 182
Reading challenges, 98
Reading Day in Our Classroom, A (middle school), 190
Reading development stages, 105-107, 185

Reading genre preferences graph, 48
*Reading with Meaning* (Miller), 14
Reading memories, curate collection of, 168-169
*Reading Zone, The* (Atwell), 3
Read to Me!
    family/caregiver instructions, 187
    program, 131-133
Rector, Rebecca Kraft, 72
Redniss, Lauren, 168
*Regarding the Fountain* (Klise and Klise), 140
Relationships, developing, with students, 32-37
Renandya, Willy A., 141
Resolutions, after winter break, 120
*Restart* (Korman), 116
Retelling stories, artsy alternative to, 158-159
Reynolds, Aaron, 151
Reynolds, Jason, 126
*Rez Dogs* (Bruchac), 116
Richardson, Jan, 81
*Ride, Roll, Run: Time for Fun* (Bolling), 151
*Rise (and Falls) of Jackie Chan, The* (Giang), 144
Robb, Laura, 65
Rosenthal, Amy Krouse, 65
Rothman, Scott, 151
Routines. *See* Literacy routines
Routman, Regie, 82, 92, 153
*Ruth and the Green Book* (Calvin), 115
Ruzzier, Sergio, 141

Salas, Laura Purdie, 66
Sayre, April Pulley, 158
Sayre, Jeff, 158
Scanlon, Liz Garton, 71
Scan the Stacks, 50, 165
Scharf, Amy, 100
Schu, John, 34, 112
Schuldt, Lorien Chambers, 140
Scoot, 162

*Seaside Stroll* (Trevino), 151

Seating, for calm reading environment, 97

Self-reflection, student
  on shared values, 120-123
  as tools for next year, 148-149

Sell, Chad, 142

Series books, 140-144

Serravallo, Jennifer, 38

*Shake Up Shared Reading* (Walther), 62

Shared reading, 158

Shared values
  converse about, 123-124
  student self-reflection on, 120-123

Shared values, collaborate on, 52-57
  classroom feel, 52-54
  take time, be creative, 57
  values chart, 56-57
  What Do We Value? list, 54-57

Sharp, Colby, 23, 112

Short texts, 51

Sibert Medal, 112

Silvestro, Annie, 38

Sims Bishop, Rudine, 15, 102

Small-group book bins, 14-17

Small groups
  collaborative conversations, 100-101
  collect reading data from, 79-80
  guided poetry reading in, 158
  topics for student-led, 81

Smith, Charles R., Jr., 144

Smith, Monique Gray, 103, 164

*Snowman – Cold = Puddle: Spring Equations* (Salas), 66

Snyder, Laurel, 142

Social-emotional learning (SEL)
  activities, 26
  gratitude, 166-167
  literacy experiences and, 104
  literacy instruction and, 52

Someday List, 49
  compile students', 166

students' review of, 165
  template, 175

Sosa, Daniela, 59

Souers, Kristin, 27

Souto-Manning, Mariana, 36

*Speak Up!* (Burgess), 126

Spring season, 139-173
  beliefs, hold true to, 149-156
  broaden supported independent reading, 140-149
  innovate on routines, 156-162
  student-to-caregiver communication, 167-171

*Squirrel's New Year's Resolution* (Miller), 120

Stages of reading development, 185

Stewart, Melissa, 15, 112, 118

Stone, Nic, 115

Stories, retelling, artsy alternative to, 158-159

StoryWalk®, 152

Strick, Alexandra, 151

Student agency and independence, 28-31

Student-led book talks, 129-130

Students
  classroom preferences, 52-54
  familiarizing with classroom library, 46-51

Students, develop relationships with, 32-37
  document observations, 37
  introduction circle, 35-37
  read-aloud experiences and, 32-35

Students, reading preferences of
  book genres and, 46-49
  Book Speed Dating and, 49-50
  short texts, 51

Student self-reflection
  on shared values, 120-123
  as tools for next year, 148-149

*Stuntboy, in the Meantime* (Reynolds), 126

Supported independent reading, 2-3
  book talks, regularly scheduled,
    114-118
  building on launch of, 46
  first day of school and, 14-20
  first semester, 78-85
  focus on the reader, 85
  ideas for remixing, 161
  multifaceted reading data for,
    78-82
  overcoming roadblocks to confer-
    ring, 82-85
  preparation for, 10
  readers inspire future readers,
    148-149
  reading beyond the classroom,
    144-148
  reenergize, after winter break,
    112-119
  series books, 140-144
  spring season, 140-149
  student-curated book bins, 118-119
  teacher's role in, 3
  three-step process for guiding
    readers, 81
  troubleshooting during, 95-96
Sutherland, Tui T., 142

Taberski, Sharon, 185
Tan, Amy, 103
Tarshis, Lauren, 95
Teach-demonstrate-practice-reflect
    cycle, 92-94
*Teaching with Intention* (Miller), 119
Telgemeier, Raina, 126
Testing
  belief-guided preparation, 152-155
  creative breaks between tests,
    155-156
  test-taking tips chart, 155
Theme, inferring, 159
Thinking About My Reading
  Response Sheet, 84, 85
  template, 179

*This Book Just Ate My Dog* (Byrne), 47
*This Is a School* (Schu), 34
*This Is Not That Kind of Book* (Healy),
    47
*This Plus That: Life's Little Equations*
    (Rosenthal), 65
Thompkins-Bigelow, Jamilah, 151
Thurman, Brittany, 100, 151
*Time Capsule* (Redniss), 168
Transitional chapter books, 142
Transitional reader, 185
Trevino, Charles, 151
Turn-and-talk, 26, 30, 50, 59, 62
*Turtle in a Tree* (Hudson), 151
*Ty's Travels: Zip, Zoom!* (Lyons), 141

*Underneath My Bed: List Poems*
    (Cleary), 159
*Underwear!* (Harney), 151
Underwood, Deborah, 163

Valdez, Patricia, 144
Values
  picture books demonstrating, 55
  shared. *See* Shared values *entries*
Values chart, 56-57
*¡Vamos! Let's Go Read* (Raúl the
    Third), 151
Varlas, Laura, 81
Vernick, Audrey, 71
Video recording
  document observations with, 37
  family/caregiver introduction,
    39-41
Visual representation
  key details in informational text,
    159
Visual schedule, 27-28
Visual signals, 32
Vo, Young, 33, 34, 151

Walk-and-talk, 162
Walther, Maria, 50, 80, 88, 158
Ward, Alessandra E., 46

Warga, Jasmine, 83

*Watch. Connect. Read.* blog (Schu), 112

*We Are the Champions* (Davis), 103

*We're in the Wrong Book* (Byrne), 47

*What About X? An Alphabet Adventure* (Houppert), 151

What Do We Value? list, 54–57

*When We Are Kind* (Smith), 164

Wiggins, Grant, 86

Willems, Mo, 141

Williams, Jennifer, 167

Willms, J. Douglas, 131

Wilson, G. W., 126

*Wings of Fire—The Dragonet Prophecy: A Graphic Novel* (Sutherland), 142

Winter break, after
    create family/caregiver engagement opportunities, 131–136
    reenergize supported independent reading, 112–119
    reintroduce routines, 124–127
    release responsibility to community members, 128–131
    revisit beliefs, actions, and goals, 124
    student reflection on shared values, 120–123

*Wonder Walkers* (Archer), 151

Woodson, Jacqueline, 100

Word cloud generator, 57

Writing about reading, 146

Yaris, Kim, 128

*Year We Learned to Fly, The* (Woodson), 100

*You Can!* (Strick), 151

Yvette, LaTonya, 151

*Zonia's Rain Forest* (Martinez-Neal), 151

*Zoobooks*, 51